Changing Teacher Professionalism

Over the past thirty years there have been significant changes in the policy and social context of teaching that have had substantial implications for teacher professionalism internationally. This period has seen both an increase in central regulation of the work of teachers and an increased role for quasi-markets centred on the ideas of choice and competition. As the influence of central regulation and marketization has increased, so the scope for professional influence on policy and practice has in many cases diminished.

This collection of work by leading international scholars in the field makes a unique contribution to understanding both how these changes are impacting on teaching and how teachers might change their practice for the better. The basic premise of the book is that if research is going to be helpful in improving professional learning and the quality of teachers' practice, the full potential of three broad approaches to research on teacher professionalism needs to be brought to bear on these issues:

- research on the changing policy and social context of professional work and practice
- research on the working lives and lived experiences of teachers
- research on how teachers' professional practices might be enhanced.

Anyone who is interested in developing a holistic understanding of the nature of contemporary teacher change with an eye both to the policy and social context of teaching and to the enhancement of professional practice will find this book an indispensable resource.

Sharon Gewirtz is Professor of Education in the Centre for Public Policy Research at King's College London, UK. **Pat Mahony** is Assistant Dean (Research) at Roehampton University, Visiting Professor at King's College London and Chair of the Universities' Council for the Education of Teachers' (UK) Research Committee. **Ian Hextall** is Senior Research Fellow at Roehampton University. **Alan Cribb** is Professor of Bioethics and Education in the Centre for Public Policy Research at King's College London, UK.

Changing Teacher Professionalism

International trends, challenges
and ways forward

**Edited by
Sharon Gewirtz, Pat Mahony,
Ian Hextall and Alan Cribb**

Foreword by Michael Apple

Routledge
Taylor & Francis Group

LONDON AND NEW YORK

First published 2009 by Routledge
2 Park Square, Milton Park, Abingdon, Oxon, OX14 4RN

Simultaneously published in the USA and Canada
by Routledge
29 West 35th Street, New York, NY 10001

Routledge is an imprint of the Taylor & Francis Group

© 2009 Sharon Gewirtz, Pat Mahony, Ian Hextall and Alan Cribb

Typeset in Times New Roman by
Florence Production Ltd, Stoodleigh, Devon
Printed and bound in Great Britain by
CPI Antony Rowe, Chippenham, Wiltshire

British Library Cataloguing in Publication Data
A catalogue record for this book is available from the British Library

Library of Congress Cataloging in Publication Data
Changing teacher professionalism: international trends, challenges,
and ways forward/edited by Sharon Gewirtz . . . [*et al.*].
    p. cm.
  1. Teachers–Professional relationships. I. Gewirtz, Sharon, 1964–
  LB1775.C5926 2008
  371.12–dc22   2008021726

ISBN10: 0–415–46777–2 (hbk)
ISBN10: 0–415–46778–0 (pbk)
ISBN10: 0–203–88726–3 (ebk)

ISBN13: 978–0–415–46777–3 (hbk)
ISBN13: 978–0–415–46778–0 (pbk)
ISBN13: 978–0–203–88726–4 (ebk)

Contents

Illustrations

Figures

Tables

Contributors

Gert Biesta is Professor of Education at the Institute of Education, University of Stirling, UK, and Visiting Professor for Education and Democratic Citizenship at Örebro University and Mälardalen University, Sweden. His research focuses on the relationships between education and democracy, adult education and lifelong learning, the philosophy of educational research, and the professional learning of teachers. Recent books include *Improving Learning Cultures in Further Education* (with David James, Routledge, 2007); *Beyond Learning: democratic education for a human future* (Paradigm Publishers, 2006); and *Pragmatism and Educational Research* (with Nicholas C. Burbules, Rowman & Littlefield, 2003).

Paul Black worked as a physicist for twenty years before moving to a Chair in Science Education. He has made many contributions in both curriculum development and in assessment research. He has served on advisory groups of the US National Research Council and as Visiting Professor at Stanford University. His work on formative assessment with colleagues at King's College London has had widespread impact.

John Clarke is a Professor of Social Policy at the Open University in the UK. His recent work has explored the political and discursive struggles involved in remaking the relationships between people, welfare and states. He is currently working with Janet Newman on a book on the conflicts surrounding changing publics and changing public services to be published by Sage in 2009.

Alan Cribb is Professor of Bioethics and Education in the Centre for Public Policy Research at King's College London. He has a particular interest in developing interdisciplinary scholarship that links philosophical, social science and professional concerns and has pursued this interest through writing about health and education.

Dona Daley became a Senior Lecturer at the Open University in the UK after a long and successful career as a schoolteacher. Her teaching and research interests were in the fields of social justice, gender and race. Before her untimely death in 2002 she was just starting to become nationally established as a writer and her last play, *Blest be the Tie* was posthumously performed at the Royal Court Theatre, London.

Jennie Davies was one of the five university based Research Fellows in the UK Economic and Social Research Council (ESRC)-funded project on Teaching and Learning Cultures in Further Education (TLC-FE) based at the University of Exeter. She is currently the lead Research Fellow for the Nuffield Foundation project, 'Improving Formative Assessment in Vocational Education and Adult Literacy, Language and Numeracy'. Before joining the TLC-FE Project, her background was in secondary, further and adult education teaching. She is a contributing author to the TLC Project collective text, *Improving Learning Cultures in Further Education*, edited by David James and Gert Biesta (RoutledgeFalmer 2007).

John Elliott is Emeritus Professor of Education in the Centre for Applied Research in Education at the University of East Anglia, Visiting Professor at Manchester Metropolitan University and an Honorary Professor at the University of Sheffield. He is well known internationally for his role in developing the theory and practice of action research in the contexts of curriculum and teacher development, and has directed a number of funded collaborative classroom research projects with teachers and schools. He was an Advisory Professor to the Hong Kong Institute of Education and a consultant to the Hong Kong Government on the strategic development of its curriculum reforms from 2001 to 2006. Recent publications include *Reflecting Where the Action Is: The selected works of John Elliott* in the Routledge World Library of Educationalists (2007).

Julia Evetts is Professor of Sociology in the School of Sociology and Social Policy at the University of Nottingham, UK. She has been researching and writing books and papers on professional occupations for several years. She has studied careers (including gender differences in careers) in teaching, in engineering and science in industrial organizations, and in banking in commercial organizations. She has written papers on the armed forces, journalists and social work. She is currently engaged in research on the internationalization of professional regulation, on the work of the UK Engineering and Scientific Institutes and on the use of professionalism as a managerial instrument of occupational control.

Sharon Gewirtz is Professor of Education in the Centre for Public Policy Research at King's College London. She has been involved in research in the sociology of education for twenty years during which time she has published extensively on the themes of policy change, teachers' work and social justice.

Denis Gleeson was one of the Directors of the ESRC-funded TLC-FE Project and one of its original designers. He is a Professor of Education at the University of Warwick and has researched and published widely in the field of further education, employment and society. His recent and current research interests focus on 14–19 reform, academy schools and professional identity. With Jennie Davies and Eunice Wheeler, he is also a contributor to the TLC-FE Project collective text.

Ian Hextall taught for many years in higher education at Goldsmiths College and also at the Institute of Education, the University of Kent, South Bank University and the Laban Centre. Policy research has been the main focus of the four ESRC projects in which he has been involved. He is currently doing research on the impact of ICT initiatives in schooling and on the dynamics of the Building Schools for the Future programme.

Heather Hodkinson is currently a Senior Research Officer in the Lifelong Learning Institute of the University of Leeds. She had an early career in secondary school geography teaching, but has worked in qualitative educational research for the past seventeen years. Her research interests include vocational education and training, teacher learning and professional development, workplace learning, life-course transitions, lifelong learning and older people's learning. She has published widely on these topics and made presentations at a number of international conferences.

Eric Hoyle is Emeritus Professor of Education and Senior Research Fellow in the Graduate School of Education at the University of Bristol. His major interests are in organization theory, the professions and professional development. He is the author of several books, including (with Mike Wallace) *Educational Leadership: Ambiguity, Professionals and Managerialism.*

Ken Jones was once a unionist activist, and a member of the National Union of Teachers' national executive, and is now Professor of Education at Keele University. His writing focuses on the cultural politics of education. In 2003 he published *Education in Britain* (Polity Press) and in 2008 co-authored *Schooling in Western Europe: the new order and its adversaries* (Palgrave).

Bob Lingard is Professional Research Fellow in the School of Education at the University of Queensland. His most recent books include *The RoutledgeFalmer Reader in Education Policy and Politics* (2007), co-edited with Jenny Ozga, *Teachers and Schooling Making a Difference* (2006), co-authored with Debra Hayes, Martin Mills and Pam Christie, and the forthcoming *Transforming Learning in Schools and Communities*, co-edited with Jon Nixon and Stewart Ranson.

Pauline Lipman is Professor of Education Policy Studies at the University of Illinois-Chicago. Her research focuses on race and class inequality in schools, globalization, and the political economy and cultural politics of race in urban education. Her current project examines the relationship between education and neo-liberal urban development. She is also a founder and active member of Chicago-area Teachers for Social Justice.

Meg Maguire is Professor of Sociology of Education in the Centre for Public Policy Studies at King's College London. Currently her teaching and research interests are in urban policy and practice, teachers' lives and age and ageism in education. With Tim Wooldridge and Simon Pratt-Adams, she recently published *The Urban Primary School* (2006, Open University/McGraw Hill).

Pat Mahony was a primary teacher before moving to Goldmiths College where she eventually became Head of the Department of Educational Studies. She took up a research post at Roehampton University and later became Assistant Dean Research. Pat is Visiting Professor at King's College London and Chair of the Universities' Council for the Education of Teachers' (UK) Research Committee. As well as nine books, Pat has written over 70 articles and book chapters.

Ian Menter is Professor of Teacher Education and Deputy Dean of the Faculty of Education, University of Glasgow. He has been President of the Scottish Educational Research Association and is an elected member of the Executive Council of the British Educational Research Association. Publications include co-authorship of *Work and Identity in the Primary School* (Open University Press, 1997) and co-editorship of *The Crisis in Teacher Supply* (Trentham Books, 2002). He is lead author of *Convergence or Divergence? Initial teacher education in Scotland and England* (Dunedon Academic Press, 2007).

Janet Newman is a Professor of Social Policy at the Open University. Her research centres on analyses of governance, policy and culture. Publications include *The Managerial State* (with John Clarke: Sage, 1997); *Modernising Governance: New Labour, Policy and Society* (Sage 2001); *Remaking Governance: peoples, politics and the public sphere* (Policy Press, 2005); *Power, Participation and Political Renewal* (with M. Barnes and H. Sullivan: Policy Press, 2007); and *Creating Citizen Consumers: changing relationships and identifications* (with John Clarke *et al*.: Sage 2007).

Jon Nixon is Professor of Professional Education at Liverpool Hope University. He has held chairs at the University of Sheffield (where he was also Head of the School of Education), Stirling University and Canterbury Christ Church University. His most recent publications include: *Towards the Virtuous University: the moral bases of academic practice* (Routledge, 2008) and (with Bob Lingard and Stewart Ranson) *Transforming Learning in Schools and Communities* (Continuum, 2008).

Jenny Reeves is currently Director of Continuing Professional Development (CPD) at the Stirling University Institute of Education and teaches on the Chartered Teacher and the Scottish Qualification for Headship programmes.

She has worked in the field of CPD, with a particular interest in leadership and management, for most of her career. Her research interests are in learning and change in organizational settings. Of late her work has centred on professional enquiry and exploring the spatiality of practice-focused learning.

Pat Sikes is Professor of Qualitative Inquiry in the School of Education, University of Sheffield. Pat has been involved in research for the best part of thirty years. During that time her focus has been on four interrelated concerns: educators' lives and careers; life history research; qualitative methodologies; and, social justice issues.

Mike Wallace is a Professor of Public Management at Cardiff University. He researches the management of change in the public services and the wider process of public policymaking and implementation. He is currently investigating the development of organization leaders as change agents in the public services. He is also Associate Director for Capacity Building within the Advanced Institute of Management Research.

Eunice Wheeler was one of four college-based Research Fellows in the ESRC TLC-FE Project team. After training in art and design she started working in further education, mainly in vocational and work-based training before moving into further education teacher training. She is currently a Teaching and Learning Development Coordinator at City of Bristol College and teaches on in-service PGCE, Cert Ed and undergraduate education programmes. Her recent research has focused on workplace observation and she continues to support practitioner-based research through teacher training and the college's own Research Group. She is also a contributing author to the TLC Project collective text *Improving Learning Cultures in Further Education*, edited by David James and Gert Biesta (RoutledgeFalmer 2007).

Foreword

A number of years ago, I argued that the very meaning of teacher professionalism was being radically transformed. Processes involving deskilling, reskilling, and intensification were increasingly evident. Ideas of professionalism long associated with managerial impulses were replacing more substantive – and more culturally, socially and educationally critical – conceptions of what it meant to be a professional. Changes in the labour process of teaching and in the ideological assemblage that placed value on it were having profound effects (Apple 1982, 1986).

It is with no sense of joy that we now recognize how widespread these transformations have become. There clearly are now major shifts in many things: in what counts as legitimate knowledge and legitimate teaching; in how such knowledge and teaching are to be evaluated; in the dominance of new managerial emphases; in the role that economic realities, as defined by the powerful, play in all this; and what these changes mean in terms of the actual experiences of people working in schools, health care, social services and other institutions.

Much of this is due to the ascendance of a new alliance – or as Gramsci would put it, a new hegemonic bloc – that combines at least three elements. Speaking broadly, these are neo-liberals who believe that private is necessarily good and public is necessarily bad, neo-conservatives who wish a return to 'discipline, tradition, and real culture', and a particular fraction of the professional and managerial middle class that is deeply committed to *audit cultures* and their accompanying and seemingly unyielding emphasis on efficiency, accountability, measurement and the constant production of evidence that one is acting 'appropriately' (Apple 2006).

A considerable number of people have critically analysed these tendencies and their damaging effects, including important volumes by many of the people included in this book. One of the things that makes *Changing Teacher Professionalism* such a valuable addition to the literature is the fact that it brings together these critical voices into one book. But the arguments that are included here are not only repetitions of what can be found elsewhere in many of these authors' other works. There is substantive new material. Taken together, these chapters provide insightful lenses that enable us to better understand the often radical changes that so many people in education are experiencing at every level of the educational system. And, at the same time, they suggest significant ways of thinking about possible interventions and interruptions to challenge what is happening.

The issue of interruption is not to only be an academic one, however. It requires something else. Let us be honest. A simple return to past practices is neither possible nor wise. As Nancy Fraser (1987, 1997) and Charles Mills (1997) have argued, most of our major institutions – indeed the entire public sphere – have historically been constructed as a gendered and raced, as well as a classed, space. The prevailing definitions of 'public' and 'private' were based on a particular assemblage of assumptions about who was a legitimate participant and who was not. Thus, we need to take the important critical analyses of what is currently happening in education that are included in this book and continue the necessary hard work of linking them to a serious discussion of what should be a more just and fair system – and we need a clear tactical sense of what needs to be done to get there. These joint agendas constitute some of the core issues around which this book is focused.

But let us be honest about something else. It is hard to specify in advance other than in broad strokes the exact character of the kinds of models of structures, practices and deliberative agency that should guide public life inside and outside of education. As Raymond Williams (1989) reminded us, the 'common' has to be continually built, since what counts as the common is the never-ending process of critical deliberation over the very question of the common itself. This more critical understanding is evacuated under the aegis of the logics of markets and audits, since we do know that what is currently being built/imposed is often destructive, even in its own terms of assuming that establishing markets and audits will restore responsiveness and even trust. Stewart Ranson (2003: 470) summarizes these arguments in the following way:

> This neo-liberal regime cannot realize its purpose of institutional achievement and public trust. Achievement grows out of the internal goods of motivation to improve (that follows recognition and the mutual deliberation of purpose) rather than the external imposition of quantifiable targets, while public trust follows deliberation of common purpose out of difference and discord, rather than the forces of competition that only create a hierarchy of class advantage and exclusion.

Ranson is not sanguine about the possibility of building a public sphere that both challenges the neo-liberal, neo-conservative and new managerial construction of an audit culture and goes beyond the limits of older versions of what counts as the public sphere. However, he does articulate a sense of what is required to do so. A reconstituted vision of the public and a set of practices and structures that support it are grounded in the following:

Trust and achievement can only emerge in a framework of public accountability that enables different accounts of public purpose and practice to be deliberated in a democratic public sphere: constituted to include difference, enable participation, voice and dissent, through to collective judgement and decision, that is in turn accountable to the public.

(2003: 476)

Such a vision is not simply utopian. Indeed, the history of higher education, for example – from early mechanics institutes, to 'people's universities', to the many attempts at creating closer cooperative connections between educational institutions and culturally, politically and economically dispossessed groups (Gandin and Apple 2003) – suggests that there is a rich storehouse of knowledge on possibilities for doing this. But this requires the restoration of memory. Thus, historical work is absolutely essential if we are to go forward. Here I do not mean a nostalgic longing for an imagined past; but an honest appraisal of the limits and possibilities of what has been done before.

The task is not only historical, however. Undoubtedly, within each and every institution of education, within the crevices and cracks so to speak, there are counter-hegemonic practices being built and defended. But they are too often isolated from each other and almost never get organized into coherent movements and strategies. Part of the task is to make public the successes in contesting the control over policies, curricula, pedagogy and evaluation – over all of our work. While public 'story-telling' may not be sufficient, it performs an important function. It keeps alive and reminds ourselves of the very possibility of difference in an age of audits and disrespect. This too is one of the reasons I welcome this book.

We have successful models for doing this, such as the book *Democratic Schools* (Apple and Beane 2007). In that book, James Beane and I saw our role as researchers very differently. We acted as 'secretaries' for socially critical educators and made public their stories of building curricula and pedagogies that expressly embodied Ranson's vision of a reconstituted public sphere based on difference, participation, voice and dissent. The book went on to sell hundreds of thousands of copies in multiple languages. This is not meant as a 'hymn' to that book. On the contrary, it is meant to remind us that large numbers of people are actively yearning for something that gives them concrete policies and practices that will enable them to actually act practically in their own institutions against the models of (de)professionalism that are being imposed on them. While *Democratic Schools* was about primary, middle and secondary schools, it does point to the ways in which such strategic interruptions can proceed in other institutional contexts. Although *Changing Teacher Professionalism* is in a different genre to *Democratic Schools*, I believe it springs out of analogous motivations. Like *Democratic Schools*, *Changing Teacher Professionalism* is concerned not only with providing a language to better understand imposed models of teacher (de)professionalism, but also with articulating policies and practices for thinking and acting differently.

In my mind, the experiences of Porto Alegre are also essential here. Critical educators at schools and universities, government officials and community activists have taken up a model of critical educational practice and of critical deliberation and dialogue based on some of the work of Paulo Freire. They have recast it to make it more inclusive of multiple dynamics of power – in both redistribution and recognition, as Fraser (1997) would put it – and have made it more sensitive to the realities of the conditions of the poor and disenfranchised. The results are striking, both in terms of the kinds of rebuilding and extending a sense of professionalism that is respectful, responsive and critical all at the same time – and especially in terms of the concrete interruptive actions that are the results of this ongoing process (see Gandin and Apple 2003; Gandin 2006; Apple and Buras 2006).

It should be clear that one of the most important steps to take in continuing the process of rebuilding and extending what it means to be a respected, responsive, and critical professional is creating compelling analyses of what is going on now. When this is linked to what the alternatives might be, our power to interrupt dominant policies and narratives is increased as well. The fact that responses to both of these tasks are found in *Changing Teacher Professionalism* is a credit to the editors and the authors of this important book. It deserves to be read.

Michael W. Apple
John Bascom Professor of Curriculum and
Instruction and Educational Policy Studies
University of Wisconsin, Madison

References

Apple, M. W. (1982) *Education and Power*, 1st edn, Boston, MA: Routledge & Kegan Paul.

—— (1986) *Teachers and Texts: a political economy of class and gender relation in education*, New York: Routledge & Kegan Paul.

—— (2006) *Educating the 'Right' Way: markets, standards, God, and inequality*, 2nd edn, New York: Routledge.

—— and Beane, J. A. (2007) *Democratic Schools: lessons in powerful education*, 2nd edn, Portsmouth, NH: Heinemann.

—— and Buras, K. L. (eds) (2006) *The Subaltern Speak: curriculum, power, and educational struggles*, New York: Routledge.

Fraser, N. (1987) *Unruly Practices*, New York: Routledge.

—— (1997) *Justice Interruptus*, New York: Routledge.

Gandin, L. A. (2006) 'Creating real alternatives to neoliberal policies in education: the citizen school project', in M. W. Apple and K. L. Buras (eds), *The Subaltern Speak: curriculum, power, and educational struggles*, New York: Routledge, pp. 217–242.

—— and Apple, M. W. (2003) 'Educating the state, democratizing knowledge: the citizen school project in Porto Alegre, Brazil', in M. W. Apple, M. P. Aasen, M. K. Cho, L. A. Gandin, A. Oliver, Y. K. Sung, H. Tavares and T. K. Wong (eds), *The State and the Politics of Knowledge*, New York: Routledge, pp. 193–220.

Mills, C. (1997) *The Racial Contract*, Ithaca, NY: Cornell University Press.

Ranson, S. (2003) 'Public accountability in the age of neo-liberal governance', *Journal of Education Policy*, 18: 459–480.

Williams, R. (1989) *Resources of Hope*, New York: Verso.

Acknowledgements

This book arose from a project called Changing Teacher Roles, Identities and Professionalism (C-TRIP) funded by the UK Economic and Social Research Council's Teaching and Learning Research Programme (ESRC-TLRP) (award ref: RES-139-25-0182). C-TRIP consisted of a literature review leading to a published annotated bibliography (Hextall *et al.* 2007) and a linked seminar series, which provided the opportunity for national and international scholars to present and debate recent research on the project theme. The work collected together in this book builds on some of the contributions made to the seminar series as well as chapters specially written for this volume. This book therefore is in large part a product of a collaborative process involving a good many colleagues and we are glad to have the chance to acknowledge them here. First, we should express our thanks to the ESRC-TLRP for funding the project. For help with the funding bid and their continuing contribution throughout the project we are especially grateful to Ian Menter, Bob Lingard, Meg Maguire and Jeremy Hodgen. For their academic guidance and sustained and much appreciated encouragement we are grateful to the TLRP directorate and critical friends, especially Mary James, Pamela Munn and Andrew Pollard. We are also glad to acknowledge the support of the project advisory group, Merryn Hutchings, Jim McNally, Jonathan Osborne and Alan Smith. We were very fortunate with the quality of administrative and logistical support we received and would particularly like to thank Kamber Bishop, Adam Terry and James O'Toole. Sincere thanks also go to Geoff Troman for working with us on the production of the annotated bibliography. Finally, we would like to offer a very heartfelt thank you to all of the authors who have contributed to this book for the very efficient and collegial way in which they have responded to our requests and suggestions thereby helping to make the editing process a smooth and enjoyable one.

Sharon Gewirtz
Pat Mahony
Ian Hextall
Alan Cribb

Reference

Hextall, I., Gewirtz, S., Cribb, A., Mahony, P. and Troman, G. (2007) *Changing Teacher Roles, Identities and Professionalism: an annotated bibliography*. Available www.tlrp.org/themes/seminar/gewirtz/papers/bibliography.pdf (accessed 20 March 2008).

Permission has been granted for reuse of material in this volume as follows:

Chapter 9 'Inventing the chartered teacher' by Jenny Reeves is an edited version of Reeves, J. (2007) 'Inventing the chartered teacher', *British Journal of Educational Studies*, 55(1): 56–76, Wiley InterScience, www.interscience. wiley.com. Reprinted by permission of the publisher.

Chapter 10 'On the making and taking of professionalism in the further education workplace' by Denis Gleeson, Jennie Davies and Eunice Wheeler is an edited version of Gleeson, D., Davies, J. and Wheeler, E. (2005) 'On the making and taking of professionalism in the further education workplace', *British Journal of Sociology of Education*, 26 (4): 445–460, Taylor & Francis Ltd, www.informaworld.com. Reprinted by permission of the publisher.

Chapter 11 'In the shadow of the Research Assessment Exercise? Working in a "new" university' by Pat Sikes is an edited version of Sikes, P. (2006) 'Working in a "new" university: in the shadow of the Research Assessment Exercise?' *Studies in Higher Education*, 3 (5): 555–568, Taylor & Francis Ltd, www.informaworld.com. Reprinted by permission of the publisher.

Chapter 13 'Improving schoolteachers' workplace learning' by Heather Hodkinson is an edited version of Hodkinson, H. and Hodkinson, P. (2005) 'Improving schoolteachers' workplace learning', *Research Papers in Education*, 20 (22): 109–131, Taylor & Francis Ltd, www.informaworld.com. Reprinted by permission of the publisher.

Chapter 16 'Education and the public good: the integrity of academic practice' by Jon Nixon is an edited version of Nixon, J. (2004) 'Education for the good society: the integrity of academic practice', *London Review of Education* 2(3): 245–252, Taylor & Francis Ltd, www.informaworld.com. Reprinted by permission of the publisher.

Introduction

1 Policy, professionalism and practice

Understanding and enhancing teachers' work

Sharon Gewirtz, Pat Mahony,
Ian Hextall and Alan Cribb

The aim of this collection is to make a contribution to understanding the changing nature of teacher professionalism. We seek to do this both as an end in itself and to inform debates about enhancing teachers' professional practice. Much has been written about the notion of professionalism and related notions such as 'profession', 'professionalization' and 'professionality', and the literature is full of all manner of overlapping distinctions and debates. We will not attempt an overview of this literature here – which would in any case take up the whole of this introduction. Nor, given the extraordinary level of contestation that surrounds the topic, will we attempt a simple 'definition' of the concept of professionalism. Nonetheless, we will offer a brief account of the broad domain we are exploring before going on to map the policy shifts that are currently shaping teachers' work and the rationale and structure of the book.

Professionalism

Professionalism is an idea that points in many different directions. At least two are worth signalling here – first, it points in the direction of 'profession', that is a category of occupational classification; and second, in the direction of 'professional virtues', that is categorizations of technical and ethical standards claimed on behalf of certain occupational roles. It is also possible, and commonplace, to see both 'professions' and 'professional virtues' in normative terms – treating them either more or less idealistically or, by contrast, more or less critically. Idealistic conceptions of professionalism emphasize the special nature of professional workers, in particular their specialist expertise, and the associated ethical virtues of trustworthiness, collegiality and service. Critical conceptions emphasize the exclusionary nature of professions and the self-interested ideologies that underpin and mask their claims to special status and influence over others.

We want to argue that in order to understand teacher professionalism we need to work with plural conceptions of professionalism that encompass all of these elements and that we need to do so dialectically. For example, we should not think of professionalism as *either* a genuine concern about standards and ethics and 'doing one's job well' *or* as a legitimating discourse that reproduces particular forms of (classed, 'raced' and gendered) identity, power and in/exclusion, but as simultaneously both of these things. Similarly, we think it is important to keep both the ideas of 'profession' and 'professionalism' in play. We say this because for those of us who are interested in teacher professionalism it can be tempting to try and separate out these two ideas. Such a separation would seem to allow us to put aside the broader symbolic connotations of labelling teachers as professionals, along with questions about whether teaching is a profession or a semi-profession (or whether it is being deprofessionalized or reprofessionalized, etc). Instead we could simply concentrate on questions about what makes a good teacher and how teaching might be enhanced. However, this is by no means an easy separation to make. Freidson's analysis of professionalism as 'The Third Logic' (2001) shows why these two sets of questions are closely interrelated and is one useful account of the glue that holds the complex and contested concept of professionalism together.

For Freidson, professions are occupational groupings that exercise relatively high degrees of control over the conditions and conduct of their work and this kind of arrangement provides a mechanism for organizing some aspects of social life in a way that properly deploys specialist knowledge. Thus professionalism, in this sense, is a mode of social coordination that competes with, and provides some insulation from, both market and bureaucratic forms of organization. Trust is a key component of the professional mode of coordination which entails a contract between professionals and the wider society – one in which professional groups provide expertise and standards and in return are trusted to do their job. To function in this way professionalism needs to be both a regime of control and an ideology – that is professional groups need a certain amount of social power and collective autonomy and need to show why professionals can and ought to be trusted. For teachers, in other words, a concern with 'doing a good job' cannot be separated out from a concern about individual and collective teacher autonomy and teacher power because 'doing a good job' involves being in a position to fully deploy one's expertise and to shape what gets done.

Hence, in this collection we are necessarily interested in both idealistic and critical readings of professionalism and in professionalism in the two senses we have just outlined – both as a mode of social coordination and as shorthand for a (shifting and contested) set of occupational virtues.

Changing landscapes

Over the past thirty years there have been significant changes in the policy and social context of teaching that have had substantial implications for both of these senses of professionalism. Under the influence of neo-liberal ideologies and associated new managerial technologies – with their privileging of cost-containment, efficiency and productivity goals – this period has seen an increase in the central regulation of the work of teachers and an increased role for quasi-markets centred on the ideas of choice and competition. As the influence of these alternative modes of coordination has increased, so, in many national settings, the scope for professional influence on policy and practice has diminished. However, as well as facing demands that stem from state regulation and competition, teachers have also had to respond to other demands stemming from broader social changes. These include greater public scepticism towards professional authority combined with a culture of consumerism, demands for public services that are more responsive to diverse cultural and social identities, and transformations in information and communications technologies.

These shifts have, of course, taken on different forms and been experienced and responded to very differently by teachers working in different settings. For example, although the trends might be similar, teachers working in the 'developing' economies of South America or Africa are obviously faced with very different kinds of demands and challenges from those working in Australia, New Zealand, Europe or the US (Day and Sachs 2004) and the scope for teachers to influence policy and shape their own practice also varies from region to region and country to country. This is illustrated by Jones' comparative study of the 'remaking of education in Europe', which has drawn attention to stark differences in the capacity for trade unions and other social movements to influence policy. Jones distinguishes between 'societies – France, Italy – where [counter-hegemonic social or ideological] blocs exist in a form strong enough still to present major obstacles to neo-liberal policy, and other societies – Spain, Germany, England – in which . . . such blocs have been weaker or have been dispersed' (Jones 2005: 231; see also, Stevenson 2007; Weis and Compton 2007).

Even within the apparently similar Nordic countries there is considerable diversity in the ways in which governments have approached the restructuring of their education systems (Hudson 2007) with diverse implications for teachers' professional and personal identities and autonomy. For instance, in Norway the day-to-day working lives of teachers are tightly regulated by a prescriptive national curriculum, whereas in Sweden much softer forms of central regulation of teachers' work are achieved via a 'goal-oriented' national curriculum. As a consequence, the *individual* autonomy that teachers have over their work is arguably much weaker in Norway than Sweden. Yet, according to Helgøy and Homme (2007), Norwegian teachers have 'a relatively strong *collective* professional identity' while Swedish teachers 'rely on a more personalized type of professionalism emphasizing teachers' knowledge, competence and performance as individual properties' (Helgøy *et al.* 2007: 200).

Nevertheless, despite such differences, it is still undoubtedly the case that the recent 'tectonic shift' (Robertson 2007) in education policy discourse – with its apparently contradictory components of regulation and standardization on the one hand and devolution, diversity and individualism on the other – is effectively a global phenomenon. As the contributions to this book will demonstrate, this discursive shift and the complex and uneven transformations in teacher identities, roles and working lives that it has generated have significant implications for conceptions of – and the possibilities for – effective professional learning and professional practice.

Rationale and content

The premise of this book is that if research is going to be helpful in informing policy and in improving professional learning and professional practice, the full potential of three broad approaches to research on teacher professionalism needs to be brought together. With the exception of this opening chapter and the concluding chapter by Ian Menter, the book is divided into three parts, broadly reflecting these three approaches. The first approach, which draws on combinations of historical, critical policy, sociological and philosophical analysis, is concerned to examine the changing political and social context of public-sector professional work. The second, largely sociological, approach is concerned to understand changes in the working lives and experiences – and roles and identities – of teachers. The third approach is concerned to explore how teachers' professional practices might be enhanced. This approach draws on and combines a wide range of disciplines and research methods. These include intervention studies, involving experimentation with different approaches to teacher development, and philosophical and critical analysis of the qualities that make up good teaching and the political and organizational conditions that are most conducive to enhancing teachers' practice.

While each approach foregrounds a different substantive concern, it is clear – not least from the contributions to this collection – that in practice all three approaches overlap and interrelate. Any analysis of the policy context of teaching and learning is inevitably going to be informed by an interest in the practices that take place within, are shaped by and shape that context; in order to understand the working lives and identities of teachers we need to pay attention to the climates within which those lives are lived and out of which those identities are constructed; and, finally, anyone interested in enhancing professional learning needs to attend to the policies, and the teacher identities and subjectivities, which can make enhanced professional learning and practice possible or constrain its realization. We hope that by bringing these three approaches together in one volume we will help to deepen understandings both of the connections between them and of the policies, working conditions and conceptions of effective professional learning and practice that are most likely to enhance the quality of teachers' lives and work.

Part 1

The four chapters in Part 1 illustrate the first of these approaches and focus on the changing context of professionalism. Those working in this tradition are concerned to map and analyse the transformations in the policy, ethical and social landscapes of professional work. This includes historical and sociological analysis of discourses of professionalism; philosophical analysis of the shifting ethical terrain within which professionals operate; and historical and contemporary accounts of the changing relationships among the state, public-sector organizations, the professionals who work in them and the people who use them.

Highly prescriptive initiatives such as the national literacy and numeracy strategies in England and mandated instructional routines in the US have arguably positioned teachers, 'as recipe-following operatives whose role is to "deliver"' (Winch and Foreman-Peck 2005: 2). However, as a number of the contributions to this book indicate, there has not been a complete erosion of autonomy. Rather, it appears to be that autonomy is increasingly only allowed to be exercised within tight limits that are determined by what policy-makers believe to be in the interests of narrowly defined notions of educational success. In Chapter 2, Julia Evetts provides a language of description that can help us to make sense of this reconfiguration of teacher autonomy. In particular she distinguishes between two ideal-types – organizational profes-sionalism (or professionalism 'from above') and occupational professionalism (or professionalism 'from within'). Evetts characterizes organizational profes-sionalism as involving:

> the increased standardization of work procedures and practices and managerialist controls. It relies on externalized forms of regulation and accountability measures such as target-setting and performance review.
>
> (Evetts, this volume)

By contrast, occupational professionalism:

> incorporates collegial authority. . . . It is based on autonomy and discretionary judgement and assessment by practitioners in complex cases. . . . Controls are operationalized by practitioners themselves who are guided by codes of professional ethics which are monitored by professional institutes and associations.
>
> (Evetts, this volume)

It would be too simplistic to suggest that what we are seeing is a wholesale shift from occupational to organizational professionalism because in reality the two kinds of professionalism are more likely to coexist (as will become evident from some of the contributions to Part 2). Nevertheless, Evetts' account helps us to see how the balance between the two conceptions might be shifting as neo-liberal approaches to educational governance increasingly take hold.

As noted above, increased central control of educational systems has been accompanied by an increased role for markets in education. This has led to concerns about the penetration of 'accounting logic' (Broadbent and Loughlin 1997) into educational processes. In Chapter 3, Alan Cribb considers what this means for the ethical climate of teaching. He argues that the result is a greater focus on narrower, extrinsic conceptions of 'success' as captured in institutional performance indicators and a diminution in the attention paid to 'more open-ended, "thicker", contested and intrinsic modes of determining' what really counts in education. However, Cribb also argues that teachers are not passive in processes of 'ethical drift'. They are active ethical agents who continually have to negotiate the dilemma-laden terrain of contemporary educational practice, and somehow reconcile conflicting ethical commitments. Cribb's analysis invites professionals to question whether, when and why 'doing my job' is the same as 'doing the right thing'.

Sitting alongside, and feeding into, centralizing and marketizing policies are social changes that have important implications for the work of teachers. Of particular relevance to teachers' work are 'multiple anti-statist and anti-professional tendencies' (Newman and Clarke 2005: 2) the implications of which are discussed by John Clarke and Janet Newman in Chapter 4. These tendencies are associated with a range of user and social movements around welfare (and education) policies and practices; forms of '"demotic" populism that have made the "voice of ordinary people" more valued'; and the rise of a culture of consumerism, reflected in various forms of 'conspicuous' and 'ethical' consumption (Newman and Clarke 2005: 2). Such tendencies have informed policies of marketization – which were designed to challenge 'producer capture' and rebalance the education and welfare systems in favour of consumers or users – but they also act as independent forces in their own right that teachers cannot ignore. In short, as Clarke and Newman put it, these tendencies mean that:

> people no longer believe – or are willing to accede to – the proposition that 'professionals know best'. In the process both the situational and wider social authority enjoyed by professionals (even public service professionals) has become fragile or contingent.
>
> (Clarke and Newman, this volume)

This change has implications for how professionals relate to their publics and, in the specific case of education, how teachers relate to parents and students. As Clarke and Newman point out, responding to 'consumers' is a complex task involving an appreciation of the unequal distribution – by class, age, ethnicity and biography – of assertiveness, knowledge and the capacity to articulate demands and interests. Responding to consumers also involves an appreciation of the fact that individual consumers are not stable, unitary entities. The same parent, for example, may be knowledgeable and assertive about some aspect of their child's educational needs but dependent on professional guidance about other aspects. Hence Clarke and Newman talk about 'unstable encounters' between professionals and their publics 'in which the possibilities of getting it wrong have multiplied as both the public and service organizations try to manage each other in more uncertain times'.

Ken Jones concludes Part 1 by reminding us in Chapter 5 that policy is modulated by local circumstance, and takes different forms in different places. To illustrate this argument he considers the contemporary international policy orthodoxy that seeks to 'modernize' the teaching profession via discourses of efficiency and effectiveness, processes of central regulation and marketization and a marginalization of teacher unionism. While these 'modernizing' tendencies are apparent across the countries of the Organisation for Economic Cooperation and Development (OECD), England has led the way. Jones asks why it is that in England 'the most comprehensive programme of reform in Western Europe has been greeted with the most pliant response'. The answer, he suggests, lies in England's distinctive historic trajectory characterized, in particular, by: a long-standing and persistent neo-conservative anti-egalitarianism; a 'New' Labour party intent on shedding its 'Old' Labour, anti-'developmental' image; and a teacher trade union movement that has, since the 1980s and unlike its Scottish counterpart, pursued a narrowly economistic strategy centred on teachers' pay at the cost of winning wider public support for an alternative vision of education based on ideas of equality and the nurturing of the 'democratic intellect' (McPherson and Raab 1988).

Part 2

Many of the themes of Part 1 are continued in Part 2, which focuses on understanding the working lives and experiences of teachers, including the social and political construction of teachers' roles and identities. In a variety of ways these chapters examine how performative, managerial and market policy formations are transforming teachers' work and their social identities and the effects of these policy formations on teacher morale and creativity, commitment and attitudes towards teaching as a career. Policy changes are seen as having effects both on teachers' subjectivities and on conceptions of 'professionalism'. Given the highly differentiated nature of teachers' work and of the teaching workforce, policy effects are mediated by teachers' gender, class, ethnic and other identifications and positionings. A further important refrain running through 'working lives' analyses has been the impact of change on teachers' emotions and other aspects of their wellbeing. There are seen to be substantial personal costs of the combination of 'performative' and 'fast' policies (in which multiple policy initiatives are tumbled out simultaneously in quick succession with limited time for debate) – costs which are not always sufficiently taken into account by policymakers.

In Chapter 6, using the city of Chicago as a paradigmatic case of neo-liberal reform, Pauline Lipman shows how accountability systems are undermining teaching as an ethical, socially just, professional practice and creating greater inequality and disempowerment of teachers. At the same time, Lipman argues, paradoxically, the market opens up spaces for socially just projects which stand in opposition to neo-liberal corporate rationality and offer examples of alternative educational ideals.

Bob Lingard in Chapter 7 draws on a large empirical study of pedagogies conducted in Queensland, Australia to examine the nature of teachers' pedagogic practice in a policy context that has a tendency 'to thin-out pedagogies and reduce the quality of the education provided'. He shows that while the teachers participating in his study tended to be very supportive of their students they tended not to sufficiently value difference, connect their teaching to the world beyond the classroom, or make substantial intellectual demands upon students. These findings, he suggests, can at least in part be explained by structural pressures including large class sizes, a 'crowded' curriculum and a policy environment that privileges basic skills and teaching to the test over and above 'cognitive demand and intellectual depth' (Luke 2006). However, Lingard also points out that the research revealed cases of what the research team called productive pedagogies characterized by supportive classroom environments, an engagement with difference, intellectual challenge and connectedness with the world outside the classroom. This was particularly the case in smaller schools as well as in early and senior year settings where in Queensland specific policies, including teacher-moderated assessment, encourage 'on-going professional conversations' about pedagogic practice.

All of this means that we need to be extremely cautious about making generalizations about the impact of policies on teachers' lives and work. We also must not forget continuity as well as change in teachers' lives. One depressing continuity powerfully illustrated by Dona Daley with Meg Maguire in Chapter 8 is the way in which teachers continue to construct their identities against racialized landscapes and, in particular, the ways in which many teachers continue to experience racism in their daily lives. The chapter explores the professional experiences of thirty African-Caribbean managers in the context of shifts in educational policy and practice over the last thirty years. All the managers Daley interviewed were working in challenging 'rough and tough' urban schools where it is harder to prove oneself as a competent manager. Added to the difficulties any manager would face in these circumstances was the pressure experienced as a consequence of the racist attitudes of some colleagues. As one of her interviewees, Yolanda, put it:

> I've got to get it right every time, because any time I make one mistake, it's – 'told you she couldn't do it . . .' People make decisions on my competence and my ability, and my capacity to work, based on the colour of my skin.
>
> (Daley with Maguire, this volume)

A key point that needs to be made about the heady mix of policies to which teachers have had to somehow respond is that the policies are built on, and in turn contribute to, a range of sometimes competing discourses about educational purposes and values. The policy mix also contains within it different versions of what is entailed in teacher professionalism. So, for example, according to Jenny Reeves in Chapter 9, the Chartered Teacher policy in Scotland, which created a new teacher status designed to allow good teachers to stay in the classroom, encompassed three competing discourses of teacher professionalism. It encompassed a 'restricted' bureau-professional form of professionalism where teachers are expected to function as experts in their own classrooms but to work within bureaucratic structures established by local authorities, a managerial form of professionalism in which teachers are constructed as closely supervised, rule-following 'operatives' and a 'new professionalism' based on notions of collaboration, knowledge sharing and 'learner-centred practice'. Tensions between these discourses, Reeves argues, create a 'space' which teachers can try to use to forge a revitalized, extended form of teacher professionalism. Reeves explores some of the conceptual and practical difficulties faced by thirty-four aspiring Chartered Teachers as they try to enact their new status in the context of these competing discourses. In doing so, she demonstrates that those with an interest in the professional development of teachers need to understand that the barriers to changing the basis of teacher professionalism are complex and multifaceted.

In Chapters 10 and 11 the focus shifts from school education to further and higher education. For teachers in further education (FE) teaching is often a second career. In Chapter 10, Denis Gleeson, Jennie Davies and Eunice Wheeler show how transition in roles and identities consequent upon employment in FE can, in some cases, generate uncertainties about:

> professional identity and status, as practitioners move from being accredited subject specialists with expertise as 'an Economist'; through higher order teaching – 'a lecturer'; followed by what some see as a slow downgrading of their professional status as it changes to being 'a teacher' of lower status courses with a welfare function.
>
> (Gleeson *et al.*, this volume)

Added to this are pressures produced by a 'reduction of resources, staffing and teaching hours' and a continuous cycle of external monitoring in which 'teaching becomes a constant struggle against rather than with students'. However, as the authors also demonstrate, FE lecturers experience and respond to the changing policy context in a range of ways, so that while the dominant picture may be one of 'high turnover and exodus' from the profession, there are tutors who are able to find 'new sources of sustenance' (Colley and James 2005) to bolster their professional identities.

Chapter 11 by Pat Sikes explores the work-related perceptions and experiences of a group of staff working in a UK university where local and national policy initiatives impact in a variety of ways. Her review of the literature on changes in academic work points to 'fragmentation . . . conflict, contestation, work overload, and widespread unhappiness'. Sikes found that increasing demands on staff initially employed as teachers to become 'research active' led to increased workloads, had implications for professional and personal identities and influenced how people felt about and enacted their work. For example, she talks about the ways in which the resulting pressures and strains leaked into other aspects of her respondents' lives, unsettling their identities and 'leaving them feeling inadequate'. However, for some the experience was positive as new career opportunities or the possibilities of promotion or enhanced status became available, or the policy shifts provided a chance to develop new courses and innovations in teaching or learning.

Part 3

The chapters in Part 3 explore how things might be different and in particular how teachers' professional practices might be enhanced. In Chapter 12, Paul Black describes two very different initiatives for teachers' professional development. Using research evidence and experience drawn from the UK and US, Black illustrates the principles and procedures that can underpin initiatives aimed at encouraging change in teachers' pedagogy leading to knowledge creation by teachers. He argues that while imposition of an innovation which has not been developed with, and by, some of the teachers for whom it is intended is sure to fail, the opposite approach – based on the belief that all innovations must arise from within the profession without external interference – is also inadequate. It is significant that the more recent UK initiative Black describes, the Formative Assessment Project, resulted in significantly enriched pedagogic practices without altering the curriculum and formal assessment structure that is widely believed to discourage innovation and the development of productive pedagogic practices. Black also explains how the initiative team modelled the pedagogic relationship they were encouraging the teachers to develop with their students, that is:

> building on the initial ideas of learners and providing feedback in response to these ideas, involving them in taking more responsibility for their own learning, helping them to understand the aims and criteria for the learning, and helping them to learn through active engagement in discussion.

(Black, this volume)

Hodkinson in Chapter 13 is also able to point to effective professional learning processes in the two English secondary schools she studied. At the level of the individual teacher, she 'found many examples of dedication to personal and professional growth and development, and to mutual support of colleagues'. Her research shows that, although current management and regulatory frameworks at local and national policy levels, and associated time and resource constraints, do limit the possibilities for effective professional learning, the dispositions of individual teachers and departmental working cultures are also important influences, which have the potential to interrupt or moderate policy constraints.

According to Hodkinson, the dominant policy approach to professional learning is inherently flawed. Contemporary policies, she argues, are based on an instrumental, technical-rational model of learning as 'acquisition'. She draws on the workplace learning literature to expose the flaws in this conception. Workplace learning is often informal, unplanned and unintentional and frequently occurs in the course of collaborative activities, within departments, across departments and across schools. Hodkinson's analysis shows how top-down, one-size-fits-all professional development courses are not responsive to the participative and constructivist ways in which teachers actually learn or to the specific interests of teachers and argues that teacher learning is best improved through the construction of more expansive learning environments.

In Chapter 14, Elliott argues that the weaknesses of the top-down approach to professional development that Hodkinson discusses are also manifest in the contemporary phenomenon of 'practitioner research', which, he suggests, involves practitioners simply testing out the applicability of the findings of school effectiveness research to their specific classroom contexts. This conception of teacher research, Elliott argues, echoes approaches that were developed in the US during the 1950s, which were shaped by an instrumentalist and objectivist rationality. He contrasts this with the work of Stenhouse, which embraced a more pragmatic, deliberative and democratic rationality, with 'action research' and 'research-based teaching' becoming aligned with anti-positivist qualitative methodologies. Elliott shows that, while contemporary UK notions of teacher research are closer to the US model, this is not the case in other countries where Stenhouse's model has been reinterpreted and adapted to accommodate different national and cultural contexts.

In countries where education academics and teachers have been 'cast out of the curriculum field' it may be time, Elliott's analysis suggests, to revisit research-based teaching and the principles underlying it: namely, a view of knowledge as open and provisional, a belief in the importance of enabling students to direct their own learning, initiate their own questions for inquiry and subject ideas to discussion and rational scrutiny, and a belief that this kind of discussion-based pedagogy, because it is alien to so many teachers, needs pedagogical experimentation and collaboration between school and university educators if it is going to stand any chance of success. This would, of course, involve a much greater degree of autonomy for teachers over how they teach and how they assess their students than is currently available in many national contexts.

As Gert Biesta argues in Chapter 15, autonomy is central to teaching because of the nature of teachers' professional knowledge. Teaching is not a narrowly technicist job that involves applying abstract rules but is one that involves making decisions informed by knowledge and understanding of the unique contexts within which teachers are working as well as by their educational values and beliefs. In short, teachers have to make technical *and* normative judgements, for example – will this approach work in the particular classroom I am working in *and* is the approach desirable and acceptable?

Biesta is interested in finding ways of enhancing teachers' capacity to reflect on the normative dimensions of their work – that is their 'ideas about what is educationally worthwhile, ideas about what it means to be an educated person, ideas about "the good life", and ideals about the "good society"'. He presents findings from an action research project in the Netherlands that reveals ways in which teachers can enhance what he calls their '"educational professionality" – i.e. their ability to make judgements about what is educationally desirable'. Certain conditions will facilitate the disposition of professionality and others will hinder or obstruct it. Biesta identified time to reflect – individually and collectively – as the most important condition for fostering this disposition. Yet in many countries contemporary policies (alongside more demands from 'consumers') have contributed to an intensification of teachers' work which squeezes out time for the kinds of professional development activities needed to enhance professionality.

Continuing the discussion of values, Jon Nixon in Chapter 16 argues that universities need to reclaim a public and inclusive language for education that reflects the moral ends and purposes of academic practice. Nixon argues that the dual processes of managerialization and commercialization have threatened the dispositions of truthfulness, respect, authenticity and magnanimity essential for universities to function in accordance with their traditional mission. This, he suggests, is to function as a civic space for people to come together to learn and engage in independent and rigorous critique. Nixon concludes by arguing that the moral conditions of academic reconstruction necessarily include a commitment by academic practitioners to the development, in themselves and others, of the dispositions he is advocating.

In the final chapter in Part 3, Chapter 17, Eric Hoyle and Mike Wallace call for a more temperate approach towards managing the teaching profession than has prevailed for decades. Their argument points to excessive leadership and management, which threaten to become self-serving and inhibit professional practice from making reforms work in contingent circumstances. Drawing on professional learning and organization theory, Hoyle and Wallace suggest that managers could do better if they were to accept that tightly controlled transformational reform is unrealistic. A more promising alternative, they say, is to expand the scope for teachers to make professional judgements.

Conclusion

In the concluding chapter of the book, Chapter 18, Ian Menter reflects on the changes in teachers' work discussed in earlier chapters, highlighting three processes shaping teachers' work, which he thinks are particularly significant: the increasing segmentation of the teaching workforce, the growth in the number of teachers now working in the expanding private sector of educational services provision (including consultancy, training and inspection) and the growing international mobility of the teaching workforce. Menter argues that what is in danger of getting lost, as teachers are increasingly recast as 'servants' of the global economy, is the role of teachers as developers of 'the human spirit and intellect', and he calls for new forms of accountability. For Menter, these:

> must start from a shared commitment to challenging assumptions and asking critical questions, questions based on the values of a democratic society, including social justice, and the value and sustaining of human life.

(Menter, this volume)

We believe that these sentiments will be shared by many of the contributors of this book and we hope that they will also be shared by many of its readers.

References

Broadbent, J. and Loughlin, R. (1997) '"Accounting logic" and controlling professionals: the case of the public sector', in J. Broadbent, M. Dietrich and J. Roberts (eds), *The End of the Professions?*, London: Routledge, pp. 33–48.

Colley, H. and James, D. (2005) 'Unbecoming tutors: towards a more dynamic notion of professional participation'. Paper presented at Changing Teacher Roles, Identities and Professionalism Seminar Series, Seminar 3: Conceptions of professionalism and professional knowledge, King's College London, 16 May 2005. Online. Available www.tir.org/themes/seminar/gewirtz/papers/seminar3/ (accessed 25 July 2008).

Day, C. and Sachs, J. (2004) 'Professionalism, performativity and empowerment: discourses in the politics, policies and purposes of continuing professional development', in C. Day and J. Sachs (eds), *International Handbook on the Continuing Professional Development of Teachers*, Maidenhead: Open University Press, pp. 3–32.

Freidson, E. (2001) *Professionalism: the third logic*, London: Polity Press.

Helgøy, I. and Homme, A. (2007) 'Towards a new professionalism in school: a comparative study of teacher autonomy in Norway and Sweden', *European Educational Research Journal*, 6 (3): 232–249.

——, Homme, A. and Gewirtz, S. (2007) 'Local autonomy or state control? Exploring the effects of new forms of regulation in education', *European Educational Research Journal*, 6 (3): 198–202.

Hudson, C. (2007) 'Governing the governance of education: the state strikes back', *European Educational Research Journal*, 6 (3): 266–282.

Jones, K. (2005) 'Remaking education in western Europe', *European Educational Research Journal*, 4 (3): 228–242.

Luke, A. (2006) 'Teaching after the market: from commodity to cosmopolitan', in L. Weis, C. McCarthy and G. Dimitriadis (eds), *Ideology, Curriculum, and the*

New Sociology of Education: revisiting the work of Michael Apple, New York: Routledge, pp. 115–143.

McPherson, A. and Raab, C. (1988) *Governing Education: a sociology of policy since 1945*, Edinburgh: Edinburgh University Press.

Newman, J. and Clarke, J. (2005) 'The rise of the citizen-consumer: implications for public service professionalism'. Paper presented at Changing Teacher Roles, Identities and Professionalism Seminar Series, Seminar 5: What can be learnt from other professions? King's College London, October 2005. Online. Available www.tlrp.org/themes/seminar/gewirtz/papers/seminar5/paper%20-%20clarke%20 &%20newman.doc (accessed 12 March 2008).

Robertson, S. (2007) '"Remaking the World": neo-liberalism and the transformation of education and teachers' labour', published by the Centre for Globalisation, Education and Societies, University of Bristol. Online. Available www.bris.ac.uk/education/people/academicstaff/edslr/publications/17slr/.

Stevenson, H. (2007) 'Guest editorial: changes in teachers' work and the challenges facing teacher unions', *International Electronic Journal for Leadership in Learning*, 11 (13). Online. Available www.ucalgary.ca/~iejll/volume11/editorial.htm (accessed 18 March 2008).

Weis, L. and Compton, M. (eds) (2007) *The Global Assault on Teachers, Teaching and their Unions*, New York: Palgrave.

Winch, C. and Foreman-Peck, L. (2005) 'What do we mean by teachers' professionalism and professional knowledge? How useful are these concepts?'. Paper presented at Changing Teacher Roles, Identities and Professionalism Seminar Series, Seminar 3: Conceptions of professionalism and professional knowledge, King's College London, 16 May 2005. Online. Available www.tlrp.org/themes/seminar/gewirtz/papers/seminar3/ (accessed 20 March 2008).

Part 1

The changing context of professionalism

2 The management of professionalism

A contemporary paradox

Julia Evetts

Profession and professionalism are increasingly being applied to work and workers in modern societies yet the conditions of trust, discretion and competence, which historically have been deemed to be necessary for professional practice, are continually being challenged, changed or 'regulated'. This represents a contemporary paradox that is important to clarify and understand.

As a sociologist of professional groups, I have been interested in knowledge-based occupational groups *other* than medicine, health and law (usually taken to be the key or archetypal professional groups). My research has focused on the study of occupational groups such as head teachers, engineers and scientists working in industrial organizations, bankers in commercial organizations, the armed forces, journalists and most recently social workers and foster carers. These occupational groups have had to develop and construct their professionalism in organizational contexts, work places and employment relations different from those in law and medicine.

Knowledge-based occupations are taken to be the expanding employment categories and the growth sectors of labour markets in developed (Lyotard 1984; Perkin 1988; Reed 1996; Frenkel *et al.* 1995), transitional (Buchner-Jeziorska 2001; Buchner-Jeziorska and Evetts 1997) and developing societies (Hiremath and Gudagunti 1998; Sautu 1998). The concept of 'profession' is not used as often outside the Anglo-American literature where it represents the category of privileged, high status, high-income occupational groups. In most societies the expansion of knowledge-based work and occupations is connected with the growing capacity of higher education systems to produce workers who are educated and trained, and the needs of employers and managers in organizations to exercise control over knowledge and service work.

In previous publications, I have argued for a shift in analytical focus, away from the concepts of profession and professionalization and towards the further analysis of the concept of professionalism and how it is being used. Of more interest and relevance in current work and employment contexts is the increased use of the *discourse of professionalism* in a wide range of occupations and organizational work places. The discourse of professionalism is used as a marketing slogan in advertising to attract customers (Fournier 1999). It is used in occupational recruitment campaigns, in company mission statements and organizational aims and objectives to motivate employees. The discourse of professionalism has entered the managerial literature and been embodied in training manuals. Even occupational regulation and control (both internal and external forms) are now explained and justified as means to improve professionalism in work.

If the focus of analysis is shifted away from the concepts of profession (as a distinct and generic category of occupational work) and professionaliza-tion (as the process to pursue, develop and maintain the closure of the occupational group) and towards the concept of professionalism, then different kinds of explanatory theory become apparent. Then the discourse of profes-sionalism can be analysed as a powerful instrument of occupational change and social control at macro, meso and micro levels and in a wide range of occupations in very different work, organizational and employment relations, contexts and conditions.

The chapter begins with an explanation of three different interpretations of professionalism that (over time) have been developed:

* professionalism as an occupational value;
* professionalism as an ideology; professionalization as market closure;
* professionalism as a discourse of occupational change and managerial control.

Then it is suggested that one consequence of current changes is the existence of two ideal typical forms of professionalism: occupational professionalism and organizational professionalism. The chapter goes on to consider some of the changes to professionalism and the consequences of the expansion of organizational forms of professionalism for aspects of trust, discretion and competence in professional work.

Professionalism and professionalization: contrasting interpretations

The concepts of profession, professionalism and professionalization have received considerable (sometimes critical) attention in sociology. In early British sociological analysis, the key concept was 'professionalism' and the emphasis was on the importance of professionalism for the stability and civility of social systems (e.g. Tawney 1921; Carr-Saunders and Wilson 1933; Marshall 1950). In these interpretations professionalism was regarded as an important and highly desirable occupational value and professional relations were characterized as collegial, cooperative and mutually supportive. Similarly, relations of trust characterized practitioner/client and practitioner/management interactions since competencies were assumed to be guaranteed by education, training and sometimes by licensing.

The early American sociological theorists of professions also developed similar interpretations and again the key concept was the occupational value of professionalism based on trust, competence, a strong occupational identity and cooperation. The best known, though perhaps most frequently misquoted, attempt to clarify the special characteristics of professionalism, its central values and its contribution to social order and stability, was that of Parsons (1939). Parsons recognized and was one of the first theorists to show how the capitalist economy, the rational–legal social order (of Weber) and the modern professions were all interrelated and mutually balancing in the maintenance and stability of a fragile normative social order. He demonstrated how the authority of the professions and of bureaucratic hierarchical organizations both rested on the same principles (for example, of functional specificity, restriction of the power domain, application of universalistic, impersonal standards). The professions, however, by means of their collegial organization and shared identity demonstrated an alternative approach (compared with the managerial hierarchy of bureaucratic organizations) towards the shared normative end.

The work of Parsons has subsequently been subject to heavy criticism mainly because of its links with functionalism (Dingwall and Lewis 1983). The differences between professionalism and rational–legal bureaucratic ways of organizing work have been returned to, however, in Freidson's (2001) recent analysis. Freidson examines the logics of three different ways of organizing work in contemporary societies (the market, organization and profession) and illustrates the respective advantages and disadvantages of each for clients and practitioners. In this analysis he demonstrates the continuing importance of maintaining professionalism (with some modifications) as the main organizing principle for public service work.

This interpretation represents what might be termed the optimistic view of what professionalism and the process of professionalization of work entails. It is based on the principle that the work is of special value either to the public or to the interests of the state or an elite (Freidson 2001: 214). According to Freidson, 'the ideal typical position of professionalism is founded on the official belief that the knowledge and skill of a particular specialization requires a foundation in abstract concepts and formal learning' (2001: 34/5). Education, training and experience are fundamental requirements but once achieved (and sometimes licensed) then the exercise of discretion based on competences is central and deserving of special status. The practitioners have special knowledge and skill and (particularly if its practice is protected by licensing) there is a need to trust professionals' intentions. As a consequence, externally imposed rules governing work are minimized and the exercise of discretion and good judgement, often in highly complex situations and circumstances, and based on recognized competences, are maximized.

There is a second more pessimistic interpretation of professionalism, however, which grew out of the more critical literature on professions which was prominent in Anglo-American analyses in the 1970s and 1980s. During this period professionalism came to be dismissed as a successful ideology (Johnson 1972) and professionalization as a process of market closure and monopoly control of work (Larson 1977) and occupational dominance (Larkin 1983). Professionalization was intended to promote professional practitioners' own occupational self-interests in terms of their salary, status and power as well as the monopoly protection of an occupational jurisdiction (Abbott 1988). This was seen to be a process largely initiated and controlled by the practitioners themselves and mainly in their own interests although it could also be argued to be in the public interest (Saks 1995).

A third and later development has involved the analysis of professionalism as a discourse of occupational change and control – this time in work organizations where the discourse is increasingly applied and utilized by managers. Fournier (1999) considers the appeal to 'professionalism' as a disciplinary mechanism in new occupational contexts. She suggests how the use of the discourse of professionalism, in a large privatized service company of managerial labour, works to inculcate 'appropriate' work identities, conducts and practices. She considers this as 'a disciplinary logic which inscribes "autonomous" professional practice within a network of account-ability and governs professional conduct at a distance' (1999: 280). It is also interesting and highly relevant to link this notion of managerial professionalism with aspects of public management – particularly in education (schools and universities) and in health (hospitals and primary care trusts).

It is also the case that the use of the discourse of professionalism varies between different occupational groups. McClelland's categorization (1990: 170) can be used (see Evetts 2003) to differentiate between professionalization 'from within' (i.e. successful manipulation of the market by the group) and 'from above' (domination of forces external to the group). In this interpretation, where the appeal to professionalism is made and used by the occupational group itself, 'from within', then the returns to the group can be substantial. In these cases, historically the group has been able to use the discourse in constructing its occupational identity, promoting its image with clients and customers, and in bargaining with states to secure and maintain its (sometimes self-) regulatory responsibilities. In these instances the occupation is using the discourse partly in its own occupational and practitioner interests but sometimes also as a way of promoting and protecting the public interest.

In the case of most contemporary public service occupations, however, professionalism is being constructed and imposed 'from above' and for the most part this means by the employers and managers of the public service organizations in which these 'professionals' work. Here the discourse (of dedicated service and autonomous decision making) is part of the appeal (or the ideology) of professionalism. When the discourse is constructed 'from above', then often it is imposed and a false or selective discourse is used to promote and facilitate occupational change (rationalization) and as a disciplinary mechanism of autonomous subjects exercising appropriate conduct. This discourse of professionalism is grasped and welcomed by the occupational group since it is perceived to be a way of improving the occupation's status and rewards, collectively and individually. However, the realities of professionalism 'from above' are very different. The effects are not the occupational control of the work by the worker/practitioners but rather control by the organizational managers and supervisors. Organizational objectives (which are sometimes political) define practitioner/client relations, set achievement targets and performance indicators. In these ways organizational objectives regulate and replace occupational control of the practitioner/ client work interactions thereby limiting the exercise of discretion and preventing the service ethic that has been so important in professional work.

In contemporary societies we seem to be witnessing the development of two different (and in many ways contrasting) forms of professionalism in knowledge-based, service-sector work: organizational and occupational professionalism (see Table 2.1). As an ideal-type *organizational professionalism* is a discourse of control used increasingly by managers in work organizations. It incorporates rational–legal forms of authority and hierarchical structures of responsibility and decision-making. It involves the increased standardization of work procedures and practices and managerialist controls. It relies on externalized forms of regulation and accountability measures such as target-setting and performance review. In contrast, and again as an ideal-type, *occupational professionalism* is a discourse constructed within professional occupational groups and incorporates collegial authority. It involves relations of practitioner trust from both employers and clients. It is based on autonomy and discretionary judgement and assessment by practitioners in complex cases. It depends on common and lengthy systems of education and vocational training and the development of strong occupational identities and work

Table 2.1 Two different forms of professionalism in knowledge-based work

Organizational professionalism	Occupational professionalsim
• discourse of control used increasingly by managers in work organizations	• discourse constructed within professional groups
• rational–legal forms of authority	• collegial authority
• standardized procedures	• discretion and occupational control of the work
• hierarchical structures of authority and decision-making	• practitioner trust by both clients and employers
• managerialism	• controls operationalized by practitioners
• accountability and externalized forms of regulation, target-setting and performance review	• professional ethics monitored by institutions and associations

cultures. Controls are operationalized by practitioners themselves who are guided by codes of professional ethics which are monitored by professional institutes and associations.

Organizational professionalism is clearly of relevance to the forms of public management currently being developed in educational institutions (schools and universities) and in UK National Health Service (NHS) hospitals and primary care practices. The appeal to professionalism can be seen as a powerful motivating force of control 'at a distance' (Miller and Rose 1990; Burchell *et al.* 1991). Essentially it is a form of inner-directed control or self-control where close managerial supervision is not required. Organizational professionalism will be achieved through increased occupational training and the certification of the workers/employees – a process labelled as credentialism by Collins (1979, 1981). In these cases the appeal to professionalism is a powerful mechanism for promoting occupational change and social control. The appeal to the discourse by managers in work organizations is to a myth or an ideology of professionalism (Evetts 2003), which includes aspects such as exclusive ownership of an area of expertise, autonomy and discretion in work practices and the occupational control of the work. But the reality of the professionalism that is actually involved is very different. The appeal to the discourse of professionalism by managers most often includes the substitution of organizational for professional values; bureaucratic, hierarchical and managerial controls rather than collegial relations; managerial and organizational objectives rather than client trust based on competencies and perhaps licensing; budgetary restrictions and financial rationalizations; the standardization of work practices rather than discretion; and performance targets, accountability and sometimes increased political controls.

The use of the discourse of professionalism is not confined to managers in work organizations. As a discourse of self-control it can also be interpreted as an ideology which enables self-motivation and sometimes even self-exploitation. Born (1995) illustrates this very well in her account of the world of French contemporary music practice. It is also clearly expressed in the work culture of artists, actors and musicians in general. Once self-defined as a *professional* artist, imposing time or other limits on one's efforts is rendered illegitimate. The expectations by self and others of the professional have no limits. For the professional, the needs and demands of pupils and students, audiences, patients, clients and customers become paramount. Professionals are expected and expect themselves to be committed, even to be morally involved in the work.

Consequences: trust, discretion, competence

What, then, are the consequences of the expansion of organizational professionalism for aspects of trust, discretion and competence which have been important in professional work. Or, alternatively, what is the significance of the increased use of professionalism as a managerial tool of occupational change and control for occupational and practitioner professionalism?

This chapter began with the contemporary paradox that the concepts of profession and professionalism are increasingly applied to work and workers in modern societies. Yet the conditions of trust, discretion and competence which historically have been deemed to be necessary for professional practice are continually being challenged or certainly changed. Does the increased use of the discourse of professionalism as a managerial instrument of occupational control mean the further decline of trust? Does the expansion of target setting and accountability mean competences can no longer be relied upon? As service and knowledge-based work expand, are professional occupational groups becoming less distinct and more like other organizational employees?

The notions of trust, competence and professionalism have been inextricably linked and interconnected. This was the case in the nineteenth century when the doctor, lawyer and clergyman, who were gentlemen, could be trusted as a result of their competence and experience to provide altruistic advice within a community of mutually dependent middle- and upper-class clients. Freidson (2001: 150) has drawn attention to the class-based nature of trust relations. This legacy, whether in fact or fiction, has provided a powerful image and incentive for many aspiring occupational groups throughout the twentieth century and helps to explain the appeal of the discourse of professionalism as a management tool.

The sociological literature on professions has also linked trust, competence, discretion and professionalism. Thus the education, training and in some cases the licence are achieved by means of a grounding or foundation in abstract concepts and followed by formal learning by experience or apprenticeship with a qualified practitioner. Once the knowledge, skill and competence are acquired then these can be applied in diverse and complex cases which necessitate the exercise of discretion. Freidson (2001: 34) has argued that the ideal-typical character of the knowledge and skill imputed to practitioners implies that they control their own work. Fox (1974: 26–35) showed in industrial work that the right of discretion implied being trusted, being committed, even being morally involved in one's work and Freidson has added (2001: 34) that 'externally imposed rules governing work are minimized' in ideal-typical professional work.

The linking of trust, competence and professionalism continues to be part of popular discourse despite a number of recent challenges to the image in the UK arising particularly from medical and legal negligence and malpractice scandals and, in the Dr Harold Shipman case in Britain, the criminal conviction of mass murder for a general practitioner doctor. However, the association of trust, competence and professionalism is now being questioned. Can we trust our public services or the people who work in them? It seems that increasingly doctors, lawyers, scientists and many others are treated with suspicion. The words of politicians and businessmen are doubted and their motives questioned. An increasingly litigious culture, fuelled by knowledge of large financial gains from negligence cases in the USA, is further undermining trust and professionalism. A related difficulty is that the suggested solution – of making professionals and service institutions such as schools and hospitals more accountable – is in fact a part of the problem in that complex systems of accountability and audit actually damage trust and reduce the time practitioners can spend with clients.

So what precisely has changed and, in particular, how is professionalism being changed in public service occupations and professions in organizational contexts? The idea of a 'new' professionalism is probably too simplistic since there are aspects of continuity as well as of change. Certainly professionalism has undergone change which could be interpreted as the state's response to the political and financial problems posed by the high financial and fiscal costs of public services or as the state's response to the difficulties of controlling and managing sometimes powerful professional groups. Professionalism can be interpreted as a tool of government intended to promote commercialized professionalism (Hanlon 1998) and/or organizational professionalism. Certainly there are strong elements of hierarchy, bureaucracy, output and performance measures and even the standardization of work practices which are characteristic of organizational forms of control of work and workers.

In addition, when service sector professionals prove enduringly difficult to manage and resistant to change, then an important part of the strategy becomes to recreate professionals as managers and to manage by normative techniques. In fact, the measurement of and attempts to demonstrate professionalism actually increase the demand for explicit accounting of professional competences. The work organization's management demands for quality control and audit, target setting and performance review become reinterpreted as the promotion of professionalism. This quest for professionalism and accountability is highly competitive (Hoggett 1996) and individualistic (Broadbent *et al.* 1999) but it is also a bureaucratic means of regaining control of a market-directed enterprise staffed by professionals.

In numerous ways, centralizing, regulatory governments intent on demonstrating value from public service budgets seem to be redefining professionalism and accountability as measurable. The control of professionals in public services is to be achieved by means of normative values and self-regulated motivation. The discourse of enterprise is fitted alongside the language of quality and customer care and the ideologies of empowerment, innovation, autonomy and discretion. In addition, this is also a discourse of individualization and competition where individual performance is linked to the success or failure of the organization. These all constitute powerful mechanisms of worker/employee control in which the occupational values of professionalism are used to promote the efficient management of the organization.

The consequences of these changes and the increased emphasis on organizational professionalism are more difficult to determine and here the analysis becomes more speculative. It might be the case that increases in organizational professionalism and accountability will further accelerate the decline in public trust and perhaps also the erosion of professional norms, values and commitment. Certainly there are complicating factors that make a causal link difficult to establish. Complicating context factors include the demystification of aspects of professional knowledge and expertise; cases of practitioner malpractice and 'unprofessional' behaviour; media exaggeration and oversimplification, and political interference; large fee and salary increases in particular professional sectors (particularly medicine) and divisions between commercial (corporate clients) and social service (state-funded) practitioners; trade union activities or threats including withdrawal of services or actions short of a strike which can indicate self- rather than the public-interest.

The expansion of organizational professionalism is then one of a number of complicating factors. It can be stated, however, that organizational techniques for controlling employees have affected the work of practitioners in professional organizations. The imposition of targets in teaching and medical work – and indeed for the police (see Boussard 2006) – have had 'unintended' consequences on the prioritization and ordering of work activities, and a focus on target achievement to the detriment or neglect of other less-measurable tasks and responsibilities. Increased regulation and form filling takes time which might arguably be devoted to pupils, students, clients and the professional task. Performance indicators, linked to future salary increases, are defined by the organization rather than the individual practitioner. The standardization of work procedures, perhaps using software programmes, is an important check on the underachieving practitioner but can be a disincentive to the creative, innovative, and inspirational professional.

It is important to remember also that the way professionals regard their service work and their working relationships are also being changed and this is an important consequence of the redefining of professionalism as an occupational value. An emphasis on internal as well as external markets, on enterprise and economic contracting, are changing professionalism. In tendering, accounting and audit management – professionalism requires practitioners to codify their competence for contracts and evaluations (du Gay and Salaman 1992; Lane 2000; Freidson 2001). 'Professional work is defined as service products to be marketed, price-tagged and individually evaluated and remunerated; it is, in that sense, commodified' (Svensson and Evetts 2003: 11). Professional service work organizations are converting into enterprises in terms of identity, hierarchy and rationality. Possible solutions to client problems and difficulties are defined by the organization (rather than the ethical codes of the professional institution) and limited by financial constraints.

The commodification of professional service work entails changes in professional work relations. When practitioners become organizational employees then the traditional relationship of employer/professional trust is changed to one necessitating supervision, assessment and audit. In turn, this affects the relations between fellow practitioners in the organization. When individual performance (e.g. of pupils and teachers, GPs and consultants) is linked to the success or failure of the organization, then this amplifies the impact of any failure. The danger in this is that professional cohesion and mutual cooperation are undermined and competition can threaten both team working and collegial support.

Relationships between professionals and clients are also being converted into customer relations through the establishment of quasi-markets, customer satisfaction surveys and evaluations, quality measures and payment by results. The production, publication and diffusion of quality and target measurements are critical indicators for changing welfare services into a market (Considine 2001). The service itself is focused, modelled on equivalents provided by other producers, shaped by the interests of the consumers and standardized. The marketing of a service organization's service product connects professionals more to their work organization than to their professional institutions and associations. Clients are converted into customers and professional work competencies become primarily related to, and defined and assessed by, the work organization.

As yet there is little firm research evidence on the links and connections between these factors and key and critical research questions need examination. The increased emphasis on professionalism in work and for workers in modern societies would obviously need to be demonstrated, not just assumed. It is also important to examine whether or not, in what ways and for which practitioners, relationships of trust, discretion and competence are being challenged and if so by whom. A related point would then be to consider to what extent trust relationships between practitioners and clients are being replaced by organizational forms of regulation such as hierarchy, bureaucracy, managerialism, target-setting, accountability and market forms of customer relations. Who is setting the targets could be a strong marker, indication or test that would indicate the construction of professionalism 'from above' rather than 'from within' the occupational group. Further questions would then need to be asked. Are we witnessing a decline in the value of professional expertise as a result of the increased availability of knowledge on the Internet? Can trust be restored by making practitioners and institutions more accountable? Or do complex systems of accountability and control themselves damage trust? And perhaps most important: how important is trust anyway in the case of knowledge-based service sector workers and experts in modern democracies with complex divisions of labour?

References

Abbott, A. (1988) *The System of Professions: an essay on the division of expert labour*, Chicago, IL: University of Chicago Press.

Born, G. (1995) *Rationalizing Culture: IRCAM, Boulez and the institutionalization of the musical avant-garde*, Berkeley, CA: University of California Press.

Boussard, V. (2006) 'Performance measurement with French national police and professional destabilization'. Paper presented at ISA World Congress, RC 52, session 1, Durban, South Africa.

Broadbent, J., Jacobs, K. and Laughlin, R. (1999) 'Comparing schools in the UK and New Zealand', *Management Accounting Research*, 10: 339–361.

Buchner-Jeziorska, A. (2001) 'Price of knowledge: the market of intellectual work in Poland in the 90s'. Paper presented in Professions Network of SASE Conference, Amsterdam, 28 June–1 July 2001.

—— and Evetts, J. (1997) 'Regulating professionals: the Polish example', *International Sociology*, 12 (1): 61–72.

Burchell, G., Gordon, C. and Miller. P. (eds) (1991) *The Foucault Effect: studies in governmentality*, Hemel Hempstead: Harvester Wheatsheaf.

Carr-Saunders, A. M. and Wilson, P. A. (1933) *The Professions*, Oxford: Clarendon Press.

Collins, R. (1979) *The Credential Society: an historical sociology of education and stratification*, New York: Academic Press.

—— (1981) 'Crises and declines in credential systems', in R. Collins *Sociology Since Midcentury: essays in theory cumulation*, New York: Academic Press.

Considine, M. (2001) *Enterprising States: the public management of welfare-to-work*, Cambridge: Cambridge University Press.

Dingwall, R. and Lewis, P. (eds) (1983) *The Sociology of the Professions: lawyers, doctors and others*, London: Macmillan.

du Gay, P. and Salaman, G. (1992) 'The cult[ure] of the customer', *Journal of Management Studies*, 29 (5): 615–633.

Evetts, J. (2003) 'The sociological analysis of professionalism: occupational change in the modern world', *International Sociology*, 18 (2): 395–415.

Fournier, V. (1999) 'The appeal to "professionalism" as a disciplinary mechanism', *Social Review*, 47 (2): 280–307.

Fox, A. (1974) *Beyond Contract: work, power and trust relationships*, London: Faber & Faber.

Freidson, E. (2001) *Professionalism: the third logic*, London: Polity Press.

Frenkel, S., Korczynski, M., Donoghue, L. and Shire, K. (1995) 'Re-constituting work: trends towards knowledge work and info-normative control', *Work, Employment and Society*, 9 (4): 773–796.

Hanlon, G. (1998) 'Professionalism as enterprise: service class politics and the redefinition of professionalism', *Sociology*, 32: 43–64.

Hiremath, S. L. and Gudagunti, R. (1998) 'Professional commitment among Indian executives'. Paper presented at ISA Congress Montreal, 26 July–1 August 1998.

Hoggett, P. (1996) 'New modes of control in the public services', *Public Administration*, 74: 9–32.

Johnson, T. (1972) *Professions and Power*, London: Macmillan.

Lane, J. E. (2000) *New Public Management*, London: Routledge & Kegan Paul.

Larkin, G. (1983) *Occupational Monopoly and Modern Medicine*, London: Tavistock.

Larson, M. S. (1977) *The Rise of Professionalism*, California: University of California Press.

Lyotard, J. F. (1984) *The Post-Modern Condition: a report on knowledge*, Manchester: Manchester University Press.

McClellend, C. E. (1990) 'Escape from freedom? Reflections on German profession-alization 1870–1933', in R. Torstendahl and M. Burrage (eds) *The Formation of Professions: knowledge, state and strategy*, London: Sage.

Marshall, T. H. (1950) *Citizenship and Social Class and Other Essays*, Cambridge: Cambridge University Press.

Miller, P. and Rose, N. (1990) 'Governing economic life', *Economy and Society*, 19 (1): 1–31.

Perkin, H. (1988) *The Rise of Professional Society*, Routledge: London.

Parsons, T. (1939) 'The professions and social structure', *Social Forces*, 17: 457–467.

Reed, M. (1996) 'Expert power and control in late modernity: an empirical review and theoretical synthesis', *Organization Studies*, 17 (4): 573–597.

Saks, M. (1995) *Professions and the Public Interest*, London: Routledge.

Sautu, R. (1998) 'The effect of the marketization of the Argentine economy on the labor market: shifts in the demand for university trained professionals'. Paper presented at ISA Congress, Montreal, 26 July–1 Aug.

Svensson, L. G. and Evetts, J. (eds) (2003) *Conceptual and Comparative Studies of Continental and Anglo-American Professions*, Goteborg Studies in Sociology No. 129, Goteborg: Goteborg University.

Tawney, R. H. (1921) *The Acquisitive Society*, New York: Harcourt Brace.

3 Professional ethics
Whose responsibility?

Alan Cribb

In this chapter I am working around two themes. First, I am exploring some descriptive and explanatory questions about professional ethics – including questions about the ways in which the ethical positions and sensibilities associated with certain occupational roles are created, sustained or transformed. Second, I am interested in some substantive ethical questions about how professionals *ought* to comport themselves and, in particular, in the question of how far our ethical stances are and ought to be defined by the roles we occupy. The first two sections of the chapter correspond, in large part, to these two themes. In the third section of the chapter I will sketch in some further exemplification of these themes, and their interactions, and in so doing highlight the central importance of role construction to professional ethics. My core purpose is to direct attention to the ways in which responsibility for professional ethics belongs with those *involved in role construction* and not just those *acting within roles*.[1] I will draw on examples from both education and healthcare.

The construction and re-construction of professional ethics

For most of this discussion I will not make any distinction between 'professional ethics' and 'occupational ethics' – that is the focus is the ethics of work roles and I am using the language of professional ethics to cover a very wide field.[2] However, it is impossible not to acknowledge the association between the ideology of professionalism and ideas of ethical distinctiveness. Professions are often deemed to be distinct from other occupations because professional cultures and modes of organization are taken to underwrite high technical and ethical standards. Different professions are also sometimes deemed to be ethically distinct from one another because they are each organized around particular sets of goods and virtues. For example, Daryl Koehn's (1994) influential defence of professional legitimacy (and hence of the basis of client trust) is based upon the public commitment of professionals to serve specific goods – in the case of doctors, for instance to serve the needs of the sick. That is, in the normal course of things, we have a reasonable expectation that when we go to see a doctor they will not only serve us but also that they will attend to us in a particular way, responding to particular signs and aiming at particular goods. Connected to this expectation, doctors have a number of distinctive powers and permissions (obviously subject to various conditions and consents) to do with access to and use of drugs, privacy, the body and so on. Many interventions that are entirely acceptable for a doctor would be inappropriate and sometimes straightforwardly unethical for a lawyer or accountant. Different kinds of roles might thus be said to occupy different ethical positions. It is this sort of ethical differentiation between roles at work (not only between occupational roles but also within occupational roles, for example, differences within a team of nurses or teachers) that I am primarily interested in here, rather than the general issue of professional demarcation – the issue of whether 'professionals' are somehow ethically special.

In healthcare one way in which the idea of role-specific ethics has been debated is in relation to the proliferation of healthcare ethics sub-disciplines: is nursing ethics something different from medical ethics? Do we need a discipline of pharmacy ethics, or psychiatric ethics (for example, see Crowden 2003) and so on? These questions obviously correspond closely to questions about the ethical positioning of individual health professionals. The question about the role-relative perspectives of medicine and nursing is the most widely discussed. It has been argued, amongst other things, that nursing is organized around a rationale of caring whereas the organizational rationale of medicine is curing. And allied to this rationale, it seems plausible to suggest, is a rather different ethical sensibility and agency.[3] It is tempting, and a valuable heuristic, to ask analogous questions of the teaching profession – such as who are the 'doctors' and 'nurses' in teaching, how are analogous role distinctions defined and how are they evolving? Many kinds of analysis are made in this context: relevant academic work is undertaken, for instance, on power and hierarchies, gender and gendered roles, professional distance and emotional labour, and on 'the ethics of care' and feminist approaches to ethics. I will not attempt to review these extensive literatures here, just underline their importance to my theme.

Another line of work that has been used to illuminate questions of role-specific ethics is MacIntyre's (1994) account of 'practices' in *After Virtue*. MacIntyre deploys the notion of 'a practice' to point to those sets of activities that embody and realize 'internal goods', that is goods that are embedded within and bound to certain practices as opposed to those 'external goods' (for example, income or status) that can be derived from a range of activities and can be pursued to some degree instrumentally and independently from the things that make activities intrinsically worth doing. Various authors have borrowed this idea to discuss particular professions, including both nursing and teaching (for example, Sellman 2000; Higgins 2003), as 'practices' (in a manner somewhat reminiscent of the idea of a 'vocation'). This device, albeit perhaps a crude one, of separating out intrinsic and extrinsic goods also allows analysts to distinguish between those things that serve institutional or policy goals and those things that are, to put it sentimentally, close to the heart of a professional practice. A teacher may, for example, talk a little longer to a distressed student or follow a line of discussion far outside the boundaries of the official curriculum, because these things are worth doing irrespective of whether or not they contribute to, or detract from, institutional performance indicators.

However, although this idea of 'a practice' can be illuminating there is a danger of it being used in a way that slides into ahistorical essentializing. Teaching roles evolve and so do the sets of goods and virtues embodied in teaching. In general it is important to see professional ethics as something that is socially constructed.[4] The history, professional traditions and evolving policy context of teaching, and the many factors that influence these things, shape and re-shape the ethics of teaching.

Recognition of the social construction of professional ethics, in this case teaching ethics, also enables analyses and critiques of educational change. In earlier work I have, along with colleagues, considered some of the effects of change on professional ethics in both healthcare and education (Cribb 1999, 2001; Molloy and Cribb 1999; Cribb and Gewirtz 2002; Cribb and Ball 2005). Here I will simply summarize one element of this work; namely some concerns about the possible effects of marketization/managerialism on professional ethics in the UK public sector. Anecdotal evidence, critical writing and qualitative research studies illuminate a whole range of ethically important issues around the changing construction of professional roles, relations and subjectivities in a climate of devolved budgets, institutional competition and increased public sector 'entrepreneurship'. These claimed changes arise directly from the ways in which managerialism and elements of marketization/privatization are expressly designed to 'reconfigure' institutional norms, and professional cultures and subjectivities.

The springs of these effects include: (a) the use of mechanisms of institutional loyalty and rivalry as means of incentivization, and the growing importance of institutional success independently of the quality of learning or 'clinical success'; (b) the accompanying pressure to 'impression manage' and pay attention to institutional image and public relations; (c) the new weight attached to performance indicators, quality indices and league tables; (d) the growth of budget consciousness, and the decrease in the insulation between professional practices and accountancy practices.

These processes have given rise to more or less deep-seated concerns about, for example:

(i) The penetration of 'accounting logic' (Broadbent and Loughlin 1997) into professional subjectivities and practices. This includes concerns about the intensification of the commodification processes that occur in professional work, but more generally a worry about an increase in narrow forms of instrumentalism or reductionist thinking. This has also been written about as a shift from more 'substantive' to more 'technical' forms of rationality (Yeatman 1987) – from more open-ended, 'thicker', contested and intrinsic modes of determining education and healthcare goods, to narrower and more extrinsic preoccupation with what is 'deemed to count', for example, in institutional performance indicators.

(ii) A reduction in collaborative or collegial working across and between institutions as a result of the structures and cultures of competition/ institutional comparison.

(iii) The creation of false or distorted priorities as artefacts of the systems of performance indicators that feed into institutional funding and comparison – including examples of 'ritual practices', encounters between professionals and 'clients' designed to affect performance indicators rather than to provide actual benefit.

(iv) The stimulation of various forms of 'cheating' for the same reason, for example, there are reports of institutions enhancing activity levels at times when they are being measured and some reports of institutions simply fiddling or fixing the figures.

(v) The growth of 'glossification' (Gewirtz *et al.* 1995), that is, institutions investing their resources and efforts on producing a surface 'gloss' for reasons of impression management, where, once again, this may not benefit (or may even detract from) the quality of service they provide.

In reviewing these concerns here I should stress that I do not want to suggest that a former period of 'pure' professional ethics has now been replaced by developments that corrode or undermine professional ethics. There is no doubt that all systems of organization and cultural climates shape professional roles, subjectivities and the possibilities of professional ethics. There are, of course, advocates of marketization/managerialism who defend them precisely in terms of their beneficial effects on professional cultures and because of the ways they foster professional responsibility in general or 'modernized virtues' in particular. Furthermore, many of the other reforms that have taken place in recent years – the growth of new professional philosophies or new professional roles – have analogous effects on professional roles (that is, they constrain or construct professional subjectivities and agency), and there is no reason to dismiss them all as forms of 'corruption'.

There is a problem in knowing what stories to tell here. There are simple, and sometimes plausible, stories of 'practices' or vocations being corrupted or destroyed, and of the *raison d'être* of certain roles being obscured or displaced by the narrowing and hardening of institutional norms. There are other, sometimes plausible, stories of professional roles evolving or being transformed and of the creation of *new* ethical positions and orientations. As always these generalizations need to be considered and combined on a case-by-case basis. But in order even to begin to make these discriminations there are some substantive ethical problems related to the idea of role-related ethics that need addressing.

'Doing my job': the division of ethical labour

What follows, ethically speaking, from the fact that there is an expectation attached to my occupational role that I will do such-and-such? In some instances we are inclined to answer, 'nothing very much'. We are rightly very wary of the 'only doing my job' response to appeals for ethical account- ability. It does not follow from the fact that my employer expects me to lie and cheat that it is right to lie and cheat. As well as having 'role agency' we have (some degree of) independent ethical agency. On the other hand work roles do seem to have *some* claim upon our ethical agency. If we assume a role such as being a teacher or a doctor we become part of a demanding and complex set of accountabilities to profession, colleagues, institutions and so on that has a prima facie claim on what we do. We may exercise conscientious objection to involvement in certain activities but surely we cannot entirely float above the network of obligations in which we have immersed ourselves. In short, much of the time we exercise our independent ethical agency partly *through* role agency. The examples I gave in the previous section suggest that ethics is interpreted differently from different vantage points; the question I am interested in now is whether it *ought* to be.

Before going on I should perhaps spell out the relevance and importance, in relation to the previous discussion, of this question about the ethical force of occupational roles. It is relevant in a number of respects but two illustrations will suffice. First, if a professional role is reshaped such that new professional or institutional obligations are inserted into it (for example, if a nurse or teacher is required to show improvement on some performance indicator) when should we describe this as reorienting ethics and when as eroding ethics? In other words, when and how do institutional and professional obligations actually amount to ethical obligations? Second, when should we embrace the demands of our occupational roles even when they require us to do things that we might otherwise regard as ethically questionable, see as incompatible with our own vocational vision or even object to in principle? I am sure that this is a question close enough to everyone's hearts not to need exemplifying. These questions about the claims of role-specific ethics are entangled with fundamental debates in personal ethics, professional ethics and ethical theory. Even if I was capable of shedding genuine light on each of these things I could not say much about them within the confines of this chapter, but I can sketch in some relevant considerations.

To start with, I would want to defend the contention, rehearsed in the first part of this chapter, that different roles occupy different positions in ethical space and that in this and other senses ethics is, and ought to be, role- relative. (Yes, there are some important qualifications to be made here also but I am not dwelling on these.) This point is sometimes made through an extended analogy with advocacy in law (see especially Applbaum 2000). Here we see a paradigm case of agents with a responsibility to support individuals about whose character and actions they have grave doubts and whose testimony they may find less than convincing. More precisely, advocacy entails a willingness not just to adopt 'the big picture', not to act entirely impartially, but to exercise socially sanctioned (and reasonable) partiality (Almond 2005) to one's client. To do one's ethical duty as an advocate can require you to do things that you might shy away from and regard as unethical outside of your professional role. This may seem like an exceptional case but the more we reflect upon it the more the continuities with a wide range of professional roles come into view. Professional roles are by their nature very often exercises in partiality of one kind or another. Again Koehn's (1994) analysis of professional ethics highlights this feature by placing the professional's special duties to their clients (e.g. 'my patients', 'my students') at the centre of her account. Indeed this idea of 'reasonable partiality' is at the centre of Nagel's (1991) brilliantly insightful analysis of *all* ethics.

For Nagel, ethics is about the continuous reconciliation of the standpoints of impartiality and partiality (within the individual, within institutions and within society at large). Although the standpoint of impartiality is definitive of ethics, it cannot be approached or practiced independently from a concern with partiality (e.g. if we want to treat the children in our family fairly we cannot do so by being blind to their individual interests, projects, commitments and relationships; quite the opposite – we need to take these things very seriously. And although fairness might involve some compromises and negotiations about these things it is certainly not about erasing them as ethically irrelevant). Nagel's account also illuminates the limitations of relying on individual motivation and capability in the pursuit of impartiality – what is needed, as in the case of advocacy, are institutional checks and balances that aim for 'global' impartiality whilst individuals do what they can in their own sphere. Hence we need what I am calling the division of ethical labour.[5]

This provides an overarching account of one dimension of the role-relative nature of occupational ethics. Advocates have a specific ethical orientation, judges have a different one, and we are all of us, some of the time, more or less like advocates or like judges depending upon what role we are operating in. If we add to this the points made above about different professions being organized around different goods and virtues, and being invested with different powers and permissions etc., then we have a reason to accept that different institutional and occupational roles *are* ethically different. What follows from this, I would argue, is that professionals cannot easily distinguish between their institutional and professional obligations and their ethical obligations pure and simple. That is to say, there can be good ethically relevant reasons to support the overall purposes of, and therefore functioning of, professions or institutions. Of course it does not follow from this that all institutional and professional obligations are ethical obligations. But in many instances there are prima facie reasons to align our ethical compass, to some degree, to directions defined by our roles. We are, as noted above, more or less immersed in, and not entirely 'above', our occupational roles.

The dilemmas associated with this analysis are very familiar ones. For example, those of us who work in higher education are accustomed to the importance of collegial working and also to the importance of sustaining the institutions of higher education. Much of the time this generates in us a disposition to take the 'bigger picture' of department or college seriously and to acknowledge some degree of ethical duty to work for these wider ends. At the same time we are conscious of the constant pressures from our employing institutions to perform in all manner of ways that we can find distasteful; with these pressures underpinned by some vague reference to the overall good. The resulting dilemmas are both chronic and serious because the exact ethical claims of our roles remain somewhat obscure. There is no simple translation between institutional obligations and ethical obligations, between 'doing my job' and 'doing the right thing'.[6] So, as well as explicitly wrestling with these dilemmas, we often find ourselves living with and working through ambivalences and resorting to ironic role distancing in order to manage the pervasive dissonances. This takes me back to some of the concerns listed at the end of the previous section about the potentially corrosive ethical effects of public sector restructuring, a topic that I don't want to explore directly any further here. Rather I will just say a little more about the underlying, the more fundamental, puzzle about roles and ethics.

We are not consumed by our roles. In any case we have a range of role-identities, and we can also speak of our role as 'citizens' or more abstractly as members of the overall moral community (however we delineate that). Thus it is always possible to stand both outside as well as within specific occupational roles or other social roles. As is characteristic of ethics, there are longstanding and plausible theoretical arguments – as well as personal inclinations – for both embracing and (partly) insulating ourselves from role-related ethical viewpoints. Julia Annas (2002), for example, sets out the way this issue was debated and determined by the Stoics. As she argues, ethics 'is never fully captured by fulfilling a given function or performing the duties of a given social role alone'. However Annas also directs our attention to the justified importance that the Stoics place upon 'our station and its duties', and their scepticism about attempts to evade our 'entrapment' by roles, attempts that may merely represent ethical failure of another hue – 'arrogance', 'vain ostentation', 'romantic self-importance':

> Trying radically to reform society . . . risks hopeless impracticality, or getting your priorities wrong if you run away from your commitments to do something grand in the name of virtue. . . . To abandon your family responsibilities in favour of doing good to more people, for example, is romantic self-importance. Stoic morality makes the harder demand, that you live the ideal in your mundane, ordinary life and make a difference there by the way you live it.
>
> (Annas 2002: 117, 120)

Once again I am not interested here in attempting to identify the correct balance that might be drawn in this balancing act. I am simply drawing attention to one side of the equation – the legitimate claim that (up to some indeterminate point) role-related ethical viewpoints and commitments have upon people in general and 'professionals' in particular.

Rethinking professional ethics

What I am arguing is that professional ethics should not be analysed or understood purely in relation to what individuals do *inside* professional roles but also – and at least as much – in relation to the ways in which roles are constructed. To put this another way and to exaggerate a little for effect: much of what is 'done' by professionals is done *by role construction* and is accomplished independently of, and so-to-speak 'before' individual professional agency kicks in. And, given that there is a prima facie reason to treat our occupational commitments with ethical seriousness, we cannot lightly dismiss the claims made upon us by changes in our roles; neither can we lightly dismiss all changes in workplace priorities, principles and cultures as ethical corrosion. We need an 'ethics of roles' – including an interest in discriminating between more or less ethically acceptable adaptations to, or extensions of, occupational roles.

There are a large number of goods at stake in public life in general and within the education and healthcare spheres specifically and not everyone can be responsible for delivering all of them. This is the basic justification for some kind of division of labour.[7] Mapping all of these goods, their interactions and their relation to the division of labour, would be absurdly complex. Here, for illustrative purposes, I can only very crudely map some axes of potential change in ethical positions in relation to professional roles in education and healthcare. I am assuming, following the discussion in the previous two sections, that ethical positions are in large measure generated through (evolving) professional traditions in interaction with (changing) policy and institutional contexts.

I am equating the ethical position of roles with the sets of goals and obligations embedded in them including the associated dispositions.[8] Evolving traditions and policies bring about changes of many kinds including, for example: in the salience of certain goals, in the nature and direction of obligations and in forms of agency. The example I used above of the possible impacts of managerialism is enough to illustrate changes to the salience of certain goals – that is, in this instance, the possibility that performance targets, tied so closely to the imperatives of institutional success, become ends in themselves and potentially distort or erase other (richer) conceptions of success. Elsewhere I have also used the example of privatization to raise questions about the effects of possible changes in the nature and direction of obligations when school staff have obligations to private sponsors or partners of various kinds which need to be weighed against, or somehow combined with, the obligations to pupils, parents, local communities and local authorities (Cribb and Ball 2005). (There is also the closely linked question of what is gained and/or lost with a shift in emphasis towards 'enterprise virtues' rather than 'teacherly virtues'.) Shifts in goals and/or obligations – as these examples suggest – can also overlap with shifts in the degree of relative autonomy experienced by, and exercised by, teachers, that is the extent to which they are able to choose and therefore to own the things they do. By talk of changes to 'forms of agency' I mean to include such changes in relative autonomy, but also to signal the extent to which professionals are expected to act as 'delegatees' or 'delegators', and the extent to which and ways in which they are expected to act in teams and/or 'interprofessionally'.

To help further specify and articulate potential changes in ethical positions I suggest it may be useful to consider any change against the following four 'value axes':

A Degree of impartiality – whose good is centre stage? How far is the focus of actions individuals or 'groups'/'publics'?
B Degree of impersonality – how far is the focus on 'subjectivity' (meanings, experiences, perceptions) rather than on non-subjective 'measurable' factors (for example, exam performance, attendance rates)?
C Degree of instrumentalism – how far are actions designed to causally bring about desirable outcomes; how far are they processes and relationships which are intrinsically related to well-being or flourishing?
D Degree of specialization – how far is the scope of attention and responsibility circumscribed around specific kinds of ends or goods? Or how far is it – in various senses – more generalist or 'holistic'?

In case there is any doubt I should stress that I do not want to valorise one end of any of these axes over the other. As rehearsed above, the division of ethical labour requires that different roles place stress in different areas (and in practice many roles will be hybrid ones with a shifting focus, although they will still represent a 'patterned' set of emphases). For example, a senior teacher working with colleagues on budget management issues will, in that respect, be working on a relatively impersonal and instrumental (as well as relatively specialist and impartial) agenda. Whereas a special needs practitioner working in a classroom setting will have a role frequently involving much more emphasis on the personal, the partial and with strong elements of non-instrumentalism and generalism. These two cases are enough to illustrate the fact that teachers' roles can change in a range of directions. Attempts to evaluate the ethical effects of teachers' role construction thus need not only to consider specific roles but also the effects of the combination and balance of roles.

I can illustrate the relevance of these axes by briefly rehearsing a concern that has been expressed about the changing ethical positioning of (some) ward nurses – namely that there is a danger of them 'distancing' themselves from patients.[9] There are two main components to this worry. It is partly a concern about the 'medicalization' of nursing – with more nurse diagnosis, prescribing and clinical intervention more generally shifting some nurses towards the instrumentalist and specialist ends of the spectrum with a potential erosion of their responsiveness to subjective well-being or more general health and comfort needs. And allied to this is a concern about the increasing 'separation' of nurses from patients by the growth in numbers of healthcare assistants. Of course, closely analogous questions arise in education, where there are continuously negotiated tensions between different conceptions of the goals of education: the correct balance between the pastoral, the academic, the vocational and the civic dimensions of teaching; the relative emphases to be placed on discipline-centred and student-centred philosophies in different settings, subjects and stages; and the proper division of labour between the classroom teacher and teaching assistants, and so on. Once again – to stick with the single issue of 'distance' – there is not necessarily an inherent ethical problem with some roles being constructed in a way that makes for 'distance'. Rather the question is what is the best balance of 'more distant' and 'closer' roles? And, looking across the division of ethical labour, how can we best analyse the ethics of teams or interprofessional ethics, and apply ethical judgements to collective, constrained or delegated agency? These issues are getting some attention within the field of healthcare ethics (Irvine, Kerridge and McPhee 2004; Dowling *et al.* 1996) but they also have considerable relevance to education and other occupational domains.

Conclusion

I should start by repeating and underlining the fact that there is no clear link between 'doing my job' and 'doing the right thing'. Very often there will be overriding ethical reasons for resisting work-role pressures. In many other cases, we might simultaneously accept an obligation to conform while using our individual and collective efforts to redefine and redraw these same role commitments. Nonetheless, there are also some good reasons for taking the demands of our occupational roles seriously, and these are not merely pragmatic reasons but are – at least in many cases – ethical reasons.[10] Roughly speaking, roles make a contribution to the broader sets of goods served by institutions and thus can legitimately require some degree of accommodation from role holders. Furthermore, role occupancy can – up to a point – provide good ethical reasons for doing things, or adopting standpoints that we might otherwise (that is, outside the role) find unacceptable. This is because roles contribute to a necessary division of ethical labour, with not everyone equally responsible for securing or enacting the global set of goods and virtues.

For any individual, the claims of their professional roles generate countless dilemmas and balancing acts which they have to find ways, hopefully with the help of colleagues, of managing. More fundamentally, I have argued that the recognition of the role-relative nature of ethics calls for new approaches to professional ethics. In particular, ethical analyses need to focus as much on role construction as on role occupancy, and ethics education needs to illuminate the ways in which ethical positions are embedded in occupational roles. At the individual and inter-personal levels, this should support professional reflexivity. At the level of professions, it provides an opportunity to examine the overall defensibility of the particular division of ethical labour in place.

Notes

1 Of course these two sets of agents overlap. To a certain extent we all shape the contours and possibilities of our roles from within.
2 For a debate about the putative distinctiveness of professional ethics see Christopher Winch's (2002) penetrating response to David Carr.
3 For one relatively early and typical exploration of this issue, see Hull (1980).
4 This does not relate in any simple way to the worthwhileness of the things that are constructed. As Searle (1995) points out, the value of a bank note is not changed by the recognition that currencies are socially constructed; rather currencies are a way of manifesting value. I would argue that, roughly speaking, the same is true for ethics – just as we have to make 'shelters' and do so from imperfect materials, we have to make ethics.
5 Nagel actually uses the expression 'moral division of labour' to refer to the overall agenda of achieving a balance between the two standpoints; 'To design institutions which serve an ideal of egalitarian impartiality without demanding a too extensive impartiality of the individuals who occupy instrumental roles in these institutions is the great unsolved problem of egalitarian political theory' (1991: 61). Applbaum (op. cit.) uses the expression 'ethical division of labor' to refer to precisely what I am interested in here, namely role-relative ethics – although his main argument is to show the limits of appeals to role position as a justification of what would otherwise be unacceptable practices. My focus is much more on what goes on *within* those limits. (I also have chosen the expression 'division of ethical labour' to refer to the way ethics is divided up as opposed to whether labour is divided up ethically – see Cribb 2005.)
6 Luban (1988) argues that there are four steps separating these things: Can we ethically justify the institution? Can we ethically defend the nature of the role (given this institution)? Can we justify this specific set of role obligations (given this role)? Can we justify this particular act (given these role obligations)? This model helps to explain the obscurity of the connection.
7 Of course we can stand back from the distinction between healthcare and education and ask about the cluster of developmental and well-being-related goods which are served in *both* healthcare and education and the inexact and overlapping division of labour between the two spheres – for example, early years work, pastoral work, patient education.
8 Where 'obligations' is being used in a very broad way to encompass corresponding powers and entitlements, and forms and directions of accountability. And where goals and obligations tend to give rise to, and be supported by (roughly) corresponding disposition sets.
9 To properly appraise the validity of this concern would require a substantial empirical and theoretical research programme. I am just rehearsing it here for illustrative purposes.
10 In the first four sentences of this paragraph (and throughout) I am attempting to draw a line between the acceptance of ethics as role-relative and the adoption of a more epistemological form of ethical relativism. While acknowledging that this is a philosophically complex subject, and while noting that there is a risk of a slide from practical relativity to epistemological relativism, I do not think

such a slide is inevitable. In crude terms, I want to affirm that the consideration of someone's role obligations is a necessary part of determining what he or she ('objectively') ought to do in specific circumstances.

References

Almond, B. (2005) 'Reasonable partiality in professional relations', *Ethical Theory and Moral Practice*, 8 (1): 155–168.

Annas, J. (2002) 'My station and its duties: ideals and the social embeddedness of virtue', *Proceedings of the Aristotelian Society*, 14 Jan, London.

Applbaum, A. I. (2000) *Ethics for Adversaries: the morality of roles in public and professional life*, New Jersey: Princeton University Press.

Broadbent, J. and Loughlin, R. (1997) '"Accounting logic" and controlling professionals: the case of the public sector', in J. Broadbent, M. Dietrich and J. Roberts (eds) *The End of the Professions?* London: Routledge.

Cribb, A. (1999) 'League tables, institutional success and professional ethics', *Journal of Medical Ethics*, 25: 413–417.

—— (2001) 'Reconfiguring professional ethics: the rise of managerialism and public health in the UK National Health Service', *HEC Forum*, 13 (2): 125–131.

—— (2005) *Health and the Good Society*, Oxford: Oxford University Press.

—— and Gewirtz, S. (2002) 'Values and schooling', in J. Dillon and M. Maguire (eds), *Becoming a Teacher*, Buckingham: Open University Press.

—— and Ball, S. (2005) 'Towards an ethical audit of the privatisation of education', *British Journal of Educational Studies*, 53 (2): 115–128.

Crowden A (2003) 'Ethically sensitive mental health care: is there a need for a unique ethics for psychiatry?' *Australian and New Zealand Journal of Psychiatry*, 37: 143–149.

Dowling, S., Martin, R., Skidmore, P., Doyal, L. Cameron, A. and Lloyd, S. (1996) 'Nurses taking on junior doctors' work: a confusion of accountability', *BMJ*, 312: 1211–1214.

Gewirtz, S., Ball, S. and Bowe, R. (1995) *Markets, Choice and Equity in Education*, Buckingham: Open University Press.

Higgins, C. (2003) 'MacIntyre's moral theory and the possibility of an aretaic ethics of teaching', *Journal of Philosophy of Education*, 37 (2): 279–292.

Hull, R. T. (1980) 'Defining nursing ethics apart from medical ethics', *Kansas Nurse* 5 (8): 20–24.

Irvine, R., Kerridge, I. and McPhee, J. (2004) 'Towards a dialogical ethics of interprofessionalism', *Journal of Postgraduate Medicine*, 50 (4): 278–280.

Koehn, D. (1994) *The Ground of Professional Ethics*, London: Routledge.

Luban, D. (1988) *Lawyers and Justice*, New Jersey: Princeton University Press.

MacIntyre, A. (1994) *After Virtue*, London: Duckworth.

Molloy, J. and Cribb, A. (1999) 'Changing values for nursing and health promotion: exploring the policy context of professional ethics', *Nursing Ethics*, 6 (5): 411–422.

Nagel, T. (1991) *Equality and Partiality*, Oxford: Oxford University Press.

Searle, J. R. (1995) *The Construction of Social Reality*, New York: Free Press.

Sellman, D. (2000) 'Alasdair MacIntyre and the professional practice of nursing', *Nursing Philosophy*, 1: 26–33.

Winch, C. (2002) 'Work, well–being and vocational education: the ethical significance of work and preparation for work', *Journal of Applied Philosophy*, 19 (3): 261–271.

Yeatman, A. (1987) 'The concept of public management and the Australian state in the 1980s', *Australian Journal of Public Administration*, XLVI (4): 334–353.

4 Elusive publics

Knowledge, power and public service reform

John Clarke and Janet Newman

This chapter draws on a research project on the relationship between images of citizens as consumers and the reform of public services in the UK.[1] We explore how 'the public' represents a problematic subject for public services and their reform (Newman 2005a). It is shape shifting, unstable and unpredictable. It embodies conflicting or ambivalent desires and doubts. This view of the public challenges accounts of public service reform that explain it as an adaptation to a more individualized or consumerist public (Office for Public Service Reform 2002) or as the creation of a more marketized set of relationships between state and citizens (Marquand 2004). In such accounts – whether enthusiastic or critical – changes towards marketized, privatized or consumerist orientations in public services are largely seen to be driven by forces beyond the national level: globalization or neo-liberalism, for example (Clarke 2004). However, our study suggested that national political projects and forces play a decisive role in shaping public service reform, not least in translating international policy and political discourses into national settings. This suggests the need for some care in 'trend spotting' in public service reform, in particular not assuming that processes of reform sharing similar orientations produce the same outcomes in different places.

At the same time, our study revealed that people using public services in England were reluctant to identify themselves as consumers or customers of public services. Respondents stressed identities as users of particular services (such as patients) or as members of publics or local communities (Clarke *et al*. 2007; Clarke and Newman 2007). This indicates something of the troublesome character of the public in relation to public services. Singular narratives of its changing identity at best obscure its recalcitrant and intractable tendencies. For us, understanding the complicated identifications of the public – and the multiple relationships to public services that they reflect – forms a critical focus for processes of public service reform, and for the place of public service professionalism within them. Professionalism has re-emerged as a central issue for debates about the further reform of public services in the UK, USA and Europe (Evetts, in this volume; see also Duyvendak *et al*. 2007; Freidson 2001).

Many of the pressures around public service professionalism have come to bear on – and are condensed in – what we have called the 'knowledge–power knot'. In this we follow Foucault in stressing the intimate, and mutually productive, relationship between forms of knowledge and modes of power. Professionalism's claim to distinctive forms of expertise seems to us to be an exemplary instance of the knowledge-power relationship. Our terminology here – linking knowledge and power in the image of a knot – is intended to convey a more tangled view of multiple threads, rather than a simple, stable and singular relationship between knowledge and power. In particular, we intend to draw attention to the ways in which multiple forms of knowledge contest dominant professional institutionalizations. We might put this crudely: people no longer believe – or are willing to accede to – the proposition that 'professionals know best'. In the process both the situational and wider social authority enjoyed by professionals (even public service professionals) has become more fragile or contingent. In exploring these issues and their implications for public service professionalism we have used the framing device of a diamond (see Figure 4.1).

The vertical axis (governmental–public) locates two of the primary sources of pressures or forces acting on professionals. Governments articulate views of reform; identify lines of social development; lay claim to particular conceptions of the public and how it is changing; and – of course – develop and administer policies for public services. In the UK, both Conservative and Labour Governments have announced themselves as the 'People's Champions' against the 'Producer Interest' (Clarke *et al.* 2007). At the other end of this axis, the public is also a complex entity. It is an 'imaginary unity' with which (some) people identify as, in our study, many people who used public services identified themselves as 'members of the public' in their relationship to public service use. But the public is also a highly differentiated entity – traversed by systems of inequality and differentiation that have been profoundly consequential for the politics, policies and practices of public services.

The horizontal axis relates more directly to the sites of professional formation in public services. Public service professionalism is formed at the conjunction of occupational and organizational dynamics (Evetts, this volume,

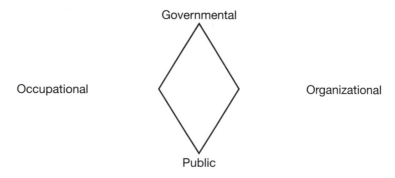

Figure 4.1 Framing knowledge/power knots

see also Johnson 1973, on the idea of 'mediating professions'). Each profession has distinctive occupational characteristics (resulting from training and both formal and informal modes of occupational socialization) and is enacted in particular organizational locations. Public service reform programmes, especially those shaped by the New Public Management, have involved struggles to unlock the power, prestige and autonomy associated with professionalism in state-based bureau-professional organizations. Managerialism involved an attempt to construct a new configuration of power along this organizational–occupational axis (Clarke and Newman 1997).

Conflicting imperatives

If we consider the logics that shape each of the four points, we might sketch three relatively clear concerns for the governmental, organizational and occupational imperatives. In doing so we can see some of the characteristic strains and potential disjunctures that make the governance of public service a field of political difficulty. When we turn to the fourth point we might see how those difficulties are deepened by a complex and unpredictable public. But first, governmental imperatives: New Labour's commitment to 'modernizing' public services has typically meant a search for a new 'organizational settlement' based on fragmented and dispersed systems of providing services organized horizontally through competition or 'quasi-competition' (league tables, and so on) and organized vertically through principal–agent models of target setting and expanded scrutiny systems (Clarke 2005).

Organizational imperatives are increasingly framed by these relationships, such that they become 'success' focused (Schram and Soss 2002). In managerial terms, they strive to become 'high performance' organizations, since both material and symbolic resources are tied to performance. This does not mean that they are simply 'implementers' of government policy – the spaces involved in 'arm's length' regulation allow the possibility of local translation and adaptation (Newman 2005b). But the management of performance (or at least the management of the representations of performance) is a key element in the organizational culture of public service provision (Clarke 2005). This directs attention inwards to the management of resources – especially the human resources of the organization. It also means attention to the environment: competitors, collaborators and the symbolic context (how the organization is seen by others). And, of course, they face the problem of managing their consumers/customers/users. Here, one key objective is to stabilize their unsettled relationships with the public. Problems include managing unpredictable and excess demand, dealing with varieties of acquiescence and assertiveness, and managing modes of access and interaction. In our study senior managers were preoccupied with the challenge of how to match demand and resources (Vidler and Clarke 2005). Managing expectations (and thus reducing some sorts of demand) was combined with processes of prioritizing some demands over others.

For occupations, we would emphasize two dominant imperatives – or at least the imperatives that command attention once the continued existence of the occupation has been secured. Autonomy has remained one critical focus of concern, whether this is the space of 'clinical judgement' for doctors or the discretion built into the 'office of the constable'. Most studies of managerialization in public services have pointed to the attempts to control, constrain and diminish the sites and forms of professional autonomy, although evaluations of the success of managerialism's impact on public service professionalism vary (for example, Exworthy and Halford 1999; Kirkpatrick *et al*. 2004). The second imperative concerns the legitimacy of public service occupations. Challenges to public services have called into question the 'public service ethos' but it remains a focal point both for public service workers and for the users of public services. Despite the decline in deference and the rise of mistrust, public service professionals tend to command a relatively high degree of public trust and confidence in surveys (especially by contrast with other occupations that sometimes claim the 'public interest' defence – politicians and journalists, for example). But legitimacy now appears more fragile and more contextually contingent, rather than being available 'en bloc' to a public service organization or occupation. As a result, the exercise of authority has become more problematic – the consent of those subjected to professional authority is more explicitly at issue in the encounters between the public and public services. These different concerns and objectives are summarized in Figure 4.2.

Of course, the most problematic element in this figure is the Public. 'Satisfaction' may mean many different things in shaping people's relationship to public services. It may include 'customer satisfaction' – which has been and remains a focus of governmental and organizational attention as a measure of performance. But satisfaction may mean a complex of other things – the satisfactory resolution of a problematic condition; the satisfaction of being taken seriously; the appreciation of well-conducted processes; the sensibility

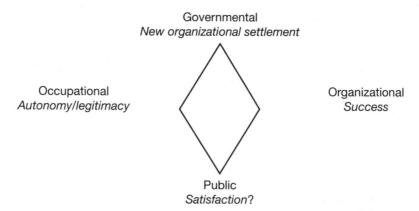

Figure 4.2 Competing concerns

of being a 'member of the public' – part of a collective identity that is being served (rather than an individualized consumer). People who use services in our study combine a concern for their own needs and desires with a complex understanding that public services have other calls on their attention and resources and a view that – at times – other people's needs and problems may be more pressing than their own. This is a key element of what we have called 'relational reasoning' about public services (Clarke 2007a).

Unsettled relationships

We now turn to the unsettled relationships formed on each of the sides of the diamond. The governmental–organizational dynamic might be said to centre on the question of 'who represents the public?' In processes of public service reform, the government has consistently claimed to act as the 'People's Champion', pursuing better quality public services through a variety of means. But organizations are not merely the passive vehicle for government action. They may inflect or interpret policy directions to fit with organizational, managerial or local predispositions. In the process, they are likely to draw on other representations of the public – or at least those sections of the public who use the service. Being 'closer to the customer' is an alternative source of legitimacy – particularly where such closeness is institutionalized in the form of participation or consultation processes. 'Local knowledge' is significant for the formation of organizational plans or strategies, but is also rhetorically vital for constructing 'wriggle room' in relation to central government.

Both central and local representations of the public lay claim to being the product of transparent processes of knowledge production, from the ballot box to customer surveys to participation exercises. Nevertheless, the public remains a troublesome collective entity in a number of ways (Newman 2005a). Its membership is uncertain (how does anyone get to be a 'member of the public'?). It may be constituted out of many different publics, counter-publics and sub-publics – and may be highly mobile as a result (Warner 2002). It is fractioned in many different ways in attempts to identify the key variables or distinctions that account for differences of interest, expectation or opinion (ranging from socio-demographic factors through to marketing derived lifestyle categorizations). It is continually sampled, surveyed and evoked in public/political discourse.

The relationship between organizations and the public involves a dynamic of unpredictability around the question 'who knows what the public wants?' Organizations have an interest in two aspects of this issue. First, they have an interest in maximizing their knowledge of what the public want, both to organize services, and to use the knowledge as leverage with central government. Second, they have an interest – in terms of managing resources and performance – in trying to stabilize their encounters with the public. Our interviews with managers are rich in concepts of 'reasonable', 'responsible' and 'informed' users of their services – through which an emphasis is placed on making the public *manageable* (Clarke *et al.* 2007: 117–120).

The public combines predictability and unpredictability in unpredictable ways. This mixture tends to outrun the modelling capacity of service organizations. It is the new 'common sense' that public service users have shifted from the deferential to the assertive; from the ignorant to the knowledgeable; from the passive to the active voice – in short, from citizens to consumers. But such shifts are profoundly uneven – they may be socially distributed (by class, by age or generation, by ethnicity); but they may also be distributed experientially (shaped by involvement in previous struggles or movements, for example). They may be distributed between different sorts of people; but people are themselves neither stable nor unitary in their encounters with services. The same person may combine being a knowledgeable expert of their own condition; a rights bearing and assertive citizen; an anxious dependent and a seeker after professional help and advice across a series of encounters with the health service. These are 'unstable encounters' (Clarke 2007b) in which the possibilities of getting it wrong have multiplied as both the public and service organizations try to manage each other in more uncertain times.

The other line of relationship at stake here is between the public and public service professionals. We can identify this as organized by the question of 'who owns needs?' Perhaps it would be more accurate to say 'who owns the definition of needs?' It is here that the contested character of knowledge/power (or combinations of authority and expertise) is most visible. Certainly in health and social care, the assumed dominance/deference relationship has been disturbed by alternative claims to be knowledgeable – the capacity to be 'an expert of one's own condition'. The extent to which such claims are made – and the extent to which they are accepted or recognized – remains highly variable. And it remains the case that, for many people, professional expertise is highly valued, although whether that also means a tolerance of professional authority (or paternalism) is more doubtful.

It will be clear that a whole range of governmental initiatives have played a part in reconfiguring these professional–public relationships – disrupting the claims of professional expertise and authority. 'Choice' – in both health and social care – has become a critical element in this, dislocating the professional control of assessment, evaluation and intervention as an integrated structure of decision-making. While we might note that the mythology of professions always overstated the integrated (and untainted) character of such decision-making, the rhetoric and institutionalization of 'choice' is (and is intended to be) disruptive. In a number of ways, the line of relationship between public service professionals and government can be characterized as a tension around 'who owns users?' Both government and professionals lay claim to be the 'patient's friend' – with government serving the user interest by challenging the knots of professional power; and professionals stressing their place close to the user that allows them to both serve and defend the user interest (against a distant and intrusive government).

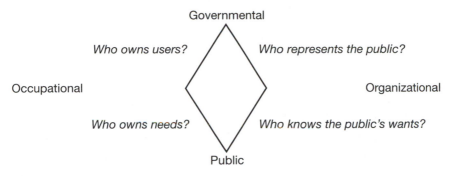

Figure 4.3 Contested relationships

We have summarized the four lines of relationship in Figure 4.3. Each of them, we suggest, remains the site of continuing contestation and uncertainty.

Knowledge–power knots: resistance, recalcitrance and tangles

In this chapter we have dealt with public service professionalism in relatively general terms. But it is clear that the formations and trajectories of specific public service professions differ greatly: in our study, the medical and related professions are characterized by sets of tensions – and particular forms of knowledge–power knot – that set them apart from the issues faced by police staff and social workers. All of them have in common governmental and organizational efforts to constrain their scope for autonomy (in part by organizational rules, or by job redefinition for these groups and related occupations). All of them have to deal with shifting knowledges – about needs, conditions and rights – that interrupt the smooth combination of professional expertise and professional authority. Equally, the organizations we have studied face some of the same challenges: how to manage their interactions with the public; and how to deal with government demands for performance, for greater consumer/customer responsiveness and other initiatives (new partnerships, new geographical boundaries) at the same time.

However, at the level of specific services, the particular tensions and tangles of the knowledge–power knot become more visible. In our study we asked people how comfortable they were about challenging providers of service (making complaints; being demanding if they felt they were not being dealt with properly). We also asked staff in the three services how comfortable they were being challenged by people using the service. The results (represented as an index of readiness to challenge/be challenged that is scaled between +100 and –100) are in Figure 4.4.

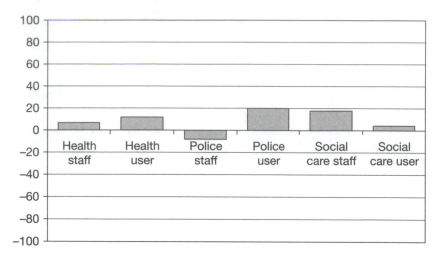

Figure 4.4 Challenge

In a questionnaire, staff and users were asked to agree/disagree (on a 5-point scale) with a series of statements about aspects of consumerism: challenge, choice, inequality and responsibility. If all respondents responded very positively to all four statements around challenge, the result would be +100.

   While the largest mismatch appears between police users and police staff, social care users seem less willing to challenge staff than in other services (despite the apparent readiness of social care staff to be challenged). Health users are slightly more willing to challenge than health staff are to be challenged.
   More broadly, we can sketch some of the particular forms taken by the current state of the knowledge–power knot in the three services. In healthcare, the knowledge problem is particularly visible around the figure of the 'expert patient'. Ideally this person is equipped with medical expertise and granted 'regulated autonomy' in the management of her own condition. But other sources of expertise may interrupt this transmission belt model (which sees knowledge being downloaded from doctor to patient). The Internet and self-help groups, for example, circulate 'unlicensed' knowledge that enables other forms of 'expert'. At the same time, the 'choice' agenda threatens to disrupt both organizational and occupational forms of control over treatment processes (and the processes of priority setting and resource allocation that are embedded in them). Nevertheless, such relatively restricted enactments of choice may satisfy neither public/patient nor professional desires for effective treatment relationships. These issues are explored more extensively in Kuhlmann and Newman (2007) and Newman and Vidler (2006).
   In policing, the tensions and tangles appear to be rather different. Although police services register a general pressure to be more 'customer friendly',

the dominant pressures are perceived to be about building new or better relationships with local communities. Both managers and front-line staff in the police see two linked problems about the relationship between knowledge and power. First, policing is seen to depend upon the application of a specific knowledge (the Law) in situations that may be contentious, conflictual or dangerous. In such contexts, authority – embodied in the person of the Constable – needs to be unchallenged. Second, the process of policing is seen to combine occupational and organizational knowledges in a way that renders it opaque to outsiders. How to police, what to police, and what priorities are to be set are seen to be largely 'internal' knowledges, though the question of priorities increasingly involves intersections with governmental demands. As a result, the problem for community 'dialogue' is how to construct a community that understands enough of the 'internal wisdom' to take part in an informed conversation (Westmarland and Smith 2004).

Finally, in social care we can see a number of contradictory tendencies that bear on the knowledge–power knot. One of these concerns the less than solid or secure status of social work as an occupation. For some time, social work has been subject to processes of splitting (especially between work with children/families and vulnerable adults); dilution (through the redefinition of many of its tasks as 'care work' rather than 'social work'); and towards organizational control (accelerating with the organizational dispersal of social work). It has been challenged 'from above' and 'from below' in many ways over the last twenty years (Clarke 1993), and is still engaged by groups and individuals arguing for a rights-based rather than needs-based approach to social care. At the same time, both organizational issues of managing resources and priorities and occupational issues of having professional judgements of 'need' and 'risk' form focal points for resisting rights-based approaches.

Yet, in some ways, social work's occupational culture precedes and prefigures some of the government's reform agenda: values of independence, autonomy and empowerment have a long history in social work theory and practice. They have been reshaped and reinvigorated as part of the profession's adaptation to some of the challenges since the 1980s (particularly from black and ethnic minority groups and disabled people). So, there is sometimes a sense that New Labour's consumerism goes with the 'grain' of social care. Nevertheless, the model of choice advanced for adult social care (Clarke *et al.* 2006) appears to place a model of individualized consumer choice into the middle of these complex occupation–organizational–user relationships, co-opting the model of 'independent living' developed in the disabled people's movement.

We have tried to sketch some of the distinctive forms and trajectories of the knowledge–power knots at the heart of the three organizational–occupational formations of public service provision in our study. Each of them is subject to forces that both untangle and re-tangle them. We think that one focal issue that they have in common is the problem of how to imagine and create the 'informed' subject of the service. Concepts of the expert patient, the informed community, and the responsible choice-maker circulate constantly through governmental, occupational and organizational discourses. Such terms point to a certain nervousness about the public in the current period. As Gabriel and Lang argued, the consumer, once evoked and brought into being, risks being an unpredictable and 'unmanageable' figure (1995). The expert patient, the informed community and the responsible consumer look like ways of trying to stabilize the knowledge–power relationship: the expert patient's expertise is to be derived from the 'real' experts; the informed community will be informed by what the police already know; and the responsible consumer will make choices that are reasonable, predictable and normalized. Whether the public is ready to be so responsible is another matter.

The future for public services, those who staff them and those who use them looks profoundly uncertain. The tendency towards services organized around mixed economies of competing Small to Medium Enterprises (whether schools, surgeries, hospitals or communities of safety), driven by models of individualized market-like choice, staffed by flexibilized employees (and/or volunteers) promises to eviscerate older conceptions of the public. It may be that there is no 'going back' – and indeed it is hard to generate much nostalgia for the mean and discriminatory paternalism of much public service provision of the 1970s. But where might we find expansive conceptions of the public and how it is to be served to set against the narrowly 'marketized' vision of New Labour?

Note

1   *Creating Citizen-Consumers: changing identifications and relationships* was funded as part of the ESRC/AHRC Cultures of Consumption research programme between March 2003 and May 2005 (Grant Number RES-143-25-0008). In addition to the authors of this chapter, the project team also included Nick Smith, Elizabeth Vidler and Louise Westmarland and was based in the Department of Social Policy at the Open University. More details about the study can be found at www.open.ac.uk/socialsciences/creating-citizen-consumers.

References

Clarke, J. (ed.) (1993) *A Crisis in Care?*, London: Sage.

Clarke, J. (2004) *Changing Welfare, Changing States: new directions in social policy*, London: Sage.

—— (2005) 'Performing for the public: doubt, desire and the evaluation of public services', in P. du Gay (ed.), *The Values of Bureaucracy*, Oxford: Oxford University Press.

—— (2007a) 'It's not like shopping: relational reasoning and public services', in M. Bevir and F. Trentmann (eds), *Governance, Citizens, and Consumers: agency and resistance in contemporary politics*, Basingstoke: Palgrave Macmillan.

—— (2007b) 'Unsettled connections: citizens, consumers and the reform of public services', *Journal of Consumer Culture*, 7 (2): 159–178.

—— and Newman, J. (1997) *The Managerial State: power, politics and ideology in the remaking of social welfare*, London: Sage.

—— and —— (2007) 'What's in a name? New Labour citizen-consumers and the remaking of public services', *Cultural Studies*, 21 (4–5): 738–757.

——, Smith, N. and Vidler, E. (2006) 'The indeterminacy of choice: political, policy and organisational implications', *Social Policy and Society*, 5 (3): 327–336.

——, Newman, J., Smith, N., Vidler, E. and Westmarland, L. (2007) *Creating Citizen-Consumers: changing publics and changing public services*, London: Sage.

Duyvendak, J., Knijn, T. and Kremer, M. (2007) *Policy, People and New Professional: de-professionalisation and re-professionalisation in care and welfare*, Amsterdam: Amsterdam University Press.

Exworthy, M. and Halford, S. (eds) (1999) *Professionals and the New Managerialism in the Public Sector*, Buckingham: Open University Press.

Freidson, E. (2001) *Professionalism: the third logic*, Cambridge: Polity Press.

Gabriel, Y. and Lang, T. (1995) *The Unmanageable Consumer*, London: Sage.

Kirkpatrick, I., Ackroyd, S. and Walker, R. (2004) *The New Managerialism and Public Service Professionals*, Basingstoke: Palgrave Macmillan.

Johnson, T. (1973) *Professions and Power*, London: Macmillan.

Kuhlmann, E. and Newman, J. (2007) 'Consumers enter the political stage: the modernisation of health care in Britain and Germany', *Journal of European Social Policy*, 17 (2): 99–111.

Marquand, D. (2004) *The Decline of the Public*, Cambridge: Polity Press.

Newman, J. (2005a) 'Going Public'. Inaugural lecture, The Open University, May 2005.

—— (2005b) 'Enter the transformational leader', *Sociology*, 39 (4): 717–734.

—— and Nutley, S. (2003) 'Transforming the Probation Service: what works, organisational change and professional identity', *Policy and Politics*, 31 (4): 547–563.

—— and Vidler, E. (2006) 'Discriminating customers, responsible patients, empowered users: consumerism and the modernisation of health care', *Journal of Social Policy*, 35 (2): 193–209.

Office of Public Services Reforms (2002) *Reforming our Services: principles into practice*, London: Office of Public Services Reforms.

Schram, S. and Soss, J. (2002) 'Success stories: welfare reform, policy discourse and the politics of research', in S. Schram, *Praxis for the Poor*, New York: New York University Press, pp. 186–200.

Vidler, E. and Clarke, J. (2005) 'Creating citizen-consumers: New Labour and the remaking of public services', *Public Policy and Administration*, 20 (2): 19–37.

Warner, M. (2002) *Publics and Counterpublics*, New York: Zone Books.

Westmarland, L. and Smith, N. (2004) 'From scumbags to consumers: customer service and the commodification of policing'. Paper presented at the British Criminological Society Annual Conference, July. Online. Available www.open.ac.uk/socialsciences/creating-citizen-consumers/ (accessed 4 April 2008).

5 An English vernacular

Teacher trade unionism and educational politics 1970–2007

Ken Jones

The transformation of the work of teachers is, of course, an international policy priority. Policy orthodoxy sees the condition of the teaching force as a major problem and its reform as a necessity. It recognizes, too, that this reform is not merely 'internal', relating to the organization of teaching and learning, but 'external', in that it must effect a change in the positioning and influence of teachers' organizations in the public arena. This chapter particularly addresses this external dimension, through a focus on the politics of teaching in England, which it hopes to grasp both in terms of what England shares with other countries in Europe, and in terms of the specific national pathway England has followed to arrive at its current, ever-ongoing process of transformation.

The road to modernization

The OECD, as part of its project for 'Attracting, Developing and Retaining Teachers', has produced a series of country reports that try, often very perceptively, to understand the teacher problem in cultural and historical dimensions.[1] Thus, in relation to Germany, an OECD review team writes of a:

> kind of malaise within the teaching profession. We heard much about lowering of social esteem, unjust criticism by politicians, increasing burdens and worsening working conditions. . . . [But] there is some evidence that teachers' psychological concerns are connected not so much with excessive situational demands but rather with the intensification of demands in the sense of forced decision-making and pressure for action . . . and [this situation] enhances a subjective feeling of being powerless.
>
> (OECD 2004: 39)

A report on Italy makes similar points. Teachers are experiencing 'widespread uneasiness, crisis of identity, deterioration of self-image and of the image offered to public opinion and, finally, the weakened trust of students and their families'. Hence the paradox of teaching: 'the more school becomes a crucially important institution in the knowledge society . . . the more teachers feel like belonging to a class the prestige of which is in decline' (OECD 2003:7, citing Cavalli 2000).

Underlying judgements like these is an historical narrative: teacher identities were formed through the experience of post-war mass education and remade through the hopes of democratization that sustained to a greater or lesser extent, the movements of the 1970s – greater in the case of Italy, France and post-Franco Spain than in that of Germany. For much of this period, teachers' work in important respects escaped overt policy direction. Even in the most regulated of systems, teachers enjoyed a kind of protected autonomy in terms of their classroom work. Autonomy was underpinned by contractual arrangements that awarded teachers, once permanently appointed, a degree of job security unusual in the workforce as a whole. This secure workforce, though often strikingly underpaid, was only lightly managed. As the OECD puts it in relation to Germany:

> Head teachers were not appointed for their managerial expertise, and had few sanctions or incentives at their disposal: salary levels related to seniority rather than 'competence' or 'performance'. Inspection regimes were not intrusive, and the absence both of market-based competition and popular involvement in school governance meant that parental demands and criticisms were not strongly felt.
>
> (OECD 2004: 16)

This situation was legitimated by teachers' claim to be uniquely capable of adapting curricula and pedagogy to student needs, and to embody the kinds of freedom that democratic societies should celebrate. Secondary teachers – especially those in selective schools – could base this claim on their specialist subject knowledge; primary teachers, less securely, could rest it on their understanding of children's learning processes. However, these claims to autonomy – though hard won against governments that had in the pre-war period possessed much stronger directive powers – provided only an ambivalent advance. Part of the problem here was the uncodifiability and uncertainty of teachers' work, in classrooms whose demands inflected the processes of teaching and learning in what were felt to be unpredictable and idiosyncratic ways. Teachers' self-image was built on such a perception; they saw teaching as an individual craft and themselves as 'lone fighters' or 'artisans', who managed uncertainty by combining unprogrammable personal qualities with a knowledge born of practical experience (Duru-Bellat and van Zanten 2006: 143–144; OECD 2004: 37). But the converse of these claims was that teaching, at least in the mass school, could not gain uncontested entry to the category of 'profession'; in the absence of a sure and authoritative knowledge base, linked to a university discipline, it lacked a measure of credibility. This later became a source of vulnerability in cases where governments turned to a policy of greater central regulation of classroom practice, but for a long period, post-war, teachers' claims were generally accepted by governments:

as Lawn puts it of England, 'teachers were professionals, fostered by the state, partners in the deliberation of policy' (Lawn 2001: 175).

It is the breakdown of this identity and the erosion of teachers' claims to be custodians and transmitters of educational knowledge that set the current parameters of the politics of teaching, creating the need for what international policy orthodoxy terms 'modernization'. Modernization has several dimensions. In terms of 'external' politics, it is an exercise in delegitimation and relegitimation, appealing to sources of legitimacy outside the realm of professional commitment and expertise – to public opinion, through staged 'great debates' like that accompanying the French Thélot report of 2004, to the judgements of 'experts' and to the deliberations of elected representatives, expressed through a plethora of legislation. Internally, as Lawn argues,

> teacher professionalism is now being redefined as a form of competent labour, flexible and multi-skilled; it operates within a regulated curriculum and internal assessment system in a decentralized external market. The dominant version (of professionalism) is now [based on] a notion of individual responsibility and incentive reward legitimised by an . . . idea of efficient service and performance incentive.
>
> (Lawn 1996: 112–113)

This reorientation, which entails assigning a new meaning to 'professionalism', is not limited to ideological advocacy; nor is it advanced only in the form of designs for the definition, management and direction of teachers' work. Important though these are, their effect depends on their interfacing with another side of policy, and strategic vision at this point combines with harsher measures. The modernization of teaching occurs in a context where managerial force and material constraint exercise a powerful influence, and where the flexibilization and in some cases casualization of teachers' work contribute to the reshaping of teacher identities. The challenge to, or eclipse of, union organization is another aspect of such change.

Teachers, like many other groups of workers, thus experience the tensions of a (neo-liberal) knowledge society, in which the exercise of new kinds of skill is accompanied by a loss of the capacity for self-definition, both in the workplace and in the political sphere. It is this double movement that can explain the symptoms of disorientation noted in the OECD's analyses – symptoms which are not unique to teachers (Sennett 1998), but are nonetheless lived by them in specific ways.

How different is England?

In the process of modernization, generalized across the EU and the countries of the OECD, where does England stand? Certainly, England is 'advanced', in the sense that policies for the reform of the teaching force were developed earlier there, and have been elaborated to a fuller extent. But the term 'advanced' can in some ways be misleading, especially in as much as it suggests a common international pathway, along which all will travel, differing merely in the pace of their journey. National distinctiveness can be better respected by thinking in terms of an 'English vernacular', a distinct local inflection of a change process that has at global level a demonstrable coherence of design but that has interacted with national circumstances to configure English educational politics in particular ways (Lingard 2000). Much more strongly than in other countries of Western Europe, the course of reform in England has been marked by conservative as well as neo-liberal influences; and much more effectively than elsewhere, neo-liberal reform has been able to link itself to a modernization project that claims to deliver social-democratic tradition from its enduring weaknesses. To begin to understand these conjunctions, we need to take a step back, to an earlier historiography.

The articles published by Tom Nairn and by Perry Anderson in *New Left Review* between 1963 and 1965 provide, as Andy Green suggested in *Education and State Formation* (1990), a productive starting point from which to interpret English educational history. The theses of these articles are starkly summarized by Anderson in the following terms:

> England experienced the first industrial revolution, in a period of international counter-revolutionary war, producing the earliest proletariat when socialist theory was least formed and available, and an industrial bourgeoisie polarised from the start towards the aristocracy . . . By the end of the nineteenth century, Britain had seized the largest empire in history . . . which saturated and 'set' British society in a matrix it has retained to this day . . . The late Victorian era and the high noon of imperialism welded aristocracy and bourgeoisie together in a single social bloc . . . The working class evolved, separate but subordinate, within the apparently unshakeable structure of British capitalism, unable . . . to transform the fundamental nature of British society.
>
> (Anderson 1964: 31, 34, 39)

From this analysis sprang both a critique of the industrial bourgeoisie, for its failure to create, along German lines, a developmental state, and for its self-imposed subordination to agrarian capital; and of the Labour Party and the trade union movement, for their like inability to address questions of social transformation, and for their blend of conservatism – in relation to the institutions of the state – and economism, in relation to the purposes and politics of trade union struggle. It is an analysis that has been challenged, both for its disparagement of working-class achievements and for what is claimed to be its implicit and unmerited valorisation of the trajectories and strategies of working-class movements in other parts of Europe, which in truth are different only in degree from those of England (Thompson 1965). Nevertheless, its theses remain in a double sense generative. They provide means with which to think about questions of national difference at several levels, political, social, cultural and educational; and they have themselves become a political resource, shaping policies and programmes.

Specifically in relation to the educational history of the last three decades, one can derive from Nairn and Anderson two kinds of understanding. The first has to do with the nature of the English 'political imaginary', and its salience to educational controversies at the founding moment of English neo-liberalism. By 'political imaginary', I mean the discursive reserve from which political strategies can draw – a reserve constituted by memory, tradition, critique and desire and expressed as much through imagery as through factual presentation. Here the influence of an anti-modernism with its origins deep in the process of aristocratic and bourgeois fusion was strong. As I have argued elsewhere (Jones 2003), between the Black Papers of 1968–1977 and the attempts of the early 1990s to turn the national curriculum further to the right (the period during which the post-1944 settlement was dissolved), the decisive force in the construction of this imaginary was an intellectual bloc which reassembled the components of Anderson's history. The nineteenth century subsumption of the values of the industrial bourgeoisie within an older humanist tradition indifferent to scientific and technical education was played over again. From Brian Cox to Roger Scruton to John Marenbon, intellectuals of the right invoked a vision not of a modernized school, but of one returned to an earlier condition, organized around a humanist culture, magically immune to the social and cultural changes of post-1960 England, and reproducing the patterns of educational segregation thought necessary to the preservation of educational standards. Opposition to multi-culturalism and an attempt to centre issues of schooling and social cohesion around a politics of national identity were central to its work; so also was its presentation of teachers as people who had undermined such an identity, at the same time as they had allowed a relapse in standards through a pursuit of child-centred and impossibly egalitarian objectives: the crisis of teaching was from this perspective a crisis of cultural order – an order imagined in terms that had little to do with the labour market, the workplace or with any but the most generalized evocations of industrial need.

The work of Anderson and Nairn enables us to understand something of the oddities and the logic of this process, in which a project of reform that instigated a wider neo-liberalization of schooling was carried forward by traditionalist intellectuals who defined themselves in terms far removed from discourses of marketization and globalization. But, as I've suggested, the Anderson/Nairn theses had more than an interpretive effect. Their insistent critique of a labour movement so wedded to economism and reformism that it was incapable of addressing the nature of the British state contributed, alongside other perspectives (those of Andrew Gamble (1988) and David Marquand (1988), for instance, who made much of the absence in Britain of a 'developmental state' capable of pushing through political and economic modernization), to the evolution of New Labour's own policy imaginary. Particularly in its first term of office (1997–2001), New Labour presented itself as a modernizing force, strengthening the powers of the central state, and sweeping away corporatist obstacles to change; hence, in education, the introduction of highly specified directives for curriculum and pedagogy – the National Literacy Strategy, for instance – and of an equally particularized regime of target-setting. In one sense, these strategies could be read as the installation of a developmental state within education. In another, they can be understood as a kind of pastiche of the developmental approach. For an analyst like Gamble, the functions of a developmental state included, centrally, responsibility for an industrial strategy and for research and development. Labour intended no such thing; instead it enacted its statism, dressed up in the Jacobin rhetoric of policymakers like Michael Barber (Barber 1996, Jones 1998) solely within a public sector shrunk by the privatizations of the Conservative years. There, its attacks on what could be presented as residual, inertial influences – Blair's famous 'forces of conservatism' – could be energetically elaborated. This 'conservatism' was not linked to what might have been presented as the archaism of English society – an educational class structure with the public schools at its apex – but was instead located among local authorities, and above all among teachers. At the same time, the modernization that was presented electorally as the antithesis of conservatism was construed in practice as an adaptation to a society and economy reshaped by financialization, in which class inequalities were more sharply present than in the immediate post-war decades.

Teachers

How did these successive discursive onslaughts alter the politics of teaching, the policies of teacher unions, and the practice of teachers? To answer the question, we need first of all to appreciate the partial radicalization of teacher politics in the 1970s in the context of political shifts in the trade union movement as a whole. Some analysts, notably Geoff Eley in his engaged and illuminating history of the left in Europe (Eley 2002), have seen this period as one in which a militant and economist sectoralism contributed strongly to the collapse of the post-war settlement and to the emergence of the neo-liberal right. As we shall see, this tendency explains part of the educational history of the 1970s – but it does not provide the whole story, which is better seen in more variegated terms. In some senses, teachers' sectoralism was lessened in this period. Educationally, teacher radicalism made a significant difference to the classroom, in ways that often sought to connect new curricula to emerging social interests – issues of gender and of race were particularly salient here (Jones 2003). In trade union terms, the two major unions, the National Union of Teachers (NUT) and National Association of Schoolmasters/Union of Women Teachers (NAS/UWT) broke with professional tradition and joined the Trades Union Congress (TUC); questions of trade union solidarity, along with social movement issues (disarmament, women's rights) became customary elements on the NUT's agenda. At the same time, in response to the cuts and job losses that affected many localities post-1976, teachers, especially through the NUT, organized strikes in decidedly non-economistic ways, with trade union action, refusing to cover the lessons of absent colleagues, and accompanied by consistent effort to build support among parents and school students. (In 1982, when teachers in the London Borough of Barking and Dagenham struck for six weeks against redundancies – the longest teachers' strike of the post-war period – parent support committees were formed in most schools (Jones 1983).) These local responses were in many cases effective, though they took their toll of union organization: in a situation where several unions competed for teacher support, there were niche recruitment opportunities for the less militant, and the NUT lost members accordingly. So far as militant teacher unionism was concerned, cutback was a process that both impelled new forms of organization and had long-term, attritional effects.

Alongside the effects of cutback, teachers and their organizations faced another difficulty, to which for a long period they failed to respond. The tradition-fuelled right-wing offensive of the 1970s and 1980s profoundly affected teachers' 'external' situation: their role as custodians of educational process was challenged, and, in the law-making that followed, two decades of effective agitation from the right was relinquished. This change was not effectively resisted. Classroom-level radicalism was too 'internally' focused to provide a resource for an 'external' politics. When teachers did attempt such an external intervention, its terms were unproductive. In 1976, at the start of Labour's 'Great Debate' – the moment at which the post-war settlement began to unravel – union leaderships centred their national response on no more than a claim of teachers' right to professional autonomy. Nothing was less likely to contribute to a popular politics of education. At local level, radical initiative at the level of the classroom was rarely linked to a politics of the public arena.

Instead, at a crucial moment, teachers in England confronted the multi-levelled Conservative offensive of the 1980s with a strategy whose central aspect was, in Nairn and Anderson's terms, economist. In 1985, just as the miners' strike was drawing to its close, teachers began a pay campaign in terms that suggested little had been learned from the miners' attempt to present the stakes of their struggle in such a way as to win wider support; the longest period of sustained industrial action by teachers in late twentieth-century Europe culminated in the most decisive defeat. Months of sporadic strike and no-cover action left the main unions weakened to the point where Mrs Thatcher's government was able to impose, in 1987, a Pay and Conditions Act which removed their right to negotiate pay, and greatly strengthened the power of school managements to direct their work. The Education Reform Act followed in 1988, introducing, through the national curriculum, a regime that further weakened teacher influence in the workplace and diminished their voice in the wider educational space. Teachers had thus been doubly undermined, both by their inability to find an educational voice through which to respond to the traditionalist right, and by the consequences of opting for an economistic campaign in circumstances where a broader educational strategy was required. Only once was such a politics challenged. The 1993–1994 boycott of national testing was a movement launched from the base – initially, by London teachers of English – that enlisted along the way the backing of union leaderships and also mobilized significant parental support. In the course of the campaign, teachers elaborated a resonant critique of the Conservative political imaginary, highlighting issues of authoritarian decision-making and attacking an impoverished traditionalism that found no place for cultural diversity. The 1993 Standard Attainment Tests (SATS) did not take place, and thus, for the first time in English education, action by teachers had affected the organization and politics of teaching, learning and assessment; its success hinted, perhaps, at what could have been achieved in the previous decade. But the campaign soon reached its limits: the opportunity to make a more lasting challenge to the new educational regime was not taken. Unions differed on the purposes of the boycott – was it intended to achieve a reduction in workload, or the defeat of a particular educational project? In the event, union leaderships preferred to settle for minor modifications of the national curriculum – an anti-climactic decision which helped determine the quiescent course of teacher response to the changes of the following decade (Jones 1994).

A Scottish comparison

This history, condensed though it is, allows some understanding of what is 'English' about the experience of teachers, and of their organizations. It suggests that national specificity has in part to do with the nature of educational conflict in the 1980s, and thus with the terms on which teachers entered the neo-liberal era. Comparison can develop the point further. In Scotland, education is very differently positioned, in relation to state and society, than it is south of the border. Lindsay Paterson (2003) is not the first to argue that the defining traditions of Scottish education, and the institutions that have sustained them, have had a strong democratic element, that though compromised by social and economic inequality, has served as a reference point for administrators, teachers and broader communities – helping to produce both a policy community more unified than in England, and a much less diverse landscape of teacher trade unionism, dominated by the Educational Institute of Scotland (EIS). The notion of the 'democratic intellect' (McPherson and Raab 1988) as a quality to be nurtured by the school system is important in this context, and the resource it afforded to egalitarian change may help explain why the reform of primary and secondary education in the 1960s was pushed further in Scotland than England, with near-universal comprehensivization and a preference for mixed-ability grouping (Jones 2003).

Thus the 'English ideology' of elitist traditionalism (and educational marketization) found no strong point of purchase in the Scotland of the 1980s;

it appeared, as Mrs Thatcher grimly noted, something of an alien intrusion (Thatcher 1993). The teachers' disputes of the period were therefore conducted on different terms, in which the national question was a strong factor. Unlike its English counterparts, the EIS, in waging its pay campaign, could summon up a potent alternative to Conservatism, in the form of a specifically national educational tradition that could serve as the basis of an effective popular response: the demands of the pay campaign may have been economic; but its conduct, in that it reached out beyond immediate issues and touched a wider constituency, escaped economism. The outcomes of the Scottish pay struggle were weighted in favour of teachers; the EIS emerged strengthened, rather than chastened, by the dispute.

Still a vernacular?

This chapter has argued that there exists a common West European crisis of teacher identity, as well as a policy orthodoxy, developed through the EU and the OECD, that has a template for resolving it. Yet, the national experience of this crisis and remaking is not uniform. The stresses of change are universally felt, but they are lived differently. As Tolstoy might have put it, every country, or every national group of teachers, is unhappy in its own way. Some research, for instance, has suggested that despite their achievements of the 1980s, subordinacy, rather than collegiality, marks the current response of Scottish teachers to reform (MacDonald 2004). Other surveys conclude that, in terms of detail and reach, the remaking of teachers' work in other European countries has not reached English proportions. Loyalties to the notion of public education provide, for teachers in some countries, a strong critical vantage point on change – as recent mobilizations in France (2006), Greece (2007) and Catalonia (2008) have shown. At the same time, for better or for worse, the practices associated with the modernization of teaching and learning have proved difficult to generalize. As one account of Spain has noted, the diffusion of a new pedagogic culture is underdeveloped (Arco Tirado and Fernandez Balboa 2003); likewise, the newer generation of teachers in France is said to be dependent upon 'survival strategies' and 'managerial techniques', rather than the comprehensive models of teaching and learning with which teachers in England are fitted out (van Zanten 2002).

I have tried to suggest that English 'unhappiness', that is to say, the remaking of teachers' 'external' situation and their 'internal' practices, has an earlier birthday and a more definite current shape than that of most other European countries. The defeats of the 1980s marked a turnaround in English teacher organization. They ensured that teachers entered the period of post-1997 modernization without strong ambitions or a distinctive project. The Labour Government, by contrast, possessed both these attributes, and has pursued over the last decade a coherent policy towards teachers, based on control of initial training, centralized direction of the curriculum and micro-management of pedagogy, and a stronger apparatus of management control, including performance pay (Hextall and Mahony 2000). No other government in Western Europe has been able to pursue so extensive a programme. On the teachers' part, the main features of Labour's developmentalism have not been challenged. Teachers' capacity for autonomous initiative, either in terms of the classroom, or in wider local or associational terms, has thus been further eroded; so far as education is concerned, the public sphere of debate is relatively empty – certainly in respect of the voicing of alternatives. In short, the most comprehensive programme of reform in Western Europe has been greeted with the most pliant response. Viewed in a comparative context, this imbalance – of voice, of influence, of political agency – is perhaps the most striking feature of the English vernacular.

Note

1   The argument of this section is extended in Jones *et al.* (2008).

References

Arco Tirado, J.-L. and Fernandez Balboa, J. M. (2003) 'Contextual barriers to school reform in Spain', *International Review of Education*, 49 (6): 585–600.

Anderson, P. (1964) 'Origins of the present crisis', *New Left Review*, 1 (23): 26–53.

Barber, M. (1996) *The Learning Game: arguments for an education revolution*, London: Gollancz.

Cavalli, A. (2000) *Gli Insegnanti Nella Scuola che Cambia*, Bologna: Il Mulino.

Eley, G. (2002) *Forging Democracy: the history of the left in Europe 1850–2000*, New York: Oxford University Press.

Duru-Bellat, M. and van Zanten, A. (2006) *Sociologie de l'école*, Paris: Armand Colin.

Gamble, A. (1988) *The Free Economy and the Strong State*, London: Macmillan.

Green, A. (1990) *Education and State Formation: the rise of education systems in England, France and the USA*, London: Macmillan.

Hextall, I. and Mahony, P. (2000) *Reconstructing Teaching: standards, performance and accountability*, London: RoutledgeFalmer.

Jones, K. (1983) *Beyond Progressive Education*, London: Macmillan.

—— (1994) 'The teachers' boycott of testing: a new kind of cultural politics?' *Changing English*, 2 (1).

—— (1998) 'The statist and the marketeer', *Education and Social Justice*, 1 (1): 35–44.

—— (2003) *Education in Britain*, Cambridge: Polity Press.

——, Cunchillos, C., Hatcher, R., Hirtt, N., Innes, R., Joshua, S. and Klausenitzer, J. (2008) *Schooling in Western Europe: the new order and its adversaries*, Basingstoke: Palgrave Macmillan.

Lawn, M. (1996) *Modern Times? Work, professionalism and citizenship in teaching*, Lewes: Falmer Press.

—— (2001) 'Borderless education: imagining a European educational space in a time of brands and networks', *Discourse*, 22 (2): 173–184.

Lingard, B. (2000) 'It is and it isn't: vernacular globalization, educational policy, and restructuring', in N. C. Burbules and C. A. Torres (eds), *Globalization and Education: critical perspectives*, New York: Routledge, pp. 79–108.

MacDonald, A. (2004) 'Collegiate or compliant? Primary teachers in post-McCrone Scotland', *British Educational Research Journal*, 30 (3): 413–433.

McPherson, A. and Raab, C. (1988) *Governing Education: a sociology of policy since 1945*, Edinburgh: Edinburgh University Press.

Marquand, D. (1988) *The Unprincipled Society: new demands and old politics*, London: Jonathan Cape.

OECD (2003) *Attracting, Developing and Retaining Effective Teachers: country background report for Italy*, Paris: OECD.

—— (2004) *Attracting, Developing and Retaining Effective Teachers: Country Note for Germany*, Paris: OECD.

Paterson, L. (2003) *Scottish Education in the Twentieth Century*, Edinburgh: Edinburgh University Press.

Sennett, R. (1998) *The Corrosion of Character: the personal consequences of work in the new capitalism*, New York: Norton.

Thatcher, M. (1993) *The Downing Street Years*, London: Harper Collins.

Thompson, E. P. (1965) 'Peculiarities of the English', *Socialist Register*, 1965, London: Merlin: 311–362.

van Zanten, A. (2002) 'Educational change and new cleavages between headteachers, teachers and parents: global and local perspectives on the French case', *Journal of Education Policy*, 17 (3): 289–304.

Part 2
Living professionalism

6   Paradoxes of teaching in neo-liberal times

Education 'reform' in Chicago

Pauline Lipman

In this chapter I draw on a study of Chicago's high-stakes education accountability system (Lipman 2004) and more recent data (2004–2007) to examine some paradoxes of teaching in neo-liberal times in the US. I define two 'moments' in neo-liberal education policy. The first moment is the centralized monitoring and regulation of schools and teaching through standards and accountability processes which began in the 1990s and continues to the present. The second, beginning also in the 1990s but accelerating in the new millennium, is the marketization of schools through school choice, privatization of education services (for example, tutoring) and public charter schools run by private operators. These two 'moments' are in fact interrelated and overlapping. However, I discuss them separately to draw out the implications of new forms of accountability for teachers' work and how that in turn influences teachers' involvement in, and experiences with, market-based reforms. Although education markets have been on the policy agenda in the US since the early 1990s, their expansion has been facilitated by high stakes accountability (Lipman and Haines 2007), particularly the federal No Child Left Behind legislation (NCLB) in 2002.[1] I use Chicago as a case study of changing teacher professionalism in the US, particularly in urban school districts, because Chicago has been a model for neo-liberal education projects. It also exemplifies the neo-liberal economic and political processes that are restructuring urban areas.

I argue that teachers' experiences in Chicago demonstrate that neo-liberal accountability systems in public education create conditions that undermine teaching as an ethical, socially just professional practice, and this pushes teachers towards the market with its promise of greater flexibility and autonomy.[2] I also argue that accountability and market reforms produce greater inequality and disempowerment of teachers in general, yet, paradoxically, the market opens up spaces for some socially just educational projects which have become sites of opposition to neo-liberal corporate rationality and demonstrations of alternative educational visions. While accountability and education markets increase stratification of schools, and thus teaching and what constitutes teacher professionalism, there are also possibilities for agency within an overall retrograde erosion of public education.

I situate my discussion in the changing nature of teachers' work in the neo-liberal context. Then I briefly describe the Chicago situation and my research. Drawing on my study of education accountability and differentiated schooling in Chicago (Lipman 2004), I summarize key implications for teaching. I go on to briefly discuss Chicago's move to a market model of school choice with the proliferation of charter schools and implications for teacher professionalism. Finally, I conclude with some thoughts about a social justice agenda.

Changing nature of teachers' work

Susan Robertson (2007: 3) notes that 'neo-liberalism has transformed, in both predictable and unpredictable ways, *how* we think and *what we do* [emphasis original] as teachers and learners'. Centralized accountability and marketization of schools and education services in the US have produced deep changes in teachers' work (for example, Apple 2001; Hursh 2007), including increased regulation and surveillance of teaching, narrowed curricula, competition through differentiated pay scales and rewards/punishments for test results, and the emergence of a new teacher subject – teacher as entrepreneur. This is part of a larger discursive shift in the purposes and processes of education from relatively complex, socially situated notions of learning and education for personal and social goals, to efficiency and economic productivity. The effects of this shift transcend preoccupations with processes of measurement and comparison. They also change what is measured, and thus taught, as teaching is driven by the idea that the only things worth teaching are those that are measured or easily tested.

The social processes involved are also mechanisms for reforming teachers' subjectivities – changing 'what it means to be a teacher' (Ball 2003: 217). In the US, in general, these shifts have undermined teaching as an ethical practice and teachers' agency and professionalism, particularly in the lowest performing schools which face the harshest accountability strictures and generally serve low-income students of colour. This amounts to a moral and political crisis in teaching as democratic and humanistic purposes of education are superseded by economic goals, and one-size-fits-all standards and high stakes testing reverse equity gains of the 1960s and 1970s. While standards and accountability have improved performance in some low-income schools of colour, the overall trend has not been to reduce disparities between white students and students of colour (Hursh 2007). For teachers, the dominance of high stakes accountability is taking a toll in increased stress, demoralization, and exit from the profession (Valli and Buese 2007).

These shifts generally mirror the changing nature of teachers' work in the UK, Australia, and elsewhere (e.g. Ball 1994, 2003; Gewirtz 1997; Mahony and Hextall 1998; Robertson 2000; Smyth 2001). However, global neo-liberal restructuring is 'path dependent' – taking different forms in different contexts shaped by specific histories, ideologies, and relations of social forces (Brenner and Theodore 2002), and education is no exception (Robertson 2007). Moreover, neo-liberalism is a *process*, not a thing, fraught with contradictions and contention that play out differently in local contexts, and teachers' responses vary (see Gewirtz 1997). It is these contradictions and aspects of contention and the possibilities they offer that are particularly instructive for those of us committed to working for more just public schools and a more just social order.

The Chicago context

In 1995, Chicago's mayor took over the public school system and appointed a corporate administration to run the schools. The new regime established a system of centralized accountability based on standardized tests, demarcated students and schools as 'failing', and meted out penalties accordingly. These included putting schools on 'probation' under direct central oversight and retaining students in grade, without regard for persistent inequities in resources and opportunity to learn, teachers' ideologies, cultural discontinuities in curriculum and instruction, or the social context of the school. Over the next twelve years, Chicago also greatly expanded educational differentiation with new highly selective enrollment schools, basic skills direct-instruction schools, public military schools, and vocational schools alongside neighbourhood schools with mostly low academic performance.

In 2004, Chicago launched a second major reform, 'Renaissance 2010'. This initiative, proposed and partly directed by the Commercial Club of Chicago, an organization of top corporate, financial, and civic leaders aimed to close at least 60–70 public schools and open over 100 new schools of choice, two thirds as charter or contract schools (Lipman and Haines 2007). Charter and contract schools are publicly funded schools run by private operators and governed by private boards. They are not required to have democratically elected local school councils and are not covered by teacher and other school employee unions. They are part of a parallel system of school options (including selective enrollment public schools) alongside traditional neighbourhood public schools. The large-scale expansion of charter and contract schools, which effectively compete for students, brings over one-sixth of the third largest school district in the US into the education market.

These initiatives reflect general trends in education policy nationally, but they are also driven by social forces shaping the neo-liberal restructuring of cities and Chicago in particular. Chicago illustrates the interconnection of neo-liberal urbanism and the restructuring of teachers' work. Brenner and Theodore (2002: 351) argue that 'cities have become strategically crucial geographic arenas in which a variety of neo-liberal initiatives . . . have been articulated', including privatization of public services, public–private ventures, restriction of democratic governance and participation, state subsidies for investment, and gentrification as a pivotal economic sector. Chicago's school policies are integral to this agenda (Lipman 2008). The city markets 'innovative' schools as anchors in gentrified and gentrifying communities. Charter schools and Renaissance 2010 are public–private partnerships, partly subsidized by the state, which give capital a direct role in the governance of public institutions, undermining democratic participation (local school councils) and public sector unions.

As economic globalization and state de-regulation have weakened the tight coupling of urban and national economies, cities compete directly in the global economy for international investment, tourism, highly skilled labour, and producer services that drive globalization (Sassen 2006). Education is crucial to this agenda. Efficient schools, demonstrated by standardized performance indicators (test scores), new selective and elite public school options alongside regulated schools for working-class youth of colour, and choice within the public school system are aspects of marketing the city. This is also true for policies designed to demonstrate that the city is 'safe' for the middle class, tourists and investors, for example, intensified surveillance, regulation and containment of low-income people of colour, and particularly youth, including through highly regulated schooling (Lipman 2004). Layered over an historically unequal education system, these new forms of stratified schooling are shaped by, and reproduce, the racialized economic and spatial inequalities that characterize the neo-liberal city (Sassen 2006). Thus the further stratification of teaching and the reconstitution of professionalism are bound up with global and local neo-liberal economic and social processes.

Teacher professionalism in the face of centralized accountability

From 1998 to 2002, I studied implications of Chicago's high stakes accountability and differentiation of schools for student learning and teachers' work (Lipman 2004). Across the school district, I found that accountability pressures, centralized regulation of schools and teaching, standards, educational 'options,' and sanctions for failure were deployed as a racialized, class specific constellation of social practices and messages. They had differential influences on student learning and notions of what constituted teacher professionalism, in, for example, academically elite selective-enrolment schools vs. direct-instruction schools.

To capture meanings of these policies for students, teachers and administrators I conducted qualitative studies of four elementary schools, which I call Grover, Westview, Brewer and Farley. Grover and Westview students were African American and were very low-income. Both schools served public housing projects. Grover, a struggling school on probation (under direct oversight of the school district and an external probation 'partner'), had high teacher turnover and a somewhat fragmented and demoralized staff. Westview was designated an 'improving school' with a core of veteran dedicated teachers, mostly African American, who interpreted teaching as a social mission. Brewer, in a Mexican immigrant community, had a core of Latino/a teachers and administrators committed to bilingual–bicultural education. They had initiated a school-wide reflection on culturally relevant (Ladson-Billings 1994) and inquiry-based teaching. Although Brewer's test scores were above the district average, it was under pressure to meet accountability goals. Farley was a multi-class, multiracial school in a mixed-income community with a strong base of professional parents and high test scores – all of which made it less subject to accountability pressures. Farley had a strong teacher culture that valued professional knowledge and judgement, and, to a greater degree than the other schools, teachers felt empowered to resist the deprofessionalizing pressures of accountability.

Regulation of teaching and narrowing the curriculum

With accountability, the state shifts responsibility for educational improvement to teachers and schools, but gives them less control over end goals, pedagogy and conceptualization (Ball 1997), stripping teachers of opportunities for professional and ethical judgement. Although accountability introduced a 'qualitatively different regime of control' of teaching (Gewirtz 1997: 222), teachers responded differently in the four schools. As the loss of control over pedagogical decisions increased for schools on, or threatened with, probation, technical rationality and measurable results were substituted (to varying degrees) for teachers' complex professional judgements and for ethical and social purposes of education. Over the course of my research, Grover and Westview teachers were increasingly monitored and the schools increasingly dominated by practices and discourses of test preparation. At the higher performing schools, Brewer and Farley, there were fewer accountability pressures. Over time, practices and discourses of test preparation, including regular test practice, routinized and formulaic instruction, emphasis on discrete (tested) skills, substitution of test-prep materials for regular texts, and differential attention to students close to passing the tests pervaded the pedagogical culture of Westview and Grover, and to some extent, Brewer. As one Westview teacher put it, '[w]e are test driven . . . everything is test driven'. Farley's more privileged position allowed teachers to eschew many of these practices, but they were fearful that district regulation would eventually redefine what it meant to teach at Farley. While some inexperienced teachers at some schools found support in the routinized and semi-scripted curricula and instructional practices encouraged by district officials and external 'partners', more experienced and self-confident teachers found the routines simplistic and professionally demeaning.

The accountability regime created and exacerbated contradictions between substantive long-term projects to improve teaching and learning, and short-term accountability-driven goals. Brewer and Grover dropped conceptual, inquiry-based mathematics in favour of procedures to quickly solve problems on standardized tests. Accountability pressures channelled Westview teachers' holistic commitment to their students into raising test scores and began to chip away at Farley teachers' sense of professional efficacy as they debated and partly revised their rich literacy curriculum to meet the state's formulaic writing template and emphasis on discrete skills. At Brewer, under the pressure of high stakes tests in English, Latino/a teachers with a deep commitment to bilingualism and biliteracy began to de-emphasize instruction in Spanish, and accountability derailed the school-wide inquiry process. At Westview, teachers were compelled to put away literature texts and projects and focus on test preparation using booklets furnished by the test maker. This de-professionalization of teachers' knowledge exemplifies the corporate rationality underlying the neoliberal restructuring of public institutions particularly in urban schools.

A racialized system of surveillance and control

Accountability is a totalizing system, permeating all aspects of school life and demanding that each level of authority, each classroom and school conform, more or less, even if not immediately threatened with sanctions. Especially in African American schools, teachers in my study expressed powerlessness, heightened stress and demoralization (see Finnigan and Gross 2007; Gewirtz 1997; Smyth 2001; Valli and Buese 2007). This was under-girded by a logic of inevitability – 'there will always be tests' – and the belief that lack of compliance would result in more surveillance. The racialized public display of individual and school failure and punishment by the state reminded teachers, as well as schools and communities of colour, that, as a Grover teacher summarized, '[y]ou really don't have too much power or say-so in what goes on'. This was particularly so at Grover where the loss of agency and demoralization was palpable as year after year Grover failed to 'get off probation' despite teachers' hard work and perhaps because of a revolving door of external mandates and imposed programmes.

A panoptic system of surveillance and an ensemble of everyday practices shape teacher as well as student identities, teaching them to discipline themselves. The separation of 'good' and 'bad' schools, that is accomplished through the testing, sorting, and ordering processes of standardized tests, distribution of stanine scores, retention of students and determination of probation lists, constructs categories of functionality and dysfunctionality, normalcy and deviance that label students, schools, neighbourhoods and their teachers. 'Deficiency' is made visible, individual, easily measured, highly stigmatized and punishable. Test scores are published in the newspaper, and teachers described the public shaming that accompanied the derision directed at teachers in schools on probation. One said, 'people don't want to shake your hand when they find out you teach at [Grover]'. By shifting responsibility for school failure from the state to individual schools, students, teachers and parents (see Gewirtz 1997), the accountability regime nurtures a culture of self-blame and shifting blame onto others. In two of the schools, test scores were posted on teachers' doors, and they were publicly rewarded or castigated accordingly. At all the schools, except Farley which was able to use its relatively privileged position to 'fly under the radar', district authorities and/or probation overseers conducted 'walk-throughs', observations that teachers described as coercive and stressful (see Valli and Buese 2007).

Accountability also worked as a discourse of containment, silencing teachers by excluding discussion of educational goals and processes and creating a climate of coercion that closed down spaces for debate (see Smyth 2001). In the schools I studied, the increased authority of the school district to surveil schools and impose sanctions reinforced already existing tendencies to avoid controversy and politically charged issues of race and culture. At Brewer, as the emphasis on test scores and central mandates grew, a budding school-wide process of collective, critical reflection on culture, race, and identity and relationships between teachers and Latino parents was relegated to the background. At Farley, African American parents initiated an inquiry into the disproportionate disciplining and lower achievement of African American male students. However, concerns by administrators and some teachers that any public controversy would draw attention from the district strengthened tendencies to depoliticize these issues, ultimately deflecting responsibility onto the students. The result was a plan to remediate individual students rather than examine school-wide practices and ideologies. At the other schools, accountability was a hegemonic discourse that diverted any questioning of its underlying logic onto technical discussions about how to accomplish mandated goals. This pervasive culture of social control typifies the de-democratization and coercion that characterizes the neo-liberal state, particularly in urban contexts (Lipman 2004).

However, across the school district surveillance was differential by race and class. Schools in low-income neighbourhoods of colour were the ones on probation and thus least in charge of their own destiny. Thus, while all teachers are, to some degree, engulfed by accountability, accumulated race and class advantages translate into very different constraints on teachers. Differences in teacher agency and professionalism are enshrined in the system of punishments and rewards. While some schools were put on probation and under strict centralized oversight, others were rewarded for their high achievement as Autonomous Management Performance Schools (AMPS) with greater autonomy from district oversight. Although there are exceptions, AMPS reproduce sedimented race and class advantages and privileged status. For example, in March 2007, Chicago Public Schools announced eighteen additional AMPS schools, bringing the total to 108 out of 625 schools. Although the school district is 92 per cent students of colour and 85 per cent low-income, of the eighteen new AMPS schools, eight are almost or more than 50 per cent white, all but three are less than 63 per cent low income and seven less than 25 per cent low income, and eleven are selective enrolment schools (requiring applications and, in some cases, admission tests).

Thus, accountability reproduces and extends race and class disparities among schools that, in turn, are reflected in the nature of teachers' work.

'Ethical retooling'

The 'ethical retooling' of the public sector (Ball 2003) emphasizes excellence, effectiveness and that which can be measured. It has changed how teachers think about teaching, what they do (Robertson 2007) and what counts as an effective teacher (Mahony and Hextall 1998). In the discourse of account-ability, teachers who were 'good' according to multidimensional and compli-cated ethical, cultural and pedagogical criteria, including those constructed by families and communities, became less so. Teachers recognized for commit-ment to children and communities, determination to help students 'read' and 'write' the world in Freire's terms, and valorization of children's languages and home cultures were ultimately judged by a single, instrumental measure – their ability to raise test scores.

Imposed pedagogical practices corrupted relations with students and ran counter to the intellectual and ethical purposes at the core of these teachers' professional identities. As teaching was redefined by test scores and teachers were encouraged to focus differentially on students who could raise the school's scores, some talked about 'a moral crisis'. Ms Jones, one of the most respected teachers at Grover, became physically ill as she felt 'under pressure because this is the first time in a long, long time since I was a child that I really feel I'm compromising my beliefs'. Test-driven language assimilation provoked a similar crisis for Brewer teachers who de-emphasized Spanish but understood from experience that language confirms one's life history and is a critical resource of community and solidarity in the face of discrimination and exploitation.

By the third year of my research, some of the most competent teachers left Grover, Brewer and Westview, or left teaching altogether. These included teacher intellectuals with explicitly critical pedagogical philosophies and committed culturally relevant and community-centred teachers – in short teachers with the capacity to provide leadership and examples for the trans-formation of teaching. Instead of supporting and extending the strengths of these teachers, the accountability regime pushed them out as it compelled others to accommodate (Finnigan and Gross 2007). After fourteen years, Ms Jones left Grover to become a special education teacher exempt from some of the accountability pressures. At Grover, between 1997 and 2001, twenty-six teachers (out of a staff of about 36) left. As one teacher put it, '[w]e have lost a lot of great teachers over the last two years who just couldn't take it anymore'. Even some Farley teachers threatened to leave for jobs in the suburbs if their school became test-driven.

At least initially, Chicago's accountability system resonated with principals, teachers, and the public concerned about uncommitted teachers, particularly in communities of colour, and about the weaknesses of novice or less-competent teachers. Accountability promised to address the perceived need for both teacher motivation and support (Finnigan and Gross 2007) through sanctions for failure, coupled with mandated instructional practices, mandated professional development and semi-scripted curricula. However, technical solutions and coercion did not enhance the capacities of teachers to develop complex pedagogical and curricular practices and judgements. Nor are they a substitute for the socio-political knowledge and ethical commitment that is crucial to culturally and politically relevant teaching. Moreover, imposed standards deny the contested nature of knowledge and evade critical discussions about what should constitute the curriculum, a good school and good teaching – a discussion that had begun at Brewer and was pushed by several teachers at Grover prior to accountability.

The technical pre-packaged practices promoted by accountability policies did not help Grover, Brewer and Westview teachers develop the strengths of Farley's rich culture of literacy. Nor did they foster the professional competencies and independent professional judgement of some Farley teachers. If anything, accountability made teaching more routinized and pushed out teachers who embodied a rich professional culture. Conversely, pigeon-holing teachers and schools as 'good' or 'bad' according to test scores did not help Farley teachers acknowledge and address weaknesses. Here I have in mind the ethical commitment to low-income African American and Latino students, culturally relevant pedagogies, and efforts to promote critical literacy that were strengths of some teachers at Grover, Westview and Brewer.

Teaching in charter schools – paradoxes and moral dilemmas

Centralized accountability without adequate resources laid the groundwork for the growth of charter schools in Chicago, presaging what is likely to happen nationally under NCLB (Lipman and Haines 2007). By normalizing a system of sorting, classifying and demarcating students, teachers and schools as 'failures,' accountability legitimates turning public schools over to private operators. NCLB introduces an additional incentive because closing public schools and reopening them as new charter schools is a way for the school district to avert state takeover for failing to meet annual NCLB benchmarks.[3] Not surprisingly, Chicago's charter schools are concentrated in low-income African American and Latino communities where public schools have been historically under-resourced and which bear the scars of years of public and private disinvestment. Thus charter schools are another arena for capital accumulation facilitated by the cycle of disinvestment, devaluation, and reinvestment in low-income urban areas (Brenner and Theodore 2002).

However, the origins and meanings of charter schools are contradictory, located in neo-liberal ideology and the logic of capital but also in the political and cultural self-determination of communities of colour and teachers' aspirations for greater professional autonomy (Wells *et al.* 2002). Overall,

charter schools open public education to the market through private management of public schools and a system of consumer choice. Authority is invested
in appointed boards which may hire for-profit educational management
organizations (EMOs) to run the schools (Ford 2005). On the other hand,
some charter schools are developed and run by community organizations or
groups of teachers seeking alternatives to the dominant practices of public
schools. In particular, some educators and communities of colour are taking
advantage of the greater flexibility offered by charter schools to develop
culturally relevant, community-centred education, in the tradition of Black
Independent Schools. The emergence of these schools is a powerful indication
of the persistent failure of public schools to provide equitable and liberatory
education in communities of colour, and it represents the urgency to counter
the criminalization, high drop-out rates, and persistent miseducation of youth
of colour in Chicago and other urban areas.

My initial investigation suggests that teachers' experiences reflect the
contradictions and multiple meanings of the charter school movement itself
(see Wells *et al.* 2005). Since charters are governed by private boards and
have varied philosophies, budgets, pay scales and administrative structures,
conditions and experiences of teaching vary. Overall, because they are not
unionized, are not required to hire certified teachers, and are subject to the
vagaries of market forces, charter schools have introduced greater insecurity
into the teaching profession. In 2004 a California for-profit EMO closed
operation of a multi-site charter school in mid-school year, leaving 10,000
students and hundreds of teachers without schools. Teachers working for
some corporate charter schools in Chicago report they have no breaks and
are afraid to challenge the administration because they have no union
protection. Because charter schools are funded at a lower rate, 'teaching'
may be redefined to include tasks typically performed by other school
personnel (Johnson and Landman 2000).

Yet, because charter schools have greater autonomy from state regulations
and local district guidelines, the educational vision, flexibility, and professional
authority offered by some charter schools can be appealing even if it means
lower pay, less security, or a greater time commitment. Importantly, a few
charter schools also open up space for ethical and politically progressive
education. The initial round of Chicago charter schools, in the 1990s, included
several started by teachers frustrated with the constraints of high stakes
accountability and motivated by visions of social justice education. Although
the vast majority are corporate (42 of 56 currently), the remainder include
Afro-centric, social justice, teacher-initiated or rigorous college preparatory
schools, most in low-income African American communities. As the space
for ethical professional practice narrows in public schools, these charter
schools attract dedicated, socially committed teachers. An example is a charter
high school, in a very low-income African American community, with a
strong college preparatory focus, intensive academic support, pre-college
experiences and a very strong rate of graduation and college matriculation.

With flexibility to develop curriculum and make pedagogical decisions, the social studies department developed a four-year course of study that begins with 'identity and difference in historical context', moves on to 'Revolution and Resistance' in the US and globally, then US foreign policy (including an examination of 'white man's burden' and 'imperialism'), and ends with impacting local government and political action.

It is one of the paradoxes of teaching in neo-liberal times that one set of neo-liberal initiatives (accountability) has begotten another (charter schools/ education markets) which, although overall regressive, opens up spaces for progressive agency. But some teachers in these schools also talk about a 'moral dilemma'. They know charter schools are part of the neo-liberal restructuring of public education that undermines the public interest and produces educational inequities. They feel complicit in this process yet guard the freedom to engage in teaching that they believe in, teaching that nurtures critical consciousness, cultural identity and political agency and a context that provides the ideological support and collaboration of like-minded colleagues. As one teacher put it, 'I know charter schools are bad for public education, but I could never teach like this in a CPS [Chicago Public] school.'

Yet, the space for agency may be limited and temporary, and the autonomy offered by school choice may be less real than it appears (Ball 1994). The state imposes accountability on charter schools even while offering them more flexibility. Some have been closed for not meeting test score targets, and others are induced to select students (formally or informally) to ensure they meet these targets. Although there are a few well-funded 'social justice' charter schools that provide teachers the time and material resources to develop the curriculum, in most, teachers work long hours at relatively low pay and shoulder administrative tasks and multiple roles. This may explain the rapid turnover of teachers, and it brings into question the viability of these schools in the long term.

Conclusion

We ought not to idealize teacher professionalism in previous periods. Schools and the conditions of teaching have always been contested and highly differentiated by social class, race and ethnicity. However, accountability and the market create new forms of inequality in teaching as well as learning (Apple 2001; Gewirtz, Ball and Bowe 1995; Hursh 2007; Lipman 2004). Indeed, this differentiation is a central feature of the market. Some, by virtue of their advantaged position (in terms of access to specific forms of social, economic and cultural capital), luck or individual initiative, benefit from market choices, but most are locked into increasingly restrictive and minimalist public schools or profit-driven corporate charter schools. Just as school choice 'appears to give more power to all parents, while systematically advantaging some and disadvantaging others' (Ball 1994: 10), options in a system of public and charter schools have a similar effect on teaching as a profession.

Chicago illustrates that teaching is increasingly stratified, competitive and insecure with growing divergence between public selective enrolment schools and a few charter schools on the one hand and corporate charters and highly regulated public schools on the other.

Although teaching is in many ways swept up in the juggernaut of neo-liberal restructuring of the city, the education market paradoxically opens a crack for opposition to neo-liberal corporate rationality and disempowerment of teachers and students. This 'freedom to teach' is what teachers in my study of accountability said they were losing. However this notion of freedom, which builds on teachers' professional autonomy, is severed from teaching as a social responsibility and articulated to the neo-liberal discourse of individual freedom to 'choose' and to be entrepreneurial – if you don't like the public system, choose to teach at a charter school. Better still, start your own. This discourse and the charter school 'option' gain potency in the face of increasing regulation of teachers' work and the seeming absence of a viable alternative. Caught in the neo-liberal discourse of inevitability – there is no alternative to neo-liberal policy and capitalism – teachers face a moral dilemma either way they turn, while a return to bureaucratic welfare state policies is not viable.

It is self-evident that what is needed is a transformative agenda for economic redistribution (restructuring of the economy), cultural recognition (transforming what counts as valorized culture and knowledge), and political representation (parity of representation) (Fraser forthcoming). Such an agenda would reframe teacher professionalism within a larger programme for social justice. It would valorize culturally centred educational projects, teacher voice and professional judgement, and educational variation within a framework of equitable redistribution of economic, cultural and political resources and power. It would value teachers' professional autonomy but articulate it to a framework of collective welfare.

One step is the emergence of various local teacher organizations and several national teacher networks and conferences centred on social justice. They include charter and public school teachers. These initiatives are motivated partly by the extreme criminalization, violence, poverty and racial oppression facing youth of colour and partly by resistance to neo-liberal policy in education and other social spheres. The evolution of these projects and a research agenda that studies and makes them visible may contribute to a counter-hegemonic discourse about teaching as a collective liberatory practice.

Notes

1   NCLB requires annual student assessment and establishes punitive measures for schools' failure to meet increasingly rigorous levels of proficiency. By 2014, 100 per cent of students are required to meet proficiency levels.
2   Charter school legislation, now passed in thirty-eight US states, allows individual schools greater autonomy from state education regulations and local district guidelines but requires them to meet accountability targets.

3   Under NCLB, school districts are eligible for state takeover after five consecutive
    years of failing to meet Adequate Yearly Progress accountability targets.

References

Apple, M. W. (2001) *Educating the 'Right' Way*, New York: Routledge.

Ball, S. J. (1994) *Education Reform: a critical and post-structural approach*,
Buckingham: Open University Press.

—— (1997) 'Policy sociology and critical social research: a personal review of recent
education policy and policy research', *British Educational Research Journal*,
23 (3): 257–274.

—— (2003) 'The teacher's soul and the terrors of performativity', *Journal of
Education Policy*, 18 (2): 215–228.

Brenner, N. and Theodore, N. (2002) 'Cities and the geographies of "Actually Existing Neoliberalism"', *Antipode*, 34 (3): 349–379.

Finnegan, K. S. and Gross, B. (2007) 'Do accountability policy sanctions influence
teacher motivation? Lessons from Chicago's low-performing schools', *American
Educational Research Journal*, 44 (3): 594–629.

Ford, B. (2005) 'The significance of charter schools and the privatization of standards:
holding the wolf by the ears', *Policy Futures in Education*, 3 (1): 16–29.

Fraser, N. (forthcoming) 'Introduction: the radical imagination between redistribution
and recognition', in N. Fraser (ed.), *Mapping the Radical Imagination*. Online.
Available www.newschool.edu/GF/polsci/faculty/fraser/ (accessed 12 July 2007).

Gewirtz, S. (1997) 'Post-welfarism and the reconstruction of teachers' work in the
UK', *Journal of Education Policy*, 12 (4): 217–231.

——, Ball, S. J. and Bowe, R. (1995) *Markets, Choice and Equity in Education*,
Buckingham: Open University Press.

Hursh, D. (2007) 'Assessing no child left behind and the rise of neoliberal education
policies', *American Educational Research Journal*, 44 (3): 493–518.

Johnson, S. M. and Landman, J. (2000) 'Sometimes bureaucracy has its charms: the
working conditions of teachers in deregulated schools', *Teachers College Record*,
102 (1): 85–124.

Ladson-Billings, G. (1994) *The Dream Deepers: successful teachers of African
American children*, San Francisco, CA: Jossey-Bass.

Lipman, P. (2004) *High Stakes Education: inequality, globalization, and urban school
reform*, New York: Routledge.

—— (2008) 'Mixed-income schools and housing: advancing the neo-liberal urban
agenda', *Journal of Education Policy*, 23 (2): 119–134.

—— and Haines, N. (2007) 'From education accountability to privatization and
African American exclusion – Chicago Public Schools' "Renaissance 2010"',
Educational Policy, 21 (3): 471–502.

Mahony, P. and Hextall, I. (1998) 'Social justice and the reconstruction of teaching',
Journal of Education Policy, 13 (4): 545–558.

Robertson, S. L. (2000) *A Class Act: changing teachers' work, the state, and globalization*, New York: Falmer.

—— (2007) '"Remaking the world": neo-liberalism and the transformation of education and teachers' labour', Centre for Globalisation, Education and Societies,
University of Bristol, Bristol BS8 1JA, UK. Online. Available at: www.bris.ac.uk/
education/people/academicStaff/edslr/publications/17slr/ (accessed 8 October 2007).

Sassen, S. (2006) *Cities in a World Economy*, 3rd edn, Thousand Oaks, CA: Pine Forge Press.

Smyth, J. (2001) *Critical Politics of Teachers' Work: an Australian perspective*, New York: Peter Lang.

Valli, L. and Buese, D. (2007) 'The changing roles of teachers in an era of high-stakes accountability', *American Educational Research Journal*, 44 (3): 519–558.

Wells, A. S., Slayton, J. and Scott, J. (2002) 'Defining democracy in the neoliberal age: charter school reform and educational consumption', *American Educational Research Journal*, 39 (2): 337–361.

Wells, A. S., Scott, J. T., Lopez, A. and Holme, J. J. (2005) 'Charter school reform and the shifting meaning of educational equity: greater voice and greater inequality?', in J. Petrovich and A. S. Wells (eds), *Bringing Equity Back: research for a new era in American educational policy*, New York: Teachers College Press, pp. 219–243.

7 Pedagogizing teacher professional identities

Bob Lingard

Over the past 150 years or so teaching as an occupation has developed as a form of state professionalism. Since the 1980s, in the context of the rise of various manifestations of global neo-liberal politics, the state has been restructured with implications for teaching as a state profession. With the 'economization' of education policy, there has been a loss of involvement of the teaching profession in the production of education policy at a macro level. Education policy production has become largely part of what Bourdieu (1998a) called 'the right hand of the state'; that is, education has been relocated within the central steering mechanisms of the Treasury and economic policy. This human capital approach has also been accompanied by a range of new policy technologies (Ball 2008) which include targets and testing regimes linked to a broader audit culture (Power 1999). The resultant culture of performativity has challenged the potential for authentic pedagogies and chiselled away at the 'soul of the teacher' (Ball 2006). Connell (1985), in his influential study of teachers' work conducted more than twenty years ago, argued that in a sense teaching was a labour process without a product. The restructured state and new forms of performative control of schools and teachers have ensured that this is no longer the case. In some policy settings this culture is also linked to the introduction of quasi-markets and discourses of parental choice.

Teachers have resented these new policy frames, which have had a deep impact on their identities and reconstituted teacher professionalism, both as a form of occupational control and as a set of traits which define the occupation. In Bourdieu's (1998a: 2) terms, teachers are part of 'the left hand of the state', 'agents of the so-called spending ministries', who reject the *raison d'être* of the right hand of the state in an attempt to hold onto some of the gains which accompanied earlier Keynesian welfare state reforms.

Within neo-liberal policy regimes, these new policy approaches in education have also tended to thin out pedagogies and reduce the quality of education, a situation documented for England by Mahony and Hextall (2000), Hartley (2003), Ranson (2003), Ball (2006) and Lingard *et al.* (2008). They have all written about the implicit pedagogization of policy in England, demonstrating its technicized and reductive character reflecting a narrow preoccupation with the goal of creating a knowledge economy. Mahony and Hextall (2000: 102) suggest that these changes have precipitated debates about the nature of teacher professionalism. Ranson (2003) shows how a regime of professional accountability in England has been replaced by a regime of neo-liberal accountability characterized by an increasing specification of curricula and classroom practices, which has reached into the pedagogic core of teachers' work. Hartley (2003) demonstrates the clear mismatch between the pedagogic effects of this neo-liberal accountability regime and what is actually required – in terms of knowledge and dispositional outcomes – from schools in today's globalized world. Hartley's argument is that the policy regime in English education ensures that the goals it desires cannot be met.

Teaching and schooling, however, have also remained part of what Bourdieu called the left hand of the state, part of the provision of welfare and care. Given the re-articulation of education policy via the right hand of the state, Bourdieu (1998a) suggests that many teachers have now become somewhat akin to social workers, who bear the weight of this neo-liberal world. At the same time, education continues to function almost as a policy garbage bin, a domain into which politicians and policymakers tip multifarious social problems for 'management' and 'mitigation', if not solutions. Further, given the strengthening of the right hand of the state in education policy production and neo-liberal assumptions about greater efficiency and effectiveness measured through outcomes accountability, teachers and schools often have to do more with less, and meet performance targets, for example, in England to maximize the numbers of pupils gaining A–C grades at GCSE.

Nonetheless, while this policy regime has real effects, there also is a way in which, drawing on Bourdieu's (1993) account of social fields, we can see that the logics of practice of the field of policy production are disjunctive with the logics of practice of teachers' work. The former logics are imperialistic in their claim to universal application. Indeed, Bourdieu (1998b: 59) saw the state as the field with the 'monopoly of the universal', which is evident in the logic of policy. However, teacher practice, pedagogy, is local, situated, specific and contingent (Coburn and Stein 2006), in stark contrast to the universalistic claims of policy. Good pedagogies are tailored to the specificities of the students in a specific class and shaped by nuanced professional readings of these specificities.

So despite the effects of the new policy regime, there is still some space for older constructions of teacher professionalism to have effects. One central aspect to strengthening this space, it is argued in this chapter, is to strengthen the place of pedagogies in teacher professional identities.

Pedagogies

Educational research and theory on pedagogies can be seen to sit within either an abstract political/theoretical frame or within an empiricist/reductive frame. As an example of the former, the critical pedagogies literature (including that informed by feminism, critical theory, neo-Marxism, post-structuralism, queer theory and, more recently, post-colonialism) is most often exhortatory in nature and not based on deep empirical accounts of classroom practices. Jennifer Gore (1993), in *The Struggle for Pedagogies*, established another binary in her Foucauldian account of critical and feminist pedagogies: between the social vision of these approaches and the more explicit instructional or pedagogical focus of the accounts against which they are often juxtaposed. However, she noted that there is at least an implicit vision in approaches that emphasize instruction or pedagogy, arguing that 'instruction and vision are analytical components of pedagogy [and] insofar as the concept implies both, each requires attention' (1993: 5). The empiricist literature, derived from actual classroom research, most often does not engage with the theoretical or critical pedagogies literature. There exist then two incommensurate traditions.

What we end up with is a divide like that described by C. Wright Mills (1959) in *The Sociological Imagination*: the divide between grand theory – it sounds significant but we do not know whether or not it is true – and abstract empiricism – where we know that what is observed is true, but is it significant? The approach taken in the Queensland School Reform Longitudinal Study (QSRLS), the research utilized in this chapter, was in some ways an attempt to provide a pedagogical theory of the middle ground, one that eschewed the grand theory/abstract empiricism and politics/pedagogies binaries and which sought to interrogate both theory and data, politics and pedagogies, accepting the imbrication of each in the other.

While conceding that the literature on critical pedagogies has been important, Apple (2000: 226) argues that, given the new 'material and ideological conditions surrounding schooling', there is a need to ensure such pedagogies are not simply romantic gestures unattached to tactical and strategic reform agendas. More recently, he has noted that critical pedagogies should not simply be about 'academic theorizing'. Rather, he states: '[c]ritical approaches are best developed in close contact with the object of one's analysis' (2006: 210). This is the position adopted by the QSRLS in seeking to construct a pedagogical theory of the middle ground.

The research

While the QSRLS was developed out of Newmann and Associates' (1996) research on 'authentic pedagogy', it was recontextualized to take account of the Australian, specifically Queensland, schooling context. The Newmann research used the concept of 'authentic pedagogy' to refer to teacher classroom practices that promoted high quality learning and boosted achievements for all students, closing to some extent the equity gap in school performance linked to gender, social class and 'race'.

In the Newmann research, authentic pedagogy incorporated the concepts of authentic instruction[1] and authentic assessment.[2] The QSRLS research differentiated between pedagogies and assessment, whilst at the same time recognizing the importance of aligning the two. Authentic instruction requires higher order thinking, deep knowledge, substantive conversations and connections to the world beyond the classroom. Authentic assessment involves students being expected to organize information, consider alternatives, demonstrate knowledge of disciplinary content and processes, perform elaborate communication, solve problems that are connected to the world beyond the classroom and present to an audience beyond the school (Newmann and Associates 1996: 46). The QSRLS augmented the concepts of authentic pedagogy and assessment so as to take account of social as well as academic outcomes. Consequently, the elements of authentic instruction were expanded into a broader grid consisting of twenty items for productive pedagogies and the elements of authentic assessment were expanded into seventeen items for productive assessment. Each item was mapped on a five-point scale in the research (see Table 7.1).

There were twenty-four carefully selected research schools, selected because of their reputations for reform, half primary, half secondary. Eight schools were studied in each year of the research, with each being visited twice for a week at a time. Classes observed in these schools were Year 6 (penultimate primary year), Year 8 and Year 11 (penultimate secondary year), in the subject areas of English, Maths, Science and Social Science.

The expanded elements of productive pedagogies were derived from a literature review. They drew on work from the sociology of education, critical readings of school effectiveness and school improvement research, socio-linguistic studies of classrooms, social psychology (including socio-cultural approaches, theories of social cognition, learning communities and constructivism), critical literacy and critical pedagogies, along with Freirean, Indigenous, post-colonial and feminist pedagogies, direct instruction and so on. These ideas were operationalized via a classroom observation manual that drew on the broader critical literatures. As indicated earlier, this was central to the attempt to constitute pedagogic theories of the middle ground, drawing on critical literatures, but also an extensive empirical base.

It was in the construction of the twenty-element model of productive pedagogies from the literature, which also formed the basis of the classroom observation manual, that the attempt was made to construct a progressive pedagogy for contemporary times. This was evident in the emphasis upon the constructed nature of knowledge and multiple perspectives and in the constructivist and collectivist approach to learning. It was also evident in the connectedness of the pedagogies to biographies, to previous knowledge, to the world in which students currently learn and play, to their everyday/every night practices. It was evident in the requirement for assessment criteria to be made explicit and in the substantive conversations which were conceived as being central to the distribution of multiple capitals to all students.

Table 7.1 Relationships between productive pedagogies and productive assessment

Dimensions	Productive pedagogies	Productive assessment
Intellectual quality	Problematic knowledge	Problematic knowledge: construction of knowledge Problematic knowledge: consideration of alternatives
	Higher order thinking	Higher order thinking
	Depth of knowledge	Depth of knowledge: disciplinary content
	Depth of students' understanding	Depth of knowledge: disciplinary processes
	Substantive conversation	Elaborated written communication
	Metalanguage	Metalanguage
Connectedness	Connectedness to the world beyond the classroom	Connectedness: problem connected to the world beyond the classroom
	Knowledge integration	Knowledge integration
	Background knowledge	Link to background knowledge
	Problem based curriculum	Problem based curriculum Connectedness: audience beyond school
Supportiveness	Students' direction	Students' direction
	Explicit quality performance criteria	Explicit quality performance criteria
	Social support	
	Academic engagement	
	Student self regulation	
Engagement with and valuing of difference	Cultural knowledges	Cultural knowledges
	Active citizenship	Active citizenship
	Narrative	
	Group identities in learning communities	Group identities in learning communities
	Representation	

Even more so, the emphasis upon working with and valuing difference attempted to take a critical 'post' perspective on differences of all sorts (ethnic, Indigenous, gender, disability, sexuality), both in terms of representation in texts and examples, but also in terms of inclusion in classroom activities, and in the goal of creating activist citizens who saw the global space as an arena for contemporary politics, but who also 'worked on' the local. This was the cosmopolitan aspect of the pedagogies, the creation of global citizens, informed by what Paul Gilroy (2004) calls 'planetary humanism' and by what Edward Said (2004) called 'democratic humanism', a non-Eurocentric, non-sexist, reflexive critical humanism, stressing similarity as well as difference. Thus, productive pedagogies sought to work with, not against, multiplicity (Dimitriadis and McCarthy 2001) and 'with a culture of respect for the history, the language and culture of the peoples represented in the classroom' (Rose, 1995: 414). Stuart Hall (2000: 216) has beautifully encapsulated the stance taken on difference in the research:

> This is not the binary form of difference between what is absolutely the same, and what is absolutely 'Other'. It is a 'weave' of similarities and differences that refuse to separate into fixed binary oppositions.

On the basis of about 1,000 classroom observations in twenty-four case study schools over three years (1998–2000) (about 250 teachers each observed four times), statistical analysis (congeneric factor analysis) has supported the development of a more complex, multidimensional model of pedagogy – what we called 'productive pedagogies'. It is important to stress here that the model was developed from observing *actual* teachers at work in *actual* classrooms.

The twenty elements of productive pedagogies fitted into four dimensions as shown in Table 7.1, which the research team named 'intellectual quality', 'connectedness', 'social support' and 'working with and valuing difference'. The latter dimension was initially called recognition of difference, but modified to working with and valuing difference to capture a more activist disposition and potentially less relativist stance.

Findings

Across the entire sample of teachers, in relation to pedagogies there was a high degree of support for students (although very few opportunities for them to affect the direction of activities in the classroom), but not enough intellectual demand, connectedness to the world or engagement with and valuing of difference. In relation to intellectual quality and connectedness, there was a high standard deviation, indicating that these dimensions were present in some classrooms. In contrast, there was a high mean and a low standard deviation for supportiveness. For the difference dimension there was a very low mean and a small standard deviation. (See Table 7.2 for statistical findings.) What we saw were very supportive and caring teachers, teachers practising an almost social-worker version of teachers' work. We believe that teachers should be praised for their commitment to providing social support for students, but that the absence of intellectual demand, connectedness and working with and valuing difference carries significant social justice concerns.

Elsewhere I have referred to the actual pedagogies identified by the research as 'pedagogies of indifference' (Lingard 2007), because of their non-connectedness, their lack of intellectual demand and their absence of working with and valuing difference. I am now a little more wary of such a descriptor, as it might seem to imply indifferent teachers.[3] It could also be seen as a criticism of teaching as a caring profession, and implicitly a critique of women teachers as well, positions I would reject. My use of the term 'pedagogies of indifference' was not meant to be read in those ways, but rather as a descriptor of the limited potential for dominant pedagogical practices to interrupt the reproduction of inequalities. However, as the evidence documented above so clearly demonstrated, what we found were caring teachers, not indifferent teachers. In line with Bourdieu's argument about teachers as social workers, there is also a way in which state policies, and more recently the impact of neo-liberal globalization mediated through the policies of the right hand of the state, almost demand that teaching be a caring profession in the face of enhanced inequalities and the need to hold some communities and lives together.

There are obviously structural explanations for the broad findings, including class sizes, policy pressures (earlier social justice policies that perhaps emphasized care over intellectual demand and contemporary testing policies), a crowded curriculum, the time and pacing demands of curriculum coverage, pressures on teachers, a focus on structural change, and so on. Allan Luke

Table 7.2 Mean ratings of dimensions of productive pedagogies from 1998 to 2000

	1998 (n = 302)		1999 (n = 343)		2000 (n = 330)		Total (n = 975)	
	Mean	Std dev.	Mean	Std dev.	Mean	Std dev.	Mean	Std dev.
Intellectual quality	2.16	0.77	2.17	0.73	2.47	0.91	2.27	0.82
Connectedness	1.84	0.77	1.97	0.79	2.39	0.97	2.07	0.88
Supportive classroom environment	2.75	0.63	3.05	0.67	3.26	0.67	3.03	0.69
Engagement with difference	1.79	0.51	1.89	0.50	2.13	0.54	1.94	0.54

(2006: 123), a member of the QSRLS research team, notes that interviews with teachers supported an explanation that 'the testing, basic skills, and accountability push had encouraged narrowing of the curriculum' and was associated with the finding of 'a shaving off of higher order and critical thinking and a lowering of cognitive demand and intellectual depth'. Here we see the effects of the restructured state.

In the context of growing inequality, we believe that teachers should be congratulated on the levels of social support and care they offer to students. We found levels of support to be particularly high in schools located in disadvantaged communities. Schools do contribute to what contemporary public policy likes to call 'social capital' – the creation of social trust, networks and community – the collective (but also dangerous) 'we' of local communities (Sennett 1998) and the imagined community of the nation (Anderson 1991). This social capital seemed, however, to be more of a defensive or ameliorative kind linked to notions of resilience, than that referred to in Bourdieu's (1986) work on capitals, where social capital suggests enduring networks, which assist in individual career preferment for the advantaged. However, the research would suggest that such support is a necessary, but not sufficient requirement for enhancing student outcomes, both social and academic, and for achieving more equality of educational opportunity. Socially just pedagogies need also to work with a more equitable distribution of cultural capital through explicitness in pedagogies and assessment practices.

The lack of intellectual demand (particularly in schools serving disadvantaged communities and in secondary schools) has social justice implications. Indeed, this absence of intellectual demand works to reproduce inequality in the way in which Bourdieu (Bourdieu and Passeron 1977) suggests; that is, by demanding of all that which they do not give, those with the requisite cultural capital are advantaged in schooling. Such a lack probably reflects the substantial amount of curriculum content teachers feel they must cover in a finite period of time; thus coverage (demanding a certain pacing) becomes more important than the pursuit of higher order thinking, citizenship goals and so on.

It is interesting that the nexus between the social class of the student body and pedagogies (particularly on the 'intellectual demandingness' dimension) appeared to be broken in some of the 'best' primary schools in the QSRLS research. By contrast, this was not so in most of the very large, working-class suburban high schools, where effective reform around good pedagogies seemed to be based more in departments, than across the whole school. School size was also an important factor here, with the smaller country high schools having better across-school pedagogies than the big city schools. It should also be noted that differences in the quality of pedagogy between primary and secondary schools evaporated when size was taken into account. There are implications here for the creation of social capital in schools.

We were also surprised how unconnected with students' lives and communities the pedagogies were, most of the time. Practice was decontextualized.

Following Bourdieu's account of the reproduction of inequality, the literature would suggest that middle-class students possessing the requisite cultural capital are better positioned to handle this decontextualized school knowledge. Bernstein's (1999) work on the distinction between vertical (in this case academic) knowledge and horizontal (connectedness to local and specific) knowledge provides insights into the difficulties faced by teachers and students in working with and across the two.

The lack – indeed absence – of engagement with difference perhaps reflected teacher doubt about what the appropriate responses were and a serious lack of effective professional development on such matters. In our view, this did not reflect so much a failure to recognize that something had to be done, but rather a not knowing what to do in an increasingly xenophobic political environment post-September 11. From 1996 until its electoral defeat in 2007, the Conservative Howard government in Australia shifted 'the public gaze and preoccupation to global events such as the War on Terror, the potential avian flu epidemic and, at the micro level, encourage[d] its population to be wary of strangers [and] to be conscious of the vulnerability of Australia and Australian shores to illegal immigrants' (Crowley and Matthews 2006: 6), provoking what Gilroy (2004) has called a 'fear of difference', rather than robust multiculturalism and robust reconciliation with Indigenous Australians.

We also found (apart from in the Aboriginal community school) an inverse relationship between the extent of engagement with and valuing of difference in pedagogical practices and the ethnic diversity of the school's population, a counterintuitive finding. In our interviews with teachers they indicated that they had no professional development in respect of difference and really did not know what to do, particularly in a context where multiculturalism had become highly politicized in a climate characterized by a fear of difference. This is why this chapter is arguing for the need for the presence of this dimension in all classroom pedagogies. Difference is even more important in the context of globalization where mobility/immobility represents an additional element of contemporary disadvantage (Bauman 1998).

The productive pedagogies research actually found pedagogies of indifference in the approximately 1,000 classrooms observed and yet also found that teachers and productive pedagogies could make a difference, in line with the findings of Coleman and colleagues (1966). The quality of the pedagogies received by all students, stretching from the pedagogy of the oppressed to the pedagogy of the elites, are very important for a political project of equality and difference. Nancy Fraser (1997), the US social theorist, has argued that a progressive politics today requires a working together of what she calls a politics of redistribution and a politics of difference. It is argued here that pedagogies in and of themselves cannot make all the difference in social justice terms. Redistributive policies and funding are necessary complements, as are certain systemic supports. However, pedagogies can make some difference, as the QSRLS demonstrated. To apply Fraser's argument to the pedagogies thesis being proffered here: socially just pedagogies, in being intellectually demanding and connected, attempt to provide a more just redistribution of intellectual capital. Furthermore, working with and valuing difference encourages a 'planetary humanism' and at the same time effects a pedagogy that makes *a* difference, particularly with respect to education as a good in and of itself.

Conclusion

The evidence reported above confirmed the significance of teacher pedagogies to student learning and the contribution of schools to equality of opportunity. The three message systems of schooling, as Bernstein (1971) called them, of curriculum, pedagogy and assessment help frame teacher identities as well as their practices. It has been the case that public policies have tended to deal explicitly with assessment and curriculum, while leaving pedagogies and pedagogical content knowledge (Shulman 1987) to teachers' professional discretion (although, as noted above, in some settings, policy has at least dealt implicitly with pedagogies – think, for example, of the Literacy Hour introduced by the then Blair government in England or of the quality pedagogy agenda in the New South Wales state system in Australia). The argument here is that teacher professional identities have to be strengthened around pedagogies, but pedagogies beyond those documented in the QSRLS. That is, they have to be strengthened around productive pedagogies as theorized in the research. This is not a criticism of teaching as a caring profession or the caring nature of the pedagogies found in the research, but rather an argument that such care is necessary but not sufficient if schools are to have the socially just effects that we would want them to. There needs to be a complementary strengthening of intellectual demand, connectedness and working with and valuing of difference in such pedagogies.

Pedagogy is the central task of teachers' work and as such the concept needs to be central to teachers' professional identities; pedagogical content knowledges need to be strengthened as core elements of teachers' shared, collective professional knowledges. Research such as the QSRLS can contribute to the strengthening of the pedagogical identities of teachers, but also always has to be re-read through the lens and specificities of practice and the collective professional conversations of teachers, and always subject to critique and subsequent research.

More than thirty years ago Lortie, in a classic sociological study of US teachers, suggested that the intellectual dependence of teachers had to be challenged, and identified stubborn obstacles to the achievement of such independence:

> the ethos of the occupation is tilted against engagement in pedagogical inquiry. Reflexive conservatism denies the significance of technical knowledge, assuming that energies should be centred on realizing conventional goals in known ways. Individualism leads to a distrust of

the concept of shared knowledge; it portrays teaching as the expression of individual personality. Presentism orientations retard making current sacrifices for later gains; inquiry rests on the opposite value.

(Lortie 1975: 240)

The argument here about the need to strengthen knowledge and collective professional talk about pedagogies as a central means of placing pedagogies at the centre of teachers' identities is, I believe, the positive model implicit in Lortie's critique and adumbration of the obstacles to greater intellectual independence for teachers.[4] It is perhaps not coincidental that the QSRLS found some of the very best pedagogies in the early years – excellent teachers identified outside the specific sample – and at the senior levels, where teachers have on-going professional conversations about pedagogies and assessment practices in response to systemic policy pressures concerning respectively a Year 2 literacy net, and school-based, teacher moderated assessment.

Currently teachers identify with the sector they work in, the year levels they teach, the subject disciplines their degrees are in, and the subjects which they teach. The argument here is that pedagogies, as central to teacher practice and idiosyncratic to the teaching profession – the specific knowledge and practice of the teaching profession, should be strengthened as an element of teacher identities. It is pedagogies that help schools make *a* difference and which *can* contribute towards schools meeting the goals of equity and social justice often articulated for them.

The paradox is that while the right hand of the state sets targets for increased retention in the last years of secondary schooling, for widening participation in university, and for strengthening the skill levels of the population, one effect of neo-liberal policy convergence globally has been the widening of inequalities within and between nations. This strengthens the pressure on teachers to enhance their care, therapeutic and social-worker role, while lessening the focus on intellectual demand and the potential for schools to achieve the sorts of outcomes in both educational and opportunity terms that the state demands of them. Further, some forms of accountability central to the audit culture, for example standardized testing, national league tables of school performance, international league tables of performance, thin out pedagogies and reduce the intellectual demand and reach of pedagogies. Better understanding of the significance and situated and specific character of pedagogies in relation to these issues is required.

As argued throughout, research and practice-based knowledges about pedagogies need to be central to teachers' professional identities. The strengthening of such identities in this way would enhance the capacity of schools to make a difference and also serve as an effective form of professional control. Pedagogical knowledges can contribute to a redefinition of teacher professionalism through strengthening the knowledge base of, and professional control over, the occupation, thus meeting the 'needs' of the profession, but at the same time also working for the broader social good.

Notes

1 We rejected the use of the word 'instruction' because of its very reductionist overtones and utilized instead the concept of 'pedagogy'.
2 The concept of 'authentic' was also rejected because of its modernist overtones and in the QSRLS pedagogy was pluralized to indicate that many pedagogical styles could be aligned with the concept of productive pedagogies.
3 This significant point was made to me by my colleagues, Jackie Marsh (University of Sheffield) and Martin Mills (University of Queensland).
4 There is an interesting discussion required here that is beyond the remit of this chapter. This is a discussion regarding the nature of educational research and its relationship to teacher professional identities, research and practices.

References

Anderson, B. (1991) *Imagined Communities*, London: Verso.
Apple, M. (2006) 'Critical education, politics and the real world', in L. Weis, C. McCarthy and G. Dimitriades (eds), *Ideology, Curriculum, and the New Sociology of Education: revisiting the work of Michael Apple*, New York: Routledge, pp. 203–217.
—— (2000) 'The shock of the real: critical pedagogies and rightist reconstructions', in P. Trifonas (ed.), *Revolutionary Pedagogies*, New York: Routledge, pp. 225–250.
Ball, S. J. (2006) *Education Policy and Social Class: the selected works of Stephen J. Ball*, London: Routledge.
—— (2008) *The Education Debate*, Bristol: Policy Press.
Bauman, Z. (1998) *Globalization: the human consequences*, Cambridge: Polity Press.
Bernstein, B. (1971) 'On the classification and framing of educational knowledge', in M. F. D. Young (ed.), *Knowledge and Control*, London: Collier-Macmillan, pp. 47–69.
—— (1999) 'Vertical and horizontal discourse: an essay', *British Journal of Sociology of Education*, 20 (2): 157–173.
Bourdieu, P. (1986) 'The forms of capital', in J. Richardson (ed.), *Handbook of Theory and Research for the Sociology of Education*, Westport, CT: Greenwood, pp. 241–258.
—— (1998a) *Acts of Resistance Against the New Myths of Our Time*, Cambridge: Polity Press.
—— (1998b) *Practical Reason*, Cambridge: Polity Press.
—— (1993) *The Field of Cultural Production*, Cambridge: Polity Press.
—— and Passeron, J. -C. (1977) *Reproduction in Education, Society and Culture*, London: Sage.
Coburn, C.E. and Stein, M.K. (2006) 'Communities of practice theory and the role of teacher professional community in policy implementation', in M. Honic (ed.), *New Directions in Education Policy Implementation: confronting complexity*, Albany, NY: State University of New York Press, pp. 25–46.
Coleman, J., Campbell, B., Hobson, C., McPartland, J., Mood, A., Winefeld, F. and York, R. (1966) *Equality of Educational Opportunity Report*, Washington, DC: US Government Printing Office.
Connell, R. W. (1985) *Teachers' Work*, Sydney: Allen & Unwin.
Crowley, V. and Matthews, J. (2006) 'Museum, memorial and mall: postcolonialism, pedagogies, racism and reconciliation', *Pedagogy, Culture and Society*, 14 (3): 263–277.

Dimitriadis, G. and McCarthy, C. (2001) *Reading and Teaching the Postcolonial: from Baldwin to Basquiat and beyond*, New York: Teachers' College Press.

Fraser, N. (1997) *Justice Interruptus*, New York: Routledge.

Gilroy, P. (2004) *After Empire: melancholia or convivial culture?*, London: Routledge.

Gore, J. (1993) *The Struggle for Pedagogies: critical and feminist discourse as regimes of truth*, New York: Routledge.

Hall, S. (2000) 'Conclusion: the multi-cultural question', in B. Hesse (ed.), *Un/settled Multiculturalism*, London: Zed Books, pp. 209–241.

Hartley, D. (2003) 'New economy, new pedagogy', *Oxford Review of Education*, 29 (1): 81–94.

Lingard, B. (2007) 'Pedagogies of indifference', *International Journal of Inclusive Education*, 11 (3): 245–266.

——, Nixon, J. and Ranson, S. (2008) 'Remaking education for a globalized world: policy and pedagogic possibilities', in B. Lingard, J. Nixon and S. Ranson (eds), *Transforming Learning in Schools and Communities*, London: Continuum, pp. 3–33.

Lortie, D. (1975) *Schoolteacher: a sociological study*, Chicago, IL: University of Chicago Press.

Luke, A. (2006) 'Teaching after the market: from commodity to cosmopolitan', in L. Weis, C. McCarthy and G. Dimitriadis (eds), *Ideology, Curriculum, and the New Sociology of Education: revisiting the work of Michael Apple*, New York: Routledge, pp. 115–141.

Mahony, P. and Hextall, I. (2000) *Reconstructing Teaching: standards, performance and accountability*, London: Routledge.

Newmann, F. and associates (1996) *Authentic Achievement: restructuring schools for intellectual quality*, San Francisco, CA: Jossey-Bass.

Power, M. (1999) *The Audit Society: the rituals of verification*, Oxford: Oxford University Press.

Ranson, S. (2003) 'Public accountability in the age of neo-liberal governance', *Journal of Education Policy*, 18 (5): 459–480.

Rose, M. (1995) *Possible Lives: the promise of public education in America*, New York: Penguin.

Said, E. W. (2004) *Humanism and Democratic Criticism*, New York: Columbia University Press.

Sennett, R. (1998) *The Corrosion of Character: the personal consequences of work in the new capitalism*, New York: Norton.

Shulman, L. (1987) 'Knowledge and teaching: foundations of the new reform', *Harvard Educational Review*, 57: 1–22.

Wright Mills, C. (1959) *The Sociological Imagination*, Harmondsworth: Penguin.

8 The lived experiences of black professionals in UK schools

Pioneers, Settlers and Inheritors

*Dona Daley with Meg Maguire**

This chapter draws on my study of thirty teachers of African Caribbean heritage who work as managers in UK schools.[1] Like these managers, I have had considerable school teaching experience and have worked as a senior manager in an urban secondary school. I also am of African Caribbean heritage and my research was based on studying people like myself (Zinn 1979). Much of the work that deals with issues of teacher professionalism has been concerned to explore the ways in which competing and conflicting discourses of professionalism have been and continue to be co-opted to manage, regulate and control the teaching force (Ozga 2000). In this chapter I want to explore a different set of questions about the lived experiences of professionals in schools that relate to their 'choice' of teaching and their progression in the profession (Daley 2001). In order to understand the professional identities of these teachers, and the racialized nature of their identity construction over the career course, it is critical to read the teachers' own accounts alongside a consideration of the part played by policy in this process. Teachers' names have been replaced with pseudonyms throughout.

'Choosing' to teach

In the UK, teaching has often been seen as a respectable and 'safe' job. For middle-class women, along with nursing, it was one of the early employment routes open to educated women. For the African Caribbean community who settled in the UK in the 1950s and 1960s, and who were predominantly working-class, becoming a teacher offered enhanced status and social mobility, as it had done for other working-class communities in the past (Burn 2001; Maguire 2005). For many of the teachers whose narratives are deployed in this chapter, becoming a teacher was, in part, scripted by long-standing discourses about 'respectable' work and 'improvement'. It was also accessible and available. However, 'choosing' to be a teacher held out an additional promise for my sample. There was and is a unique role for black teachers

---

* Dona Daley undertook this research for her Ph.D. She died in 2002. Her supervisor, Meg Maguire, has compiled this chapter from her dissertation.

in the UK – becoming role models for others and being advocates for black children and their families in the school system (Irvine 1989; King 1993; Pole 1999).

This is a distinctive aspect of teaching as a career that has always inflected the professional identities of minority-ethnic teachers in the UK (Siraj-Blatchford 1993; Jones and Maguire 1998; Roberts *et al.* 2002). My respondents testify to the tensions, complexities and difficulties associated with this particular inflection. Drawing on the work of Mama (1995) and Rassool (1999), I argue that the subjectivities and flexible identities of people who are educational managers, who are women or men, who are of African Caribbean descent and who are British mean that, when they inhabit their professional roles as teachers and managers, they do not operate outside their identities as black women or men. Mama suggests that:

> Black people living in Britain often develop the skill of moving in and out of various subject positions with great alacrity in the course of their social relationships and interactions with a diverse array of groups in their personal, political and working lives.
>
> (Mama 1995: 120)

One outcome of inhabiting these various subject positions is that the teachers sometimes had to 'choose' to act, or not to act in relation to their 'racialized' selves. Their embodied identities meant that many of the sample reported that they were expected to take on the role of 'black teacher' very early on in their training by 'sorting out the black kids' (Martin). Being a white teacher does not carry the same responsibilities, demands and contradictions: 'You know if things are too up front [about race issues] they think you are making a case and trying to rock the boat' (Barry).

It seems that black teachers and managers need to carefully consider which situations they should intervene in or draw attention to. Not to speak about certain matters can amount to collusion with poor practice; yet to talk about every incident that is of concern to them can mean that the teacher's voice might lose its impact in relation to the most critical incidents. These sorts of 'choice' pressures can have an impact on the professional relationships that managers form and maintain with the staff and other adults with whom they interact. Their role as leaders and managers and in particular their role as black leaders and managers adds another dimension to the already complex micro-relationships within an institution (Ball 1987):

> I think it was to do with this notion of having a black person telling them how to do their job, telling them that they're not doing it as well as they might be ... basically being in charge. Now think about it in this country, how many people in their wildest dreams think that one day that's going to happen to them?
>
> (Sonia)

'Choosing' to teach may well call up a series of shifts in subject positions; achieving progress in the teaching profession might involve equally complex manoeuvres.

Progression in a teaching career

All the managers in my sample were aware that they would have to fulfil a complex role in their professional lives. They were and are aware that their identity as black people in British society is sometimes in tension with their professional role. Their reasons for becoming managers are typified by Fay's comment and are probably not that different from the reasons that would be offered by many other teachers seeking promotion:

> I was frustrated in the classroom, I wanted to do more – when you are in the classroom you have access to thirty children and that's it. If you are in management you have access to the whole school.

But, if the initial 'choice' to become a teacher was, in part, scripted by what was available in terms of education, training and employment, as well as in terms of what was seen as desirable in terms of offering a degree of social mobility, progression was another story. I do not wish to contribute towards a pathologizing of black managers but at the same time I do not want to romanticize their progression. Undoubtedly these black teachers experienced obstacles that were not the lot of their white peers.

Before considering some of the obstacles reported by the black managers, it is necessary to highlight the structural location of these thirty teachers who have progressed in their careers. All of these managers were working in 'rough and tough' urban schools. This finding is itself worthy of further exploration. Is this because black managers themselves select to work in these schools? Is it because policy sometimes valorizes the unique contributions that minority-ethnic teachers can make in urban settings? Is it because it is difficult for black managers to obtain promotion in less challenging schools? Whatever the reasons, the outcomes have to be recognized – black managers in UK schools may well be placed in schools where it is hardest to 'prove' their efficiency and effectiveness – high stakes work indeed! Three of the five secondary black headteachers that I interviewed were managing schools that were under 'special measures'.[2]

All but one of the respondents talked about the pressures of working in 'challenging' urban schools, in particular, having to meet centrally derived targets, whilst working with children and young people who sometimes arrived in their schools with 'below average' scores. Yolanda, a head in a school under special measures, highlighted this issue:

> Eighty per cent of my year 7 [11–12-year-olds] has reading ages of 6–9. Two years from now, someone is going to publish a statistic that says

that [the] school is failing. The miracle is that I beat up on the staff and enable them to produce the percentages they do.

(Yolanda)

Yolanda was under pressure to improve the attainment of the students in her school. She recognized that she 'beat up on the staff'. This behaviour could produce tensions between her and some staff members. She was personally aware that her staff were working in difficult circumstances, yet professionally she needed to ensure that everything was being done to improve the academic standing of the school. An added dimension to the difficulties that these managers encounter is the fact they are black teachers running schools that are beset by difficulties and so as individuals these managers are very 'high-profile'. As Yolanda recounts:

Well, I think my problem here is that, as a black headteacher, people don't judge me as a headteacher; they judge me as a black headteacher. I don't have any room to get it wrong. I've got to get it right every time, I'm not allowed to get it wrong ever. I've got to get it right every time, because any time I make one mistake, it's – 'told you she couldn't do it'.

(Yolanda)

Martin sees the tension between his role and social identity in similar terms:

I was conscious of the fact that being a black person in a school with lots of black kids – they want me to straighten these kids out. But I realized that in any position of responsibility and management as a black person, you are setting yourself up for people to shoot you.

(Martin)

While the headteachers in the sample keenly felt the weight of their responsibilities as black headteachers, they were, to some extent, insulated by their role as leaders of large institutions. Black teachers who work as middle managers have more day-to-day contact with staff and more direct association with students. When a teacher has attained a middle-management post in a UK school, such as head of a subject department in a secondary school, or a curriculum leader in a primary school (Ruding 2000), they are likely to be preparing for further promotion. Many of the black middle managers reported personal 'obstacles' to their progression; they reported a lack of guidance about career development and a lack of support in their current posts. Some reported times when they believed that they were treated differently from their white peers.

In her first post, Maxine had wanted to attend a management course and had been refused permission to go but discovered that other – white – members of staff were being sent on the course although they were not keen to go.

There may have been a number of reasons why Maxine was not allowed to go on the course that she was not aware of, but nonetheless her perception was that she and other black staff always had a hard time when trying to access additional training:

> We [the black teachers] wanted to know the criteria being used to select people for the [middle managers] course. Apparently they had used information such as attendance and punctuality to make their final decisions, but still that didn't add up because there were several of us who had met those criteria – we were told that there would be no further discussion about the decisions made and the matter was closed. That was that!
>
> (Maxine)

All of my thirty respondents reported experiencing difficulties of one kind or another in progressing in their careers. Many of the sample had applied for large numbers of jobs in order to attain a position of influence. All the respondents' management positions had been hard won, similarly to black people in other occupations (Davidson 1997). But what typified my sample was their enormous capacity to overcome obstacles. Many of the managers in my study reported being 'the first' and sometimes 'the only' black teacher or manager in their school or local education authority. Self-sustaining strategies were critical in these contexts. These managers are used to dealing with the obstacles they face as black people living in the UK. On more than one occasion respondents made reference to the strength they gained from being practising Christians and having support from their local community (Channer 1995). Beverley talked about the 'legacy of slavery' and how this awareness has made her resilient. By this, she means that struggle and difficulty are hallmarks of her life; they are a part of her existence and the black experience which she has witnessed for as long as she can remember (see hooks 1993 and Angelou 1993). This history has afforded her fortitude and resilience to overcome whatever life may throw at her.

So far, what I have suggested is that, as with other working-class communities in the UK, teaching as a career has offered black teachers a 'step up' into a professional occupation and, for this sample, into an occupation that has historically carried high status in the Caribbean. What is distinctive about this progression is that alongside an individual desire for social mobility and enhanced status, there is a strong collective commitment towards the black community – not just in terms of becoming role models but, more powerfully, working as advocates to offer support and challenge social injustice (Foster 1997). Black teachers are expected to take on complex racialized identifications in relation to their professional roles in school teaching. These identifications pattern their professional experiences and play a part in 'producing' 'the black manager'.

The Pioneers – being among the first

The older respondents in my sample had completed their training in the UK at a time when there were very few black teachers in the UK (mid to late 1960s/early 1970s) (Braithwaite 1962). Many trained in rural colleges often doing their teaching practices in all-white schools. All of these respondents had some of their education outside Britain. Some of 'the Pioneers' reported a desire to teach from an early age:

> For me teaching was an honourable profession, it was making a massive contribution to society, and it was something which I could contribute towards if, and when I returned to the Caribbean, to Jamaica where I was born.
>
> (Martin)

Armed with a teaching qualification, the Pioneers started to look for jobs. They all reported that they expected to work in the communities where they lived (Gilroy 1976). The Pioneers all talked about being supported by 'significant people' early on in their teaching careers. Sometimes the 'supporter' was another Pioneer. Yolanda talks about a time when she worked with Alan:

> He was at that point a Head of Year . . . and just his very presence gave me confidence because I was very unconfident . . . So, in a way, I walked in his shadow . . . I told him that if I could find the courage one day, I wanted to be a Head of Year, and he said, 'Well you can be my deputy'.

Because there were few black teachers in the profession when they started, all the Pioneers know of each other or have worked together at some point in their careers. The Pioneers were clear about their role in education and chose to work in schools where there were relatively large numbers of what were termed 'immigrant pupils' when they started teaching.

Martin had expected to follow an academic career but he was offered a management post, which he could see carried enormous potential. He talks about being sent black boys to discipline by his colleagues. The Pioneers got promoted 'through the ranks' (i.e. they spent a great deal of time working in a number of middle-management posts with varying degrees of responsibility) and spent all their careers in mainstream schools, usually gaining further qualifications along the way. Their career progress is characterized by the notion of purpose, in that they had a desire to work in schools where they could be 'useful' and be influential in the lives of the young people with whom they came into contact:

> So far, I've tended to work with those people who are from the most vulnerable sections of the community. So to be able to make a difference

in their lives – you change peoples' lives, it's a wonderful power to be able to do that, it's just a tremendous power to do that.

(Alan)

The Pioneers all have strong roots in the Caribbean. For them, teaching has always been an 'honourable profession' that was respected in the community. Some of them qualified to teach in the Caribbean and expected to make the same sort of career progression in the UK as would have occurred had they stayed at home (Gilroy 1976).[3] The Pioneers were among the first to 'arrive' in teaching in the UK (Foner 1979). They commonly reported being the 'only black' child, student, trainee teacher or teacher in their educational progress through the system (Philips and Philips 1998). However, their presence in education was characterized by being 'wanted' by a number of urban educational authorities in the UK. For the first time, a group of black teachers existed in appreciable numbers, so much so that the Caribbean Teachers Association was formed in London in the early 1970s with over 300 members (Gibbes 1980). In a period when assimilation was being advocated, these pioneers were often involved in early agitation to develop more appropriate ways of working with newly arrived children from the Caribbean. The Pioneers were active in their communities and active in rejecting the 'deficit' views of the black child that were in circulation in this period in the UK (Coard 1971).

The Settlers – being needed

All the teachers in this cohort received the majority of their education in the UK. The majority of the Settlers, in contrast to the Pioneers, gained rapid promotion. Many of this second group of teachers rarely stayed in one position for more than four years. All the Settlers trained in the mid to late 1970s during what Barber (1996) describes as the 'last expansion of education'. Like the Pioneers, the Settlers do not report negative training experiences. Their careers began in a similar fashion to the 'Pioneers'; they gained jobs in the inner city after their training:

My teaching practices were in very good schools that gave me the opportunity to really develop my skills as a teacher. In fact, both my teaching practice schools wanted me when I left college but I felt it was important to work in multi-ethnic schools.

(Kwame)

What characterizes the professional lives of this group of teachers is that these teachers seemed to be able to make informed career choices rather than proceed in the 'ad hoc' style of the Pioneers. All the Settlers talked about working in the community to which they belonged (i.e. the inner-city or places where there was a considerable representation of black people).

The Settlers were determined to make a difference in the communities they worked in. Two members of this group were able to spend time abroad on secondments that enhanced their professional development:

> I stumbled across the scheme and realized that white teachers, who had gone on an exchange for a year to the Caribbean, came back as 'experts' about black children. I felt that I should go to have the experience and bring back a different perspective. After all I was an expert in a different way, yet at times it felt what I had to say wasn't valid because I hadn't had the same experience as white colleagues who had worked in the country for a whole year.
>
> (Wilma)

Wilma had been working in schools for about five years when a 'window of opportunity' became available for her cohort of black teachers. The issues of multi-ethnic education, equal opportunities and antiracist teaching were being firmly placed on the UK education agenda for a number of reasons (Grosvenor 1997; Tomlinson 1998). Because of their 'lived experience', this group of teachers was able to contribute to debates on multicultural and antiracist education. The Settlers were well positioned, in terms of their cultural capital, to offer expertise and leadership in the area of anti-racisist/multicultural provision. All of this group were determined to have a career and knew what was necessary to progress in education (Hart 1995). The Settlers enjoyed a fulfilling time professionally but recognized that to further their careers they had to 'go back into the mainstream'. As a consequence of their experience, many of them were able to attain posts in senior management teams and headships in urban schools relatively early on in their careers.

The settlers were educated against a background of growing politicization and confidence in the British black communities whose members were demanding equal rights and were angry about the discrimination and oppression they continued to face (Pryce 1979; Fryer 1984; Ramdin 1987). National and local policies (Swann Report 1985; Troyna and Williams 1986) were pressing for changes in the curriculum and pedagogy of schooling. The Settlers were uniquely placed. There was no one else who could do the job as effectively as these teachers. Policy had opened a window for the Settlers to make progress in their professional careers.

The Inheritors – being tolerated?

The Inheritors do not seem to have had the same opportunities as their 'brothers and sisters' in the Settlers cohort. This group trained during the mid to late 1980s. The Inheritors are the only group who report having experienced racism in their training (Pole 1999; Jones and Maguire 1998). Marilyn was the only black student on an education course at a prestigious college:

We did this thing on language and we all sat in a circle, and the lecturer came in, apparently he was some big lecturer ... he was going to tell us about language and all this kind of stuff, and he said, 'Hands up all of you who speak a language or have a background in another language'. And I put my hand up and this other girl put her hand up ... So first of all he asked the girl what her language was and I think she said Spanish or Italian. He turned to me and said, 'What's yours?' I said it's a French Creole spoken in the Caribbean. He said, 'Oh no that's not a language'. Imagine how I felt.

The Pioneers, in the vanguard of change, knew that struggle would characterize their progression but they were organizing for change and fighting against policies that excluded their communities and positioned them as a 'problem'. They were fighting against assimilationist and integrationist education policies (Troyna and Williams 1986). The Settlers were needed and wanted in the multicultural and antiracist policy context, and perhaps, superficially, this was a time of some positive changes – although mainly in urban, ethnically diverse settings. The third 'group' inherited a situation where they were frequently made to feel 'other' and unwelcome.

Maxine eventually became Head of a Religious Education department in an inner-city school where almost half of the staff are black, there is a black headteacher, and the majority of children are of minority-ethnic descent. On the one hand, there was an opportunity to work in a proactive way and affirm the experience of black school students through the curriculum, but on the other, there were problems in the staffroom. Maxine describes her first day at the school:

A caucus of people [i.e. white staff] were looking at me as if to say, 'here's another one' – that's what I was reading from them. Having heard things before I'd arrived I suppose it was easy for me to work out what that was all about.

From interviews with this cohort, I identified a sense of frustration at not being able to gain positions of real influence. This group reported feeling unable to progress in their careers and were more ready to describe situations which they construed as discriminatory (Osler 1997a). They reported feeling overlooked for internal and external promotion. Barry occupies a middle-management role and is in a position to develop a number of initiatives, if the resources are made available, but he is frustrated in his role as a teacher because:

The head doesn't trust me. Why? I'm black. Nothing that I have ever done should lead him to that conclusion ... He doesn't allow me to do things ... he has to check and double check. If there is anything I want to do, organize a day trip or something then he should empower me.

Now maybe he doesn't empower anybody, but that is not the impression I get. The impression I get is that other people can set things up and run with them.

Another factor that may have an adverse effect on the Inheritors is the type of school in which they are able to gain posts of responsibility. Marilyn believes that:

Any school that was [a] very 'nice', high academic type, I didn't get a look in. But any school that was inner city, or was based in an environment where the children would be challenging, then my application would be accepted and I would be invited to be interviewed.

Marilyn went on to describe three instances where she had applied to suburban schools and did not get the job. She describes a situation in her debriefing where the advisor didn't give any reason why she didn't get a post but simply said: 'There are particular people for particular schools' and invited her to apply for several jobs in the inner-city area of the same authority. Blair (1994) has claimed that black teachers and students are structurally positioned less favourably than their white peers with regard to the education market. Black students and black teachers are perhaps 'less desirable' commodities in the race for dominance in the league tables (Tomlinson 1998). As black teachers, the Inheritors, like the Pioneers and the Settlers, see their role as working with black pupils in schools (Gordon 2000). However, currently the majority of black children are located in schools that face the most difficulty.

Conclusion

This chapter has focused on the lived experiences of black professionals. They could all be described as successful professionals; they have entered the teaching profession and achieved promotion. What is also evident is that these black managers have experienced a lack of mobility. Gaining depth of experience in the inner city might, paradoxically, contribute to their inability to work anywhere else, potentially curtailing the breadth of their professional lives. These teachers want to make a difference, not just to 'fill the gaps' in 'rough tough' schools. They want the same opportunities that other (white) educational professionals have in terms of career progression (Osler 1997b). What has emerged from this study is that their capacity to achieve this ambition is mediated by the policy context in which they are located as well as the racialized nature of their professional identity construction over the career course:

I say to the children that they are worth something . . . I say that I want something better for them . . . Because you are black children, people will define you by the colour of your skin, because they do it to me.

(Yolanda)

Notes

1   In the UK school system, teachers can apply for promotion into management and senior leadership positions in schools. All of the participants in the study are qualified teachers.
2   In the UK, a school is put under 'special measures' when inspectors have judged it to be failing, or at risk of failing to provide an adequate standard of education. Schools in special measures must be in regular contact with inspectors and are expected to meet termly targets.
3   Beryl Gilroy came to the UK in 1951 from Guyana as an experienced teacher. She was forced to take a series of unskilled jobs before being able to resume her career in teaching.

References

Angelou, M. (1993) *Wouldn't Take Anything for My Journey Now*, London: Virago.

Ball, S. J. (1987) *The Micro Politics of the School*, London: Routledge.

Barber, M. (1996) *The Learning Game – arguments for an education revolution*, London: Victor Gollancz.

Blair, M. (1994) 'Black teachers, black students and education markets', *Cambridge Journal of Education*, 24 (2): 277–292.

Braithwaite, E. R. (1962) *To Sir, With Love*, London: Four Square Edition.

Burn, E. (2001) 'Battling through the system: a working class teacher in an inner city school', *International Journal of Inclusive Education*, 5 (1): 85–92.

Channer, Y. (1995) *I Am a Promise: the school achievement of British African Caribbeans*, Stoke-on-Trent: Trentham Books.

Coard, B. (1971) *How the West Indian Child is Made Educationally Subnormal in the British Education System: the scandal of the black child in schools in Britain*, London: New Beacon for the Caribbean Education and Community Workers' Association.

Daley, D. M. (2001) 'The experience of the African Caribbean manager in the British school system', unpublished Ph.D. thesis, London: King's College London.

Davidson, M. (1997) *The Black and Ethnic Minority Woman Manager: cracking the concrete ceiling*, London: Paul Chapman.

Foner, N. (1979) *Jamaica Farewell: Jamaican migrants in London*, London: Routledge & Kegan Paul.

Foster, M. (1997) *Black Teachers on Teaching*, New York: New Press.

Fryer, P. (1984) *Staying Power: the history of Black people in Britain*, London: Pluto Press.

Gibbes, N. (1980) *West Indian Teachers Speak Out*, London: Caribbean Teachers' Association and the Lewisham Council for Community Relations.

Gilroy, B. (1976) *Black Teacher*, London: Cassell.

Gordon, J. A. (2000) *The Color of Teaching*, London: RoutledgeFalmer.

Grosvenor, I. (1997) *Assimilating Identities: racism and educational policy in post 1945 Britain*, London: Lawrence & Wishart.

Hart, A. (1995) 'Going for careers – not just for jobs', *NATFHE Journal*, 20 (3): 16–17.

hooks, b. (1994) *Teaching to Transgress: education as the practice of freedom*, New York & London: Routledge.

Irvine, J. (1989) 'Beyond role models: an evaluation of cultural influences on the pedagogical perspectives of black teachers', *Peabody Journal of Education*, 66 (4): 51–63.

Jones, C. and Maguire, M. (1998) 'Needed and wanted? The school experiences of some minority ethnic trainee teachers', *UK European Journal of Intercultural Studies*, 9 (1): 79–91.

King, S. H. (1993) 'Why did we choose teaching careers and what will enable us to stay? Insights from one cohort of the African American teaching pool', *Journal of Negro Education*, 62 (4): 475–492.

Maguire, M. (2005) '"Not footprints behind but footsteps forward": working class women who teach', *Gender and Education*, 17 (1): 3–18.

Mama, A. (1995) *Beyond the Masks: race gender and subjectivity*, London: Routledge.

Osler, A. (1997a) 'Black teachers as professionals: survival success and subversion', *Forum*, 39 (2): 55–59.

—— (1997b) *The Education and Careers of Black Teachers: changing identities changing lives*, Buckingham: Open University Press.

Ozga, J. (2000) *Policy Research in Educational Settings: contested terrain*, Buckingham and Philadelphia, PA: Open University Press.

Phillips, M. and Phillips, S. T. (1998) *Windrush: the irresistible rise of multi-racial Britain*, London: Harper Collins.

Pole, C. (1999) 'Black teachers giving voice: choosing and experiencing teaching', *Teacher Development*, 3 (3): 313–328.

Pryce, K. (1979) *Endless Pressure*, Bristol: Bristol Classical Press.

Rassool, N. (1999) 'Flexible identities: exploring race and gender issues among a group of immigrant pupils in an inner-city comprehensive school', *British Journal of Sociology of Education*, 20 (1): 23–36.

Ramdin, R. (1987) *The Making of the Black Working Class in Britain*, Aldershot: Wildwood House.

Roberts, L., McNamara, O., Basit, T. N. and Hatch, G. (2002) 'It's like black people are still aliens'. Paper presented at BERA Conference, University of Exeter, September 2002.

Ruding, E. (2000) *Middle Management in Action: practical approaches to school improvement*, London: RoutledgeFalmer.

Siraj-Blatchford, I. (1993) *'Race', Gender and the Education of Teachers*, Buckingham: Open University Press.

Swann Report (Committee of Inquiry into the Education of Children from Ethnic Minority Groups) (1985) *Education for All*, London: HMSO.

Tomlinson, S. (1998) 'New inequalities? Educational markets and ethnic minorities', *'Race', Ethnicity and Education*, 2 (2): 207–223.

Troyna, B. and Williams, J. (1986) *Racism, Education and the State*, London: Croom Helm.

Zinn, M. B. (1979) 'Field research in minority communities: ethical, methodological and political observations by an insider', *Social Problems*, 27 (2): 209–219.

9   Inventing the Chartered Teacher

Jenny Reeves

For several decades successive governments in the West have set about reforming public services through establishing and elaborating new forms of governance. In education the goal of these reforms has been to make schools more effective by increasing the accountability of those who work in the sector using frameworks of standards and targets. In the UK, Australia and the US these developments, which emphasize compliance with centrally determined directives, are seen by many commentators as counterproductive in terms of student learning (e.g. Smyth and Shacklock 1998; Apple and Beane 1999; Mahony and Hextall 2000; Gewirtz 2002). For example, Harris and Lambert (2003) have argued that school improvement is neither feasible nor sustainable without the full and active participation of teachers in the change process, an argument that has been extended to reassert the case for professional autonomy in the form of distributed, or shared, leadership where problems of learning are solved locally by teachers and their school communities (Watkins *et al.* 2007). The institutionalization of values of 'reflective practice, collegiality and critical pedagogy' (Sachs 2003: 21) is linked in this discourse to establishing a commitment to the collaborative creation of knowledge about student learning by teachers and their managers (Street and Temperley 2005). Professional trust, it is claimed, can be re-established if educational practice is built on an evidence-informed approach to pedagogy on the part of all teachers (Hargreaves 1999) – although this too can be based on a reductionist view of teaching and learning (Pressley *et al.* 2004; Hammersley 2007).

Such arguments have fed into calls for the development of a 'new' professionalism on the part of teachers, a call that is beginning to have an influence on some areas of policy in some national settings. This chapter explores the issues that arose when some of the principles of the 'new' professionalism were introduced in Scotland via what came to be known as the Chartered Teacher initiative and considers the implications of the experiences of Chartered Teachers for the pursuit of school improvement.

Teacher professionalisms

Up until the mid 1980s teachers in Scotland, like those elsewhere in the UK and other parts of the world, were largely operating within a framework that Clarke and Newman (1997) have described as bureau professional. In this framework public sector professionals were granted a measure of autonomy to enable them to exercise their expertise within limits set by the organizations for which they worked. Thus teachers exercised their expertise in their own classrooms within bureaucratic frameworks laid down by their local authorities and administered by their headteachers, resulting, according to Hoyle (1974:15), in the dominance of a restricted form of professionalism where teaching was seen as an intuitive practice developed through classroom experience. In Scotland this was compounded by a traditional concern for uniformity of educational provision (Anderson 1999) embedded within a complex hierarchy for administering and managing the profession.

A significant change in the official conception of teacher professionalism was marked, during the first half of the 1990s, by the production of a series of performance indicators for schools culminating in the publication in 1996 by Her Majesty's Inspectorate (HMI) of *How good is our school? Self-evaluation using performance indicators* (HGIOS). The most important alteration that HGIOS signalled was in the relationship between senior managers and teachers. Under the heading, *Management, leadership and quality assurance*, the role of senior staff was recast so as to include the practice of school development planning, the setting of targets and the monitoring and evaluation of teachers' work (HMI 1996: 64–68). Headteachers and promoted staff were to act as line managers operationalizing national and local authority priorities in schools. Good teaching was represented as the display of certain prescribed behaviours that should be used to grade teacher performance as a prerequisite for identifying targets for improvement. This formulation represents the extension of the 'hard' end of managerialism into the public services with an emphasis on accountability and control achieved through the detailed prescription and supervision of performance. It was combined with the implementation of a centrally determined curriculum, thus setting clear restrictions on the exercise of practitioner judgement and agency. An important element in this injection of managerialism across the UK was the development of a framework of occupational standards for teachers (DfES 2001; SEED 2002b) and, in England and Wales, the introduction of performance-related pay. Smyth and Shacklock (1998) characterized changes in teacher 'professionalism' under similar conditions in Australia as reducing teachers to the status of educational operatives, a judgement that many UK educationalists endorsed (e.g. Mahony and Hextall 2000).

The delineation of teachers as compliant operatives shares certain commonalities with the positioning of teachers within bureau professional regimes, particularly with regard to teachers' lack of say over organizational goals and governance and the hierarchical nature of power relations in the education system. However, 'educational operationalism' does make for a very marked increase in both the range of mechanisms for controlling teachers' work and the intensity of their impact. It signals a material alteration of relationships within the hierarchy resulting in a loss of trust in and autonomy for teachers.

The government in Scotland followed much the same path; however, there were substantive differences. From 1998 to 2002 a similar framework of occupational standards was developed, but these differed from those south of the border in that the Scottish standards were based on a model of action (Reeves *et al.* 1998) which included professional values. Using Mahony and Hextall's classification, these standards were conceived as having a developmental as well as a regulatory function (2000: 31). Nor did the restructuring of the profession in Scotland based on the report of the McCrone Committee[1] (SEED 2001) introduce performance related pay. In the list of teacher duties described in the report there was an emphasis on collaboration and shared responsibility for the education offered to pupils (SEED 2001: 45). The continuing professional development of teachers, coupled with an improved career structure and a reduction in workload, was identified as the main engine for school improvement.

The Scottish proposals were compatible with a form of 'soft' managerialism associated with the idea of the learning organization (Senge 1990). Such organizations supposedly allow the pursuit of both shared objectives and projects of individual self-actualization on the part of organizational members. This emphasis on the reflective and collegial role of organizational members has much in common with notions of professionalism advocated by educationalists and variously described as 'extended', 'new' and 'activist' (Stenhouse 1975; Hargreaves 1999; Sachs 2003). Within this descriptive range common features of the 'new' professionalism are:

*   learner-centred practice;
*   clarity about moral and social purpose;
*   commitment to evidence-informed practice and critical reflection;
*   discretionary judgement exercised both collectively and singly;
*   collegiality and collaboration with colleagues, other professionals, pupils and parents; and
*   commitment to continuing professional development and knowledge creation.

Thus the introduction of the status of Chartered Teacher in Scotland occurred within a field where 'teacher professionalism' is subject to contesting and contrasting paradigms held and championed by different interests. This has resulted in the issue and use of policy texts by a variety of institutions that 'speak' in a mixture of 'tongues' and in which there are both internal inconsistencies as well as statements laid out in one document that are directly contradicted by another (e.g., as in the case of HMIE 2002 and SEED 2002a).

The Chartered Teacher

From 2001 to 2003 teachers' working conditions in Scotland were restructured. The consultation paper, *Targeting Excellence* (SOEID 1999), heralded most of the changes brought about by this restructuring. The paper placed these changes within a wider agenda for the reform of the education service, proposing the modernization of the teaching force through the creation of 'a more highly qualified, more effective profession which would acquire higher status' within the community. As a key element in this project the McCrone Report (SEED 2000) recommended the establishment of two new statuses: the Chartered Teacher and the Advanced Chartered Teacher, each of which signified a level of excellence in teaching. Chartered Teacher status was to be achieved by a majority of established teachers whereas fewer would attain the advanced status. While Chartered Teachers would remain in the classroom and serve as a role model for junior colleagues, the Advanced Chartered Teacher was envisaged as fulfilling a more demanding role and serving as 'a resource for the nation in driving forward educational standards' (SEED 2000: 22–23). Both statuses were to be achieved through the completion of an appropriate, accredited programme of CPD (SEED 2000: 66).

Between the McCrone Report and the McCrone Agreement[2] (SEED 2001) Advanced Chartered Teacher status disappeared to leave Chartered Teacher as the only means of pursuing a classroom-based teaching career. In the process, two contrasting interpretations of the status appeared in policy documents. The first of these presented Chartered Teacher status 'as a means of rewarding experienced high quality teachers who seek a challenging career without having to pursue school management posts' (SEED 2002b). This was, and still is, understood to mean that the status would be achieved by good classroom teachers for doing much as they had always done, a view that was strongly advocated by the teacher unions. However, the Standard for Chartered Teachers (SEED, 2002a) presents a rather different conception. It delineates a role that is closer to the McCrone Report's description of an Advanced Chartered teacher:

> The consultation process confirms support for identifying nine forms of professional action. These can be categorized to correspond to the four professional values and personal commitments, namely, Effectiveness in promoting learning in the classroom; Critical reflection, self-evaluation and development; Collaboration and influence; and Educational and social values.
>
> (SEED 2002a: 8)

Educational and social values are listed as 'concern for truth, personal responsibility, equality, social justice and inclusion'. In the more detailed exemplars the Chartered Teacher is to be:

- 'innovative and creative';
- an 'initiator and advocate of change';
- engaged in 'professional enquiry and action research';
- involved in identifying and challenging 'negative aspects of school culture – stimulating colleagues to bring about improvement'; and
- involved in contributing 'to the literature on, and public discussion of, teaching and learning and education' and 'articulating a personal, independent and critical stance in relation to contrasting perspectives on educational issues, policies and developments.'

What this text affords for both providers of Chartered Teacher programmes and those teachers who wish to achieve the status is a space in which to assert a form of teacher professionalism which is in marked contrast to educational operationalism.

The outcome of this particular policy initiative was that those attempting to enact Chartered Teacher status found themselves having to invent what it means in a context where the kind of teacher professionalism advocated by the Standard is both contested and, arguably, dysfunctional.

Inventing the Chartered Teacher

In order to illuminate teacher perceptions of enacting teacher leadership and collaborative enquiry as a basis for improving students' learning, this chapter draws on the experiences of participants on a Chartered Teacher programme (Reeves 2007). The General Teaching Council for Scotland accredited programmes leading to Chartered Teacher status in 2002. One of these was the MEd in Professional Enquiry, which was conceived as a practice-based course that drew on the outcomes of research into learning processes on the Scottish Qualification for Headship (Reeves *et al.* 2003). The programme requires participants to undertake two action enquiry projects. The first of these takes place in their own classrooms, while the second requires that they work collaboratively on a project to improve students' learning with a group of colleagues. Course participants have generally experienced the individual projects as a reaffirmation of professional identity and autonomy but the experience of undertaking the collaborative projects has been rather different.

Teachers' reactions

Once participants had managed to secure a group to work with they found dealing with uncertainty and lack of control difficult. The contrast between acting as an individual and as part of a group was experienced as disturbing. It was difficult to cope with the length of time it took to reach some form of alignment of purpose and understanding with their colleagues. As one participant put it:

Even after careful negotiation and agreement getting going can be problematic because of differences of understanding – particularly where there's been the gap of the summer holidays in between. It is very slow working with others as they start without any idea of what action enquiry is.

In nearly all cases participants reported that their fellow teachers expected them to take the lead, at least during the initial stages. This played unhelpfully with an instinctive inclination to keep control of the project because colleagues might not 'do things properly'. It was very hard for participants to know how to position themselves, not least because a number of them wished to enact a more democratic model of professionalism where everyone in the group had an equal voice in decision-making. For example, one participant commented:

> Some people are keen to 'help' you but they do not really have any ideas about what they want for themselves. How do you get the others in your group really engaged? They want you to act as leader/manager and simply tell them what to do.

In particular, participants found establishing discussion and debate problematic. Their observations matched those of Hargreaves (2003) that there are norms of interaction among teachers that suppress risk-taking, criticality and 'grown-up' professional relationships. Getting colleagues to bring along examples of pupils' work was often the best way of developing discussion but in many settings it took time to establish sufficient trust for teachers to do this. As one participant explained:

> It has taken time to get people to really take ownership of the enquiries. Now people are getting into practicalities and gathering data in class, they're getting more interested and beginning to come forward with their own ideas.

Many of the collaborating teachers only took an interest in the project at the level of their own classrooms and showed little curiosity in taking any wider overview (Hancock 2001). They often wanted to apply ideas without engaging in any detailed diagnosis of learners' problems (Nuthall 2004) or an exploration of possible solutions. The practice of articulating desired outcomes and establishing a baseline before trialling a new approach was also felt to be very foreign:

> How do you get a decent baseline because teachers get enthusiastic and rush off and start things rather than proceeding with an orderly enquiry and doing the groundwork for the measurement of outcomes?

One participant observed that she had often collaborated with her colleagues on working parties in the past and that it came as a shock to her to realize just how different action enquiry was from their normal way of working.

One interpretation of these experiences is to point to the discontinuities arising from the interplay and clash of different constructions of teacher professionalism. Enactment of collaborative enquiry showed the course group that they had their own difficulties with the notion of collaboration because for them, as for their colleagues, the dominant framing remained the old bureau professionalism with some of the 'educational operationalism' paradigm mixed in. While acting as a more autonomous individual had not caused problems, sharing practice and crossing individual classroom boundaries was a very different matter for both programme participants and their colleagues. These teachers were not used to being asked to engage in joint diagnostic reflection on their own classroom evidence. Working together in circumstances where they had not been given a clear task to undertake was also experienced as strange. It was difficult for both participants and their colleagues to cope with the notion of a teacher as someone who initiates change within a school (Sachs 2003), rather than complying with an agenda passed down by management. 'Traditional' expectations about decision-making processes were hard to shift. Given a degree of personal and professional credibility, participants felt they were then framed as quasi-leader/managers and expected to mimic a hierarchical and directive form of behaviour that conformed with teachers' expectations of working groups. Nixon *et al.*'s (1997) notion of 'new' professionalism as emergent, localized and negotiated took on a stark reality. Extending professional enquiry beyond an individual classroom raised a number of issues about the practicality of the implementation and sustainability of the collegiate ideals expressed in the Chartered Teacher Standard (Huberman 2001) and, by analogy, those advocating distributed leadership in schools.

Managers' reactions

The enactment of collaborative professional enquiry also caused problems for participants in relation to their interactions with their managers. As with their teaching colleagues, many of the participants' managers were inclined to regard a display of 'activism' on the part of a class teacher as surprising and, in some cases, highly inappropriate. Even where participants gained the verbal backing of their line manager, some still felt frustrated at having to negotiate and gain permission on a piecemeal basis for resources. What they felt this signalled to them and their colleagues was that they should not suppose that teachers will be treated in the same way as a member of the management team. Other line managers were extremely suspicious and wanted to keep a very tight rein on what was happening, which made it difficult for participants to apply collaborative principles in their work with colleagues. These difficulties could be interpreted as a clash with the norms of bureau professionalism in that these difficulties suggested that it was not viewed as 'proper' for an ordinary teacher to display behaviour reserved for those in management posts. One participant described the difficulties as follows:

[There is] quite a lively debate about how far the whole notion of teacher-led action enquiry represents a radical challenge to the system. Clearly there are quite wide variations in terms of response. Most people are experiencing some difficulty in managing the group/manager interface – something that has to be constantly worked on.

A second source of discomfort arose from the difference in principles underpinning the process of action enquiry and school improvement planning. While managers might agree to let participants lead an initiative that related to the school's priorities, they wanted it 'actioned' as a discrete task not an open enquiry focusing on the experiences and responses of learners. There was impatience on the part of managers with regard to time being taken to investigate and debate ideas. Participants felt this was attributable to the short-termism of the model of change embedded in development planning and the concern of their managers to comply with targets. As one participant put it:

There is a difference between our understanding of collaboration and the SMT's [senior management team's] definition of collaboration. The SMT find it quite scary that teachers will come up with the content of the project and they are nervous about the whole thing because they don't feel they have control.

However, one of the authorities whose staff was involved in the programme had adopted an organizational learning strategy that championed action enquiry as the basis for school improvement (Reeves and Boreham 2006). Teachers from this authority found this provided them with an important source of legitimation so that their programme-related activities were generally regarded in a more positive light by senior managers than those of participants from other authorities. This contrast gives an indication of how strong the operational link between school managers and local and central government has become.

The participants' difficulties with managers were shaped by both a bureau-professional mindset and, equally strongly, by educational operationalism. School managers, as those charged with responsibility for school development planning, are tightly tied into the quality assurance system and the various technologies of compliance and control associated with it. Arguably, the 'boundary' problems between school managers and Chartered Teachers could have been predicted on the basis of the fact that the two groups are using two tools: *How Good is Our School?* and the *Standard for Chartered Teacher*, which position teachers very differently.

There was little that prepared the teachers for the political work involved in attempting to change practice in collaboration with colleagues. Chartered Teachers, with no formal status in the school hierarchy, were reliant on their personal credibility and skills when trying to secure the permissions and resources they needed to act. Initiating collaborative enquiry in their schools required an ability to persuade and influence others and a combination of flexibility and persistence in interaction with staff at various levels within the school hierarchy. This was an unfamiliar form of practice for both the participants and their colleagues and it was therefore hard to secure a space for it to happen (Reeves and Forde 2004). It was also evident from discussions with participants that would-be collaborators needed a sound understanding of the way in which their schools worked. A lack of work-process knowledge was a significant barrier to negotiating both initiation and the ongoing functioning of groups (Boreham 2002).

Implications

It seems that all three versions of teacher professionalism – that is, bureau professionalism, educational operationalism and the 'new' professionalism – are actively in play in schools, embedded in multilevelled and mixed practices where the 'old' bureau professionalism appears to be strong at teacher level but is overlayered by the greater penetration of educational operationalism at school manager level. Clarke and Newman identify this complex layering and mixing of paradigms as typical of the impact of public service reform (1997: 95). Our sample of Chartered Teachers, as promoters of a particular form of 'new' professionalism, appeared to be running up against the structures and cultures that had been put in place to support earlier forms of teachers' work practices. In many ways the story I have presented could be understood as representing the second round in a discursive battle, the first round of which had gone to the 'hard' school when it captured development planning, supposedly a 'soft' technique for legitimizing local decision-making, as the means of operationalizing central directives. Without wider systemic changes that support collaborative interaction and evidence-informed practice, class teachers face formidable barriers to engaging in the kind of activities that the authors of the McCrone Report and other supporters of the 'soft' managerial approach see as critical to school improvement.

While it may seem that this analysis is essentially pessimistic, it does afford grounds for hope. Whether Chartered Teacher status becomes a successful Trojan Horse for the collaborative, enquiry-based model of professionalism outlined in the Standard or it is hybridized or swamped by one or both of the other versions of professionalism discussed in this chapter will depend on the outcome of the complex politics of the system. It is open to Chartered Teachers and others who support the implementation of the 'new' professionalism to engage in what Brienes (1980: 421) has termed 'prefigurative politics' which 'seeks to create and sustain within lived practice

. . . relationships and political forms that "prefigure" and embody the desired society'. Developments in Scotland indicate that those who believe that greater reliance on research-led teaching and collaborative local approaches to improving the quality of education provide the best way forward need to be prepared to position themselves as political actors. This could form the basis for actively inventing new forms of teacher professionalism through action, argument and alliances within the field of practice that could offer the possibility of greater engagement and success in learning for all.

Notes

1   A committee established by the Scottish Executive in 1999 to make recommendations about the future of the teaching profession in Scotland. The Committee's recommendations were published in the McCrone Report (SEED 2000).
2   Following the publication of the McCrone Report (SEED 2000), an implementation group comprising representatives of government, employers and teacher unions was established to negotiate an agreement on how to take forward the Report's recommendations. The McCrone Agreement was published in 2001 (SEED 2001).

References

Anderson, R. (1999) 'The history of Scottish education, pre-1980', in T. Bryce and W. Humes (eds), *Scottish Education*, Edinburgh: Edinburgh University Press, pp. 215–224.

Apple, M. and Beane, J. A. (eds) (1999) *Democratic Schools: lessons from the chalkface*, Buckingham: Open University Press.

Boreham, N. (2002) 'Work process knowledge in technological and organisational development', in N. Boreham, R. Samurcay and M. Fischer (eds), *Work Process Knowledge*, London: Routledge, pp. 1–14.

Brienes, W. (1980) 'Community and organisation: the New Left and Michels' "Iron Law"', *Social Problems*, 27 (4): 419–429.

Clarke, J. and Newman, J. (1997) *The Managerial State: power, politics and ideology in the remaking of social welfare*, London: Sage.

Department for Education and Skills (2001) *Teachers' Standards Framework*, London: DfES.

Gewirtz, S. (2002) *The Managerial School: post-welfarism and social justice in education*, London: Routledge.

Hammersley, M. (ed.) (2007) *Educational Research and Evidence-Based Practice*, London: Sage.

Hancock, R. (2001) 'Why are class teachers reluctant to become researchers?', in J. Soler, A. Craft and H. Burgess (eds), *Teacher Development: exploring our own practice*, London: Paul Chapman, pp. 119–132.

Hargreaves, A. (2003) *Teaching in the Knowledge Society: education in the age of insecurity*, Maidenhead: Open University Press.

Hargreaves, D. (1999) 'The knowledge creating school', *British Journal of Educational Studies*, 47 (2): 122–144.

Harris, A. and Lambert, L. (2003) *Building Leadership Capacity for School Improvement*, Maidenhead: Open University Press.

Hoyle, E. (1974) 'Professionality, professionalism and control in teaching', *London Educational Review*, 3 (2): 13–19.

Huberman, M. (2001) 'Networks that alter teaching: conceptualisation, exchanges and experiments', in J. Soler, A. Craft and H. Burgess (eds), *Teacher Development: exploring our own practice*, London: Paul Chapman, pp. 141–159.

HMI (1996) *How Good is Our School? Self-evaluation using performance indicators*, Edinburgh: Audit Unit.

HMIE (2002) *How Good is Our School? Self-evaluation using performance indicators*, Edinburgh: Audit Unit.

Mahony, P. and Hextall, I. (2000) *Reconstructing Teaching: standards, performance and accountability*, London: RoutledgeFalmer.

Nixon, J. Martin, J. McKeown, P. and Ranson, S. (1997) 'Towards a learning profession: changing codes of occupational practice within the new management of education', *British Journal of Sociology in Education*, 18 (1): 5–28.

Nuthall, G. (2004) 'Relating classroom teaching to student learning: a critical analysis of why research has failed to bridge the theory-practice divide', *Harvard Educational Review*, 74 (3): 273–306.

Pressley, M., Duke, N. K. and Boling, E. C. (2004) 'The educational science and scientifically based instruction we need: lessons from reading research and policymaking', *Harvard Educational Review*, 74 (1): 30–61.

Reeves, J. (2007) 'Inventing the Chartered Teacher', *British Journal of Educational Studies*, 55 (1): 56–76.

—— and Forde, C. (2004) 'The social dynamics of changing practice', *Cambridge Journal of Education*, 34 (1): 85–102.

—— and Boreham, N. (2006) 'What's in a vision? Introducing an organisational learning strategy in a local authority's education service', *Oxford Review of Education*, 32 (4): 467–486.

——, Forde, C., Casteel, V. and Lynas, R. (1998) 'A model of professional action', *School Leadership and Management*, 18 (2): 185–196.

——, Forde, C. Morris, B. and Turner, E. (2003) 'Social processes and work-based learning in the Scottish Qualification for headship', in L. Kidd, L. Anderson and W. Newton (eds), *Leading People and Teams in Education*, London: Paul Chapman Publishing, pp. 57–70.

Sachs, J. (2003) *The Activist Teaching Profession*, Buckingham: Open University Press.

Scottish Executive Education Department (2000) *A Teaching Profession for the 21st Century: the report of the Committee of Inquiry into professional conditions of service for teachers*, Edinburgh: The Stationery Office.

—— (2001) *A Teaching Profession for the 21st Century: the agreement following the recommendations of the McCrone Report*, Edinburgh: Scottish Executive.

—— (2002a) *Standard for Chartered Teacher*, Edinburgh: Scottish Executive.

—— (2002b) *Continuing Professional Development*, Edinburgh: Scottish Executive.

Scottish Office Education and Industry Department (1999) *Targeting Excellence: modernising Scotland's schools*, Edinburgh: The Stationery Office.

Senge, P. (1990) *The Fifth Discipline: the art and practice of the learning organisation*, New York: Currency Doubleday.

Smyth, J. and Shacklock, G. (1998) *Re-making Teaching: ideology, policy and practice*, London: Routledge.

Stenhouse, L. (1975) *Introduction to Curriculum Research and Development*, London: Heineman.

Street, H. and Temperley, J. (eds) (2005) *Improving Schools through Collaborative Enquiry*, London: Continuum.

Watkins, C. Carnell, E. and Lodge, C. (2007) *Effective Learning in Classrooms*, London: Paul Chapman Publishers.

10 On the making and taking of professionalism in the further education workplace[1]

Denis Gleeson, Jennie Davies and Eunice Wheeler

Traditional attempts to define professionalism, removed from the context of its practice, offer limited insight to its meaning. This chapter looks at the further education (FE) practitioner as a 'case in point' (Robson 1998). It explores two contrasting notions of the FE professional, as either the recipient or agent of change, reflecting the wider positioning of professionalism as a socially defined or situationally constructed process. The former denotes issues of structure, in terms of how the professional is 'framed' by external factors and the latter focuses on agency in the way professionals construct meaning in the situated contexts of their work (Hoyle 1995). While the two are not mutually exclusive categories, there exists a *dualism* in sociological thinking between agency and structure around the way professionalism is understood (Grace 1995). In addressing this dualism the chapter critically examines various ways in which FE professionals intersect agency and structure in their work. All names are pseudonyms.

In essence, FE is unified by being different (Gleeson and Mardle 1980). It provides work-based training but is not like private training organizations (it is more professional but is nonetheless *the*, not *a*, 'Cinderella' Service). It is not like higher education (it has its feet on the ground, works with difficult learners, offers proper 'on the job' teacher training, serves the local community, and is misunderstood). It is not like schools (it works with adults, part-time students, 'rescues' school failures, offers diverse academic/vocational programmes, and has strong industry–business links).

But there is justifiable reason for treating FE as a 'case in point'. Despite its particularities and peculiarly English connotation, FE has much in common with attempts by governments worldwide to reform post-compulsory education and training within a global discourse of economic improvement, re-skilling and social inclusion (Elliott 1996). In this context English FE represents a 'prototype' of one of the most market tested sectors of public education provision in which quasi-market interventions have radically altered democratic accountability in favour of government, business and corporate interests (Ranson 2003). While ostensibly FE colleges are independent of government control, the sector operates within a context of licensed autonomy and its professionals are treated as 'trusted servants rather than as empowered professionals' (Avis 2003: 329). This market has been bolstered by the introduction of a national learning and skills strategy, reinforced by an audit and inspection regime through which standards of FE provision are judged and assessed (Holloway 1999; Hyland and Merrill 2003).

The professionalism of FE practitioners remains largely unresearched. Much of the prevailing literature has tended to focus on organizational and policy issues rather than on pedagogy and professionalism reflecting entrenched distinctions between the management of FE, and its practice at classroom and workshop level (Gleeson and Mardle, 1980). In addressing the *relational* aspects between the two this chapter focuses on who FE practitioners are and how they make sense of both dimensions in the context of their work.

Becoming an FE practitioner

Early research in the field associates FE professionalism with practitioners' former trade and occupational identities that find expression in the instrumental and pragmatic culture of FE (Gleeson and Mardle 1980). More recent evidence indicates, however, that this prevailing culture is being challenged as residues of old and new FE cultures sit alongside one another.

According to Guile and Lucas (1999) a paradigm shift is taking place reflected in the emergence of a new 'learning professional' working across academic and vocational divisions, in a more polycontextual environment. This change in professional status is by no means complete or unchallenged. Tension remains between the complex demands of the learning professional and the traditional forms of FE practice left unchanged and, as some argue, 'proletarianized' by the recent passage of managerial reforms (Randle and Brady 1994, 1997). A recurring contradiction identified in the research literature is that traditional forms of professional socialization and practice sit uneasily with the multi-skilled nature of FE practitioners' work, in an increasingly prescribed performance environment. Few FE practitioners, for example, can trace the roots of their professionalism to an established desire to teach in FE. Entering FE is, for many, less a career choice than an opportunity at a particular moment in time. As Ruth notes:

> nobody leaves school saying, Oh I want to be a basic skills teacher. It's something you come to via a variety of routes.

The transition into FE is not a smooth one. It often coincides with lifestyle changes, career breaks, redundancy, divorce and relocation. Rachel, for example, talks of 'sliding' into FE after a divorce. Following a successful career in the travel and tourism industry she pursued a second career in FE, gaining the City and Guilds 730 and Certificate in Education (FE) qualification. Her decision to join FE was initially a pragmatic one:

It's not a vocation for me and in fact if I didn't have the children I don't think I'd be here today.

Such 'sliding' into FE is also associated with prior forms of part-time teaching which tempers the accidental nature of transition into FE teaching. John, for example, started teaching when the college needed urgent cover:

I got to know a few people . . . and so eventually I sort of spent time sitting on the boss's doorstep, 'til he knew me well enough and I got a yearly contract, and then finally a full-time contract.

This experience of starting with a few part-time hours is typical. Gwen, for example, remembers making a critical decision about leaving a secure job to enter FE teaching:

Shall I take a chance? Because you can't get a job at any of the Colleges, well certainly not in our faculty, you can't just get a full-time job off the streets. You have to be tried and tested, and so I gave up my job, and I went part-time [teaching].

Despite the risks involved, Gwen subsequently worked part-time at three different colleges before two years later being offered full-time work. In a quite different context Paul used the opportunity to teach part-time to support his dual interests:

[I] liked [teaching], and I suppose when I was near the end of my photography course I just thought, oh yes, do a couple of evening classes and see what happens and also have a go at doing this photography business, and one was a bit more lucrative than the other. Now I do photography for me and, because I teach, I've got the luxury of not having to sell anything if I don't want to.

Such 'entryism' into FE teaching is not new and, whilst mirroring national fluctuations in local labour markets, reflects FE's voluntaristic and entrepreneurial legacy (Gleeson and Mardle 1980). Far from being challenged by modernization, traditional patterns of recruitment and induction, overlaid by national reforms which emphasize labour 'flexibility', reinforce casualization in the sector. While the nature of such flexibility can initially work to the benefit of both college and practitioner, in the long term it has proved damaging to labour relations and professional development (Hodge 1998). If part-time and contractual work offers a flexible response to market fluctuations it also increases distinctions between core and periphery practitioners with knock-on effects in terms of pay, pension and conditions of service. For the college this can perpetuate the uncertainty around recruitment, retention and morale of staff and, for practitioners, there is the tension about whether the 'long interview' through part-time work is worth it.

In such circumstances teacher education and development in FE have tended to remain of secondary consideration. Despite recent government attempts to re-professionalize FE teachers through the acquisition of new professional skills, standards and qualifications,[2] recurring problems of recruitment, retention and casualization have weakened the impact of such initiatives. While subject knowledge and prior work experience often act to sustain new recruits entering FE, many are not prepared for the fragmented working conditions that await them. John, for example, recalls feeling vulnerable in being asked to teach a unit on microprocessors which was not his area of expertise:

> I found it a painful experience really because you were so isolated. You were never quite sure whether you were doing it right or not . . . So you made it up as best yourself and hoped that no one would disapprove.

From this initial experience more part-time work followed with John eventually becoming a full-time lecturer. Like John, Paul was also asked to teach an area beyond his expertise but, as a full-time member of staff and with student numbers falling, he felt vulnerable:

> I ended up running media courses because someone had to and I was one of the more flexible folk around . . . and I ended up flexing myself out of what I like doing best.

FE practitioners encompass change readily in a sector where college mergers, reorganization and redundancy are now features of everyday professional life. As Paul recalls, there are trade offs to be made:

> I was very, very pissed off and we were having big fights over all this: he [Paul's line manager] said, when the opportunity arises you'll be back you know, and that's what happened and I'm back and I'm running the HE side of things now which is very good. If I could do anything in the faculty it would be that.

If Paul stuck around to get the job he really wanted, Gwen's experience was different. Initially she spoke about her enthusiasm for the freedom her 'one to one' working relations with students allowed, and of her car and her home 'as more office than college':

> It's probably the most interesting job I've had because things change all the time. You can take on new things as you like and my line manager is very good at allowing me to do this.

By our second interview with her there had been changes in the funding mechanisms for NVQs[3], which led to a college review of how work-based assessors should work with students. The upshot of it was to reduce the time spent working face to face with students, and the development of distance learning and 'e:type' assessment materials. According to Gwen:

> it does worry me because it would mean a lot more sitting in front of a computer and marking things on computer, and emailing people . . . all that sort of thing, and I'm not sure whether that's the way I want to go at all.

Professional engagement with flexibility is then contingent upon a variety of experiences, sometimes punitive, enhancing or strategic. In this context 'being flexible' represents a type of risk taking (James and Diment 2003).

Such contrasting fortunes can be likened to a pair of balance scales: on the one side are the structural frustrations with the job and, on the other, the compensatory aspects of working with colleagues and students (Gleeson and Shain 1999). There are times when one side will weigh heavier than the other, and also times when the two sides will be in balance with one another. Rachel, for example, provides an example of both the restrictive and expansive elements of this dimension:

> I think as I get more into [the job] I find it more and more difficult . . . to think of apportioning your time between what you think you're here for and what you actually end up doing.
>
> The joys are of course the students that you can see you've, or feel you've made a difference with, the ones that have really come on. You know their confidence builds and so on. However you look at it you've got to have had some part in that.

Despite her earlier denial of vocation, Rachel expresses values and attitudes traditionally associated with professional commitment and engagement. The subtle ways in which agency and structure surface in practitioner narratives is, however, revealing, as we go on to argue. Analysis of more than thirty plus interviews with participating practitioners reveals, on the one hand, disenchantment with pay, inspection and administration and, on the other, a strong commitment to teaching and student development. While the background and interpretations of this process vary among practitioners, they share much in common. Noticeable is the way in which tutors handle 'duality' both in terms of expressing frustration with the structures that affect the conditions and contexts in which they work, and optimism about working with students and colleagues which is seen to count for more (agency).

Yet there are contradictions around this avowed commitment to students. It found expression, for example, among trade practitioners in the 1980s concerned about their status and what they termed 'Mickey Mouse' courses that did not measure up to apprenticeship programmes deskilled by recession. Then (under Thatcherism) and now with FE being used as a vehicle of New

Labour's social inclusion policy there is controversy over the way government intervention in welfare policy is restructuring the goals of public policy among FE professionals. As Ecclestone (2004) has noted, therapeutic assumptions about low self-esteem among 'learners at risk', or 'hard to reach' students with 'fragile identities', are becoming more prevalent in policymakers' and professionals' everyday terminology. It is to this that we now turn.

Pedagogy and inclusion

As FE increasingly absorbs 'hard to reach' students as part of the Government's wider social inclusion agenda, provision has been skewed by audit, inspection and performance management regimes which result in a number of unintended consequences (Hyland and Merrill 2003). While the desire to promote individualized student learning remains a strongly expressed core value among FE practitioners, there are tensions around its delivery. One such tension is in the relationship between 'biography' and 'baggage', which eschews subject expertise in favour of a craft of 'empathy' towards students (Ecclestone 2004). A current belief in FE is that it is essential for tutors to understand the biography of disadvantaged students (their prior experience and what their problems are) so that issues can be addressed to support effective learning which, in turn, feeds into more reflexive professional practice (Wahlberg and Gleeson 2003). Addressing biography is another way in which FE practitioners both define their professionalism and, at the same time, feel threatened by it. As the following comment from Tessa indicates, there are lines to be drawn between biography and baggage:

> Yes, if they've got all this baggage that they really can't get through, we're going to have to try and do something about it before we can free up their mind . . . [T]hey come with a lot of baggage and you're always going to get the ones that want to offload that . . .You can't take all their bags and baggage. . . . [I]f you feel they need referring somewhere then you can do that.

The argument is taken a step further by George, a Business Studies tutor who points out that 'with the younger kids' he is now hardly a teacher, and feels more like a welfare officer. This shift, from 'teaching to welfare', arose in a number of interviews. It is seen as one of the consequences of a social inclusion policy which has involved the college in recruiting ever younger, and ever more 'marginal' and vulnerable students into a variety of vocational programmes that are inappropriate to their needs (Ainley and Bailey 1997). The nature of such inclusion has become codified by practitioners in terms of interpretations of what 'the old' and 'the new' FE is about: between principles of teaching one's subject to motivated students and issues of social justice and inclusion. The issue of professionalism raised here is about more than just 'biography and baggage'. It relates to uncertainties about losing a sense of professional identity and status, as practitioners move from being accredited subject specialists with expertise as 'an Economist'; through higher order teaching – 'a lecturer'; followed by what some see as a slow downgrading of their professional status as it changes to being 'a teacher' of lower status courses with a welfare function, as tutors increasingly need to address the personal problems of new types of 'included' student. According to George, the floor will be reached if and when they become untrained 'welfare officers', or even worse, 'key skills trainers'.

If such responses appear defensive they are also indicative of a reaction among tutors to uncertainty in the sector, often associated with reduction in resources, staffing and teaching hours. Whether universal or not, the data here highlights the sense of marginality through which FE practitioners often define themselves. They feel caught up in a fast changing policy-practice dynamic in which their identity and status has been 'casualized' and curtailed by a procession of market, funding-led and managerialist reforms (Gleeson and Shain 1999).

Another such ambiguity finds expression, ironically, in students' definitions of 'good' tutors as being the ones who know their subject and can 'deliver'. The students look for the professionality of the staff in a different place from that which the staff define themselves as now occupying. This deepens the contradictory forces around the way professionality refracts into the learning context, creating what Bathmaker (2001a) calls 'dupes' and 'devils'. Increasingly, many tutors and students are tied to a hegemony of performance that binds them to an externally monitored cycle of recruitment, retention and certification linked to college funding, resource and remuneration (Bathmaker 2001b; Bloomer 1998). In such circumstances teaching becomes a constant struggle against rather than with students.

The ever-present concern among practitioners is that they will be 'blamed' by blinkered thinking in a world of inspection, audit and surveillance. Rachel, for example, expresses the view that external inspection appears more focused on teacher performance than student learning. Here she describes a lesson that had been observed by a senior colleague as part of a practice observation in preparation for a forthcoming inspection:

> a lesson in which I did absolutely no teaching but the outcomes were great in learning terms . . . It was amusing to be told that as no teaching had taken place she [senior tutor] could not give me adequate feedback on the 'lesson' as a whole, although she could not fault the activities, the students' commitment and dedication to the task, and the outcome was clearly that a high degree of learning had taken place. This latter was endorsed by the students who said that they had enjoyed the activity and felt they had learned a lot.
>
> (Journal extract)

Alongside external inspection runs an insatiable audit trail linked to the funding of colleges. For Paul, who works in a highly flexible working environment, where adult students sign themselves in for registration at different points in the day and week, keeping track of their attendance is difficult. He reflects here that students sometimes forget to register and that constantly registering 'hard to reach' students (though their attendance is often good) is not conducive to a high trust working relationship:

> It feels to me like the audit process assumes a certain mode of learning, the students turn up and sit in classrooms, which we simply don't do.

This tension between auditing systems and the flexible nature of programmes is at the root of an accountability system where discrepancies can lead to cuts in teaching hours, resources and staffing (Holloway 1999). At the same time practitioners are conscious that their jobs may be on the line if student recruitment and retention is not maintained. This is notably the case for practitioners working with so-called 'hard to reach' students. Celia, for example, has been using text messaging with her students as a way of improving communications with the college 'on their terms'. To date most of her tutor group use the text message system to communicate about lateness or absence, though not exclusively so as the following clips indicate:

- assessment issues and crises, for example, *'we r waitin outside staff rm 2 give our assignments but there is no1 there what shall we do'*;
- family 'policing', for example, *'Hi it is X's brother would it be possible to come see you'* followed by a message from X *'my bro don't know ive got a fone or a bfriend he fink im in college all week & the days off ive had he don't know about them'*;
- academic worries, for example, *'I am so worried about this presentation .. pl tell me u r not goin to ask questions sorry abt txtn u on weekend'*;
- complaints, for example, *'(she) shouted at me in front of every1 only bcuz we were laffin in leson, I did all my wrk & she flipped at me'*.

Text messaging has enabled Celia to produce a register that is less threatening to her students, but which meets registration and audit criteria. This is also a way for her to reconcile the conflict between her sense of professionalism as a tutor (knowing about and effectively helping her tutees), and the bureaucratization of the tutor's role (its reduction to the tick boxes on the register showing 'notified' absences). While Celia is aware that a number of the reasons given for lateness may be invented, this is not the issue. What matters is that the students have recognized their responsibility for reporting absence or lateness. This is a 'success' that can be chalked up. Moreover, once in touch, Celia feels that she can watch out for students who are in difficulty and offer help in a more meaningful way than scheduled 'progress' tutorials allow.

As Bathmaker's (2001b) research indicates, the relationship between students and staff is critical to addressing the low self-esteem of the student, and addressing failure. The text-messaging example reveals a creative way of dealing with pragmatic and professional issues (Gale 2001). Thus it would be a mistake to assume that FE practitioners are passive when dealing with inspection and audit cultures. What we have sought to illustrate here are the ways in which practitioners seek to resolve 'duality' in the contradictions between agency and structure experienced in the context of their work (Colley and Hodkinson 2003). In the next section we return to the broader sociological implications of such analysis with reference to FE professionalism in the wider context of public accountability.

FE professionalism in and beyond regulation

From the evidence so far, the idea that there exists a 'community of professional practice' in FE is a misnomer (Lave and Wenger 1991). The challenge is to build one around recognition of the types of high trust working practices that have informed this chapter. Building professional capacity in FE requires new *theories* of professionalism which can guide pedagogy and policy since the empiricism of FE practice is incapable of achieving such change alone. It also requires forms of research that challenge the prevailing culture of technicism. In the current volatile environment of FE the way in which research might influence FE practice is limited:

> college reactions to the national policy and funding situation have predominantly negative impacts upon learning quality. Examples include increased group sizes, serious reductions in resources and contact time, and the loss of high quality teaching staff, for example, through redundancy. In some circumstances, learning cultures and the quality of learning are only sustained because tutors put in significant amounts of extra time and effort. The current climate in the FE sector as a whole is generally hostile to research capacity building, though unintentionally so. Except for a few pockets, research is seen as a luxury.
>
> (Hodkinson *et al.* 2004: 4)

The narratives in this study reveal a disjuncture between the policy rhetoric of FE as a high skill vocational route, characterized by greater social inclusion and opportunity, and the reality as it is experienced by professionals 'on the ground'. We have sought to demonstrate that professional knowledge is constructed, changed and sustained through the working out of tensions experienced between external criteria of performance and those 'ecologies of practice' (Stronach *et al.* 2002) that frame reality making among FE professionals. This situational and constructionist view of professional knowledge contrasts sharply with disembodied conceptions of the FE professional as the harbinger of technical skills and competencies, delivering units and responding to targets in a technicist fashion. It emphasizes the importance of agency, context and creativity, including issues of culture and identity in constructing the vocational habitus of practitioners (Engeström and Young 2001).

Such a perspective suggests that professional knowledge is not fixed but situated in unstable conditions, in a variety of localized circumstances. The creative tensions involved cannot, therefore, be reduced to either/or oppositions (dupes or devils) but rather find expression in the dual identities that practitioners experience in the contradictions of their everyday work. As we have argued, at one level, coalition through audit fosters pathologies of defensiveness in response to performance cultures. At another, it can evoke either resistance or strategic compliance where performance targets are considered unworkable or in danger of collapse (Gleeson and Husbands 2001).

Another possibility is to understand issues of identity as a basis for rethinking how professionalism can be reworked in preferred ways. Seddon *et al.* (2003), for example, emphasize the way that liberal market reform is changing the boundaries of professional practice, challenging occupational standards and reshaping the workplace, including broader articulations of power, knowledge and community in the wider politics of civil society. At the same time, it is through such 'living tensions' that multiplicity in professional roles and identities are experienced and developed in transformative ways (Zucas and Malcolm 2002). In their study *Management Lives*, Knights and Wilmott (1999) demonstrate how practitioners define their professionality through such lived experience, rather than interpreting their experiences as eroding creativity and autonomy. This view draws attention to the ways in which professionalism is constructed from *within* the cracks, crevices and contradictions of practice, rather than imposed by external sources such as government, policymakers, corporations and media. As the more disembodied elements of performance management come under scrutiny, the intriguing question is raised whether marketization has had the paradoxical effect of restoring professional power by reconstructing professionalism through resistance and contestation (Ranson 2003). According to Stronach *et al.* (2002), such identity formation constitutes a powerful narrative ethic which allows professionals to 're-story' themselves in and against the audit culture.

If, as we have argued, one form of accountability, professional self-regulation, has been replaced by another based on neo-liberal principles, where do we look for new signs of professionalism? Neither form constitutes an adequate model of public accountability. Yet, regulative accountability has had the paradoxical effect of drawing attention to failures and contradictions associated with managerialism and audit regimes (missed targets, contestation and compliance). The issue is, then, more complicated than simply calling for a renewal of independent professionalism or 'restorying' professionals. It also involves reference to wider forms of power, governance and accountability necessary to promote democratic professionalism.

Evidence from different sector and workplace studies reveals that professionals experience contradiction between agency and structure in their work (Shain and Gleeson 1999). At one level this manifests itself in creative and routinized compliance, rule following or rule breaking, resulting in the fabrication of activities designed to meet targets. At another, it involves mediation, contestation and redefinition among professionals negotiating or exploiting contradictions where audit cultures do little more than hold professionals and clients to account. As Ranson (2003) notes, such activity is embodied in spaces of local governance which offer professionals, agencies and community groups the opportunity to work together, in *localized* interventions. For Seddon *et al.* (2003: 18) this brings into relief the 'bigger picture' for social partnership work and workers, including 'their relationship with various political rationalities and political projects, and the way these activities map across the wider social structures in terms of gender, ethnicity, class and in relation to the state'. In this context the transformative potential of professionals 'restorying themselves' is contingent on the restoration of wider forms of democratic governance and accountability, which grow out of cultural capital and citizenship and transcend economized market and consumerized concerns imposed from above (Bourdieu and Wacquant 1992). If part of this process involves social partnerships and self-governing institutions, it is also dependent on more transparent forms of plurality, contestation and accountability at the centre of the public sphere. According to Marquand (2000), a priority for modern, social democracy is to both retrieve and reinvent the public domain, which erects barriers against unaccountable incursions of the market. Central to this restructuring is a balancing of 'agreement making' (Nixon and Ranson 1997) between government, professionals and local communities concerning the objectives, strategies and forms of accountability that is part of a wider democratic conversation (Lauder *et al.* 2004). In other words it involves relational aspects of both agency and structure:

> Notions of agency and structure are potentially important in drawing attention to power relationships that lead to inequalities in life chances ... and equally to explanations of how the individual relates to society and to citizens' social and democratic understanding of their place in the world, what has been called reflexive solidarity.
>
> (Lauder *et al.* 2004: 19)

Reflexive solidarity in FE is easier said than done. It involves the ability of professionals to reflect on their actions and conditions, to change and modify these in the light of practice and experience, and to exercise independent judgement accordingly (Bourdieu 1977). This is not a process driven by empiricism but rather one that articulates a *theory* of professional authority grounded in the consent of civic society through which more robust forms of professionalism can expose political rhetoric to public scrutiny.

Conclusion

Such an argument turns on *relational* forms of discourse that position professionalism alongside more transparent democratic forms of accountability at the centre of civic society. If this sounds a familiar argument in support of strengthening professionalism against 'private' market interests, it is more than that. It addresses wider forms of 'duality' around which both structure and agency challenge *dualism* and, in the current context of professional practice, give voice to critique and ideas emerging from the contradictions between education policy and practice. In this context FE professionals, as experts and citizens, prowl the boundaries of public and private spaces in brokering the interface between citizen, state and consumer interests. In a multi-million pound sector, linking school F/HE and work – incorporating over 4 million students of all ages and backgrounds – FE practitioners are well placed to engage with this process. In this respect restorying professional narratives becomes inseparable from a more communicative discourse of public accountability, fashioning more authentic forms of authority and voice linked to local conditions of governance and public accountability. This in turn, Crouch (2003) argues, requires that both policy and professional agendas inform one another which, in principle, allows local contexts (colleges, schools, hospitals, welfare and community organizations) to mediate between central and global agendas. This, we argue, brings FE professionalism in from the cold by challenging the conditions of *dualism* that have constrained professional practice as either self-serving or in the service of a performance society, and move it toward a more transformative view of its role in public life.

Notes

1 This chapter is an edited version of Gleeson *et al.* (2005). It draws on data from the Transforming Learning Cultures in Further Education Project (2001–2005). The TLC–FE Project is part of the wider ESRC Teaching and Learning Research Programme (TLRP) www.ex.ac.uk/sell/tlc. We acknowledge funding received from the Economic and Social Research Council (ESRC) (award no: L139251025).
2 E.g. those stipulated by the Further Education National Training Organisation, DFES Standards Unit, Lifelong Learning UK, Institute for Lifelong Learning.
3 National Vocational Qualifications.

References

Ainley, P. and Bailey, B. (1997) *The Business of Learning*, London: Cassell.
Avis, J. (2003) 'Rethinking trust in a performative culture: the case of post compulsory education', *Journal of Education Policy*, 18 (3): 315–332.
Bathmaker, A.-M. (2001a) 'Neither dupes or devils: teachers' constructions of their changing role in further education'. Paper presented at the Learning and Skills Research Network Conference, Robinson College, Cambridge, December 2001.
—— (2001b) 'It's the perfect education: lifelong learning and the experience of Foundation Level GNVQ students', *Journal of Vocational Education and Training*, 53 (1): 81–100.

Bloomer, M. (1998) 'They tell you what to do and then they let you get on with it,' *Journal of Education and Work*, 11 (2): 167–186.

Bourdieu, P. (1977) *Outline of a Theory of Practice*, Cambridge: Cambridge University Press.

—— and Wacquant, L. J. D. (1992) *An Invitation to Reflexive Sociology*, Cambridge: Polity Press.

Colley, H. and Hodkinson, P. (2001) 'Problems with "bridging the gap": the reversal of structure and agency in addressing social exclusion', *Critical Social Policy*, 21 (3): 337–361.

Crouch, C. (2003) *Commercialism or Citizenship*, London: Fabian Society.

Ecclestone, K. (2004) 'Learning or therapy? The demoralisation of education', *British Journal of Education Studies*, 57 (3): 127–141.

Elliott, G. (1996) *Crisis and Change in Vocational Education and Training*, London: Jessica Kingsley.

Engeström, Y. and Young, M. F. D. (2001) 'Expansive learning at work', unpublished paper, London: Institute of Education.

Fuller, A. and Unwin, L. (2002) 'Context and meaning in apprenticeships'. Paper presented at Teaching and Learning Research Programme Conference, Nene, University College Northampton, November 2002.

Gale, K. (2003) 'Creative pedagogies of resistance in post compulsory teacher education', in J. Satterwaite, E. Atkinson and K. Gale (eds), *Discourse, Power and Resistance*, London: Trentham Books.

Gleeson, D. and Shain, F. (1999) 'Managing ambiguity: between markets and managerialism', *Sociological Review*, 47 (3): 461–490.

—— and Husbands, C. (2001) (eds) *The Performing School*, London: Routledge Falmer.

—— and Mardle, G. (with the assistance of McCourt, J.) (1980) *Further Education or Training?*, London: Routledge & Kegan Paul.

——, Davies, J. and Wheeler, E. (2005) 'On the making and taking of professionalism in the further education workplace', *British Journal of Sociology of Education*, 26 (4): 445–460.

Grace, G. (1995) *School Leadership: beyond educational management: an essay in policy scholarship*, London: Falmer.

Guile, D. and Lucas, N. (1999) 'Rethinking initial FE teacher education and development', in A. Green and N. Lucas (eds), *FE and Lifelong Learning*, London: Institute of Education.

Hodge. M. (1998) *House of Commons Select Committee Report on Education and Employment*, London: The Stationery Office.

Hodkinson, P., Gleeson, D., James, D. and Postlethwaite, K. (2004) *TLC-FE End of Year Project Report to ESRC*, Swindon: ESRC.

Holloway, D. (1999) 'The Audit Commission, managerialism and the Further Education sector', *Journal of Vocational Education and Training*, 51 (2): 229–243.

Hoyle, E. (1995) 'Changing conceptions of a profession', in H. Busher and R. Saran (eds), *Managing Teachers and Professionals in Schools*, London: Kogan Page.

Hyland, T. and Merrill, B. (2003) *The Changing Face of Further Education*, London: RoutledgeFalmer.

James, D. and Diment, K. (2003) 'Going underground? Learning and assessment in an ambiguous space', *Journal of Vocational Education and Training*, 55 (4): 407–422.

Knights, D. and Wilmott, H. (1999*) Management Lives*, London: Sage.

Lauder, H., Brown, P. and Halsey, A. H. (2004) 'Sociology: some principles of a new policy science', *British Journal of Sociology*, 55 (1): 3–22.

Lave, J. and Wenger, E. (1991) *Situated Learning*, Cambridge: Cambridge University Press.

Marquand, D. (2000) 'The fall of civic culture', *New Statesman*, 13 November.

Nixon, J. and Ranson, S. (1997) 'Theorising agreement: the moral basis of the emergent professionalism within the new management of education', *Discourse*, 18 (2): 197–214.

Randle, K. and Brady, N. (1994) 'Further education and the new managerialism', *Journal of Further and Higher Education*, 21 (2): 229–239.

—— (1997) 'Managerialism and professionalism in the cinderella service', *Journal of Vocational Education and Training*, 49 (1): 121–139.

Ranson, S. (2003) 'Public accountability in the age of neo-liberal governance', *Journal of Education Policy*, 18 (5): 459–480.

Robson, J. (1998) 'A profession in crisis: status, culture and identity in the further education college', *Journal of Vocational Education and Training*, 50 (4): 585–607.

Seddon, T., Billett, S. and Clemens, A. (2003) 'Politics of social partnerships: a framework for learning', unpublished paper, Melbourne: Monash University.

Shain, F. and Gleeson, D. (1999) 'Under new management: changing conceptions of teacher professionalism and policy in the further education sector', *Journal of Education Policy*, 14 (4): 445–462.

Stronach, I., Corbin, B., McNamara, O., Stark, S. and Warne, T. (2002) 'Towards an uncertain politics of professionalism', *Journal of Education Policy*, 17 (1): 109–138.

Wahlberg, M. and Gleeson, D. (2003) 'Doing the business: paradox and irony in vocational education', *Journal of Vocational Education and Training*, 55 (4): 423–446.

Zucas, M. and Malcolm, J. (2002) '"Playing the game": regulation, scrutiny and pedagogic identities in post-compulsory education', unpublished mimeo, Leeds: Centre for Lifelong Learning, University of Leeds.

11 In the shadow of the Research Assessment Exercise?

Working in a 'new' university[1]

Pat Sikes

I was appointed to teach on the Post Compulsory Education and Training course but since I came here, research has come to be much more of a priority. Whereas before it was optional, it's definitely expected that you do it now.

(Ron)

I was a schoolteacher for twenty odd years and that's how I automatically identify, as a teacher or lecturer.

(Carole)

I've got a Ph.D. But I haven't tended to see myself as a researcher until recently, since I've been involved in various projects and had some papers published. Most of what I do is related to the courses I'm responsible for and the 100 hours research time gets swallowed up in marking and admin.

(Kath)

Ron, Carole and Kath (all pseudonyms) are employed as permanent, full-time members of the academic staff in the School of Education at New University. All have responsibility for the advertising, marketing, recruitment, administration, curriculum design and assessment of a range of teaching programmes (up to Masters level) catering for student numbers in the high hundreds. The majority of these students are part-timers and many programmes are taught as evening sessions in venues up to 200 miles away. Kath, for instance, has a specified workload of 550 hours (p.a.) rising to 800 plus when she adds in travel. Within the School, this is not unusual: most people have job specifications of 450 hours 'teaching', with 100 hours for 'research', although this frequently gets taken up by course-related activities.

In the 2001, UK Research Assessment Exercise (RAE)[2], Education at New University improved on the rating achieved in 1996. Around the time this result was announced, a new Vice-Chancellor (VC), committed to raising the research profile of the institution, was appointed. The message was that

New University was to become a research focused institution and that all staff were expected to be research active in RAE returnable terms, publishing in peer-reviewed journals and obtaining research funding from external sources. The general feeling within the School was that the VC had 'wannabee' (Marginson 1998) aspirations, which had led to a shift in emphasis, realising Taylor's (1999: 47) observation that 'the reality is that for the majority of academics, the emergent job demands are not the demands described or implied in the "job descriptions" of the positions for which they were originally employed'. This is the 'reality' for many workers these days and academics are by no means in a unique position. However, while there may be some comfort in knowing you are not alone, the impact upon conditions of work, job content, and personal and professional identities is still felt – for better or worse. And how people feel about their work has implications for how they go about doing it: with individual and institutional consequences.

This chapter considers how some staff at New University perceived and experienced being academics, focusing particularly upon the demand that they become research active. Looking at what individuals had to say may give some insights into interactions between identity, especially 'academic identity' (Henkel 2000), personal agency and biography, and structural force. Although the RAE is a UK phenomenon, other countries have their equivalents (Greenwood and Levin 2005; Rogers 2005). Indeed Middleton (2005) describes a similar situation for academics in Education Departments in New Zealand faced with their Performance-Based Research Fund Quality Evaluation (PBRF).

The chapter draws on a fraction of the rich data from interviews, conversations, discussions and documents accumulated during an ongoing collaborative, autoethnographic (Ellis and Bochner 2000; Roth 2005), critical action research project involving myself and staff in the School of Education at New University. The key aim has been to support those engaging in research and writing, rather than to boost RAE performance. Thus, over the last seven years I have come into the institution as a 'consultant' and have worked alongside colleagues developing research projects and providing input on research related topics. Simultaneously, I have recorded and reflected on my perceptions and experiences. Although it may sound grandiose, I consider this work to be in the critical action tradition (Foley and Valenzuela 2005) since my intention has been to 'make a difference'.

What does it mean to be an academic at New University?

In 1997 Henkel argued that British academics held values embodying the assumptions that they should experience,

> security of tenure, relatively generous allocations of time, relatively low levels of administration, a common salary structure, the interdependence of at least teaching and research, an emphasis on equality issues in the

allocation of work and the idea that academic specialization is discipline, rather than functionally, based.

(1997: 134)

This was the ideal. Writing in 2007, academic tenure was abolished over 18 years ago; time is generally at a premium; administration is ever increasing; academic salaries are rated as relatively low; the official view favours a split between research and teaching (DfES 2003); equality in work distribution is, frequently, more rhetoric than substance; and even within identifiable disciplines, what discipline means and what it entails, is contested (Becher and Trowler 2001; Neumann *et al*. 2002; Scott *et al*. 2005).

Many staff in the School of Education described themselves primarily as 'teachers'. There was even some reluctance to identify as academics – although the definition of the word 'as one studying or teaching at a university' (Chambers 1972: 6) is undoubtedly applicable:

I'm not comfortable calling myself an academic. It seems to imply someone whose been working away for centuries on some arcane and esoteric topic.

(Brian)

An academic? Well I suppose I am, technically. But it's not how I see or describe myself.

(Sally)

It may be that what Thomas said reflected what underlay other people's considerations of whether or not New University staff were academics:

To be honest the environment here is not steeped in an intellectual, scholarly, academic ethos: it's not like Balliol College, where I imagine it is taken for granted that everyone is an intellectual.

(Thomas)

But even at Balliol and in 'traditional' universities, things are no longer as they were – or as Golden Age thinking might lead one to believe they once were (Clegg 2005). Pressure to publish in peer-reviewed journals has become a characteristic of academic life (Henkel 2000), and a career that does not involve this is likely to be increasingly difficult to sustain unless one has a teaching-only contract.

Academic work in changing/present times

A review of literature dealing with academic work emphasizes change, 'fragmentation' (Rowland 2002), conflict, contestation, work overload and widespread unhappiness. Beck and Young talk of 'alienation and anomie' and describe 'a generation of practitioners (*who*) have experienced what is, to some, a sense of crisis and of loss. Cherished identities and commitments have been undermined and, for some, this has been experienced as an assault on their professionalism' (2005: 184). Again, this is an observation that equally applies to workers in other occupations. Regardless of one's job, changes which affect it potentially challenge 'fundamental conceptions of self and self-worth' (Lee and Boud 2003: 188). And also, change is a constant, though it may be possible to argue that present day change is more pervasive and radical and is happening at a faster pace than previously. Indeed, Becher and Trowler characterize change in higher education as 'turbulent' (2001: 1). Simon and Jessica's comments echo this:

> Plus ça change, le même chose. It seems that there's always something new to do, new administrative procedures, new technology, new concerns, new intelligences even. I decided to stop being a head when I was having to spend more and more of my time on things I did not see as legitimate tasks for an educationist. I come here and almost immediately I'm back in response mode.
>
> (Simon)

> Things change overnight as it were. You get used to one set of require-ments and before you know it they've been abolished and there are new ones in place.
>
> (Jessica)

Some readers of this chapter are likely to be employed in higher education and will, therefore, be well aware of the origins, nature and personal and professional consequences of the changes that have occurred. Barnett (2003) talks of the malign influence of 'pernicious ideologies', including those of quality and audit and managerialism, and most academics presently in service will have been touched, in some way or other, by institutional and national policies and imperatives associated with, for instance:

*   the restructuring and reorganization of HE: including the granting of university status to polytechnics and some colleges of HE, and the amalgamation and affiliation of previously independent institutions;
*   increased accountability: for teaching and learning (e.g. QAA,[3] Ofsted,[4] FENTO[5]), for research activity (RAE), for use of resources, and so on;
*   strategies aimed at widening participation: such as attracting 'non-traditional' students and offering different types of programme;
*   pressure to generate income and to develop and market courses in competition with other providers (see Henkel 1997);
*   changing notions of the role and nature of higher education in general and its relation to business and the economy in particular (see DfES 2003);

- the introduction of tuition fees and student loans;
- changes to funding arrangements instituted by the higher education funding councils;
- the introduction of prescribed content and pedagogy: for instance in initial teacher education and for those in receipt of ESRC studentships.

Silver depicts such changes in a negative light noting that

> conflict, uncertainty and the difficulties of response have penetrated the daily lives of academic staff. They have difficult commitments and decisions to make regarding unwelcome or confusing national or institutional policies that affect their daily lives and concerns, and their longer-term professional implications.
>
> (2003: 165)

My own knowledge and experience of academic climates suggests that the feelings Silver is talking about are shared, to some degree, by the majority of people working in universities. However, at the same time, there are those for whom the changes have had positive effects (see Morley 2003). For instance: as well as redundancy and changes to job specifications which are experienced negatively by existing incumbents, restructuring and reorganization can create new positions open to people with different qualifications and backgrounds than has traditionally been the case. Career opportunities and promotion may become available – as may the option to take early retirement on advantageous terms. There may be exciting chances to develop new courses, curricula, and approaches to teaching, learning and assessment. Moves to widen participation may enable some to pursue commitments to social justice concerns, bringing about a closer match between personal, professional and political values and job content.

Putting the emphasis on research

> Of the recent changes in higher education, it is arguably the expectation for all academics to undertake research that has generated the greatest threat, as well as some of the greatest opportunities for change.
>
> (Lee and Boud 2003: 188)

Although Lee and Boud are writing about Australia, what they have to say is relevant to the UK and other countries with similar funding policies. Certainly, at New University, there were those who felt that the RAE offered possibilities. For these people the exercise has had 'high identity value' (Hartley 2002: 197) in that greater emphasis on research, where previously teaching was seen as paramount, has brought recognition and self-affirmation for those who wanted to be, and be seen as being, researchers.

In response to the RAE climate I'm conscious that I'm now spending more time than ever before in research related activities. I'm still engaged in the usual pedagogical research, the kind of stuff that supports my day-to-day teaching activities and without which my teaching would suffer. However, I'm now spending much more time doing research for outcomes other than this. And I welcome it.

(Ron)

Some people, however, felt that the emphasis on RAE returns devalued their identities as teachers:

If the impetus is towards research and all the status and brownie points are attached to research then what does that say about teaching? I'm a teacher, I like to think that I'm a good teacher and I am proud to be a teacher but that doesn't seem to count for much any more.

(Val)

Others took ambivalent or reflectively critical or even cynical positions:

What is odd about the pressure to be researchers is that this is put to us as the *sine qua non* of our professional identity. Anything else you do is of little interest – or so it seems.

(Ambrose)

No matter how well we do we're not going to get a 5*.[6] It is impossible. So there will be no money attached. I think that we should just give up and maintain our integrity. It's irrelevant to us.

(Barry)

Division and polarization of 'teachers' and 'researchers' is an almost inevitable consequence of the RAE (for example, McNay 1997, 1998; Murray *et al.* 2005). This could be discerned at New University where a policy of giving more resources and time for research and activities expected to meet RAE criteria to those deemed likely to be productive had been adopted:

If people are going to be research active they will be supported. We'll pay for them to go to conferences if they give a paper which can then be submitted to a journal, and we'll give them more research time. . . . If people aren't going to produce the RAE goods they are going to have to do more teaching.

(Sam)

This strategy inevitably means that others have increased teaching and administrative loads and are, therefore, even less likely to become research active themselves:

If you're not seen as a researcher then you get more teaching so you lose the time that you might have had for research and writing, and so it goes on.

(Amina)

Identity and context: structure and agency

How individuals perceived and experienced (RAE returnable) research and teaching, in relation to their work as academics, seemed to depend upon: the identities they held and were comfortable with within their specific work situations (their 'situational self' (Nias, 1989)); what they were required to do in their jobs; and where they were in their lives and careers.

Personal identities are 'never gained and maintained once and for all' (Sikes *et al.* 1985: 155) but are formed and informed, 'forged, rehearsed and remade' (Lee and Boud 2003: 188) through discursive practices and social interactions, 'established in the response' (Rolling 2004: 876) and 'subject to the volatile logic of iterability' (Butler 1993: 105). Identities are constructed out of 'the categories which people cho[o]se in order to explain themselves' (MacLure 1993: 316). How people experience change depends on how change is (officially) conceptualized and realized within specific contexts and upon how they understand and experience the change and those contexts in terms of their own biographies. This explains why people in the same situation can experience it in very different ways and why an individual can attribute alternative meanings to the same experience at, and from, various points and positions in their lives. We each have persisting, core identities – 'substantial selves' (Nias 1989) – which endure throughout or for long periods of, our lives, and identities that are far more contextually and circumstantially dependent. Stronach *et al.* talk of professionals 'mobilizing a complex of occasional identities in response to shifting contexts' (2002: 117). Day *et al.* comment that,

> such mobilizations occur in the space between the 'structure' (of the relations between power and status) and 'agency' (in the influence which we and others can have); and it is the interaction between these which influences how teachers see themselves i.e. their personal and professional identities.
>
> (2005: 24)

When contexts change and priorities shift, keeping hold of comfortable identities is not easy since the tensions, contradictions and complexities in any altered situation are inherent in the space between structure and agency. Anxieties and pressures occasioned by striving to meet changed and intensified professional priorities and demands can spill over into other areas of people's lives and lead to them questioning their identities and what they are doing, as well as leaving them feeling inadequate. A number of the women I spoke with also questioned whether there was a gender effect at work here (see Acker and Armenti 2004; Devos 2004; Hartley 2003; Morley and Walsh 1995). For example:

> I'm feeling that my professional identity is in flux and am confused about what to prioritize . . . I feel pulled in different directions . . . [and] inadequate to the task. I feel de-skilled as if what I/we do is not valued or is easy or could somehow be done quicker. I feel as if there's something wrong with me that I cannot manage my time to achieve what is required. Any progress I make [in my research and writing] is in the evenings or weekends, and that is when I am up-to-date and not marking. The result of this lack of separate times for rest and recreation . . . is that I never fully escape . . . I suspect that we keep much of this from each other and from those in power in institutions for fear of seeming weak or inadequate etc. I wonder if some of this is a feminist issue especially when looking at priorities?
>
> (Doreen)

> The pressure comes in waves of angst that I'm not fulfilling the demands expected of me, and that I'm therefore failing in my role as 'senior lecturer'. This job is so closely related to 'who I am', and what helps me make sense of who I am in the world, that I feel the pressure to meet the expectations, but feel concern that I am not necessarily able to be the academic researching University lecturer that is encouraged by the Faculty.
>
> (Sara)

These women approach their jobs in a committed, conscientious and effective manner. Both undertake research and have published in peer-reviewed outlets. The feelings of inadequacy they express are, logically, inappropriate. That they feel as they do is the consequence of a range of factors: however, I would suggest that, the way in which the requirement to be research active was being managed within the School was significantly contributing to the tensions between, and challenges to, their identities that they describe.

End thoughts

Staff at the School of Education at New University were facing imperatives which often conflicted, making it difficult for them to be the sort of professionals they wanted to be and to be seen as being. People worked more hours than were officially allocated to meet their perceived commitments to their students. The pressure to meet RAE demands was an additional source of stress, as research and writing had to be done in 'personal' time, thereby impinging on other identities.

Since the RAE was introduced, questions have been raised concerning its equity and possible deleterious effects on research generally (Becher and Trowler 2001). With reference to those responsible for introducing and enacting research assessment mechanisms, Middleton pertinently quotes Foucault's observation that they often 'know what they do; they frequently know why they do what they do; but what they don't know is what what they do does' (Foucault, cited in Dreyfus and Rabinow 1982: 187). Education is an applied field where a primary intention is to develop and improve practice and it has been argued, with limited success, that dissemination aimed at practitioners should be given equal value to peer-reviewed journal papers (Furlong 2004; Oancea 2004). It has also been pointed out (e.g. by Thornton 2003) that it is inappropriate to treat 'old' and 'new' universities the same, given their different missions, conditions and clientele.

No one questioned that New University should be a research institution; nor did anyone advocate differentiated institutions (see DfES 2003). It was the fact that people now felt pressurized to produce RAE returnable publications on top of everything else that was in contention:

> The RAE casts a shadow over everything we do. Research is crucial but this way it's inimical to good practice, and to good scholarship.
>
> (Ambrose)

Hartley writes,

> a defensive concern to secure identity is often accomplished through a negation of the other, and this is particularly the case during periods of organizational change which privilege some organizational members at the expense of others. . . . In this sense, universities have become sites of contested identity, where, for example, research professors and the 'research active' become the other in relation to whom the less research active defend their previously constituted selves in terms of now devalued criteria.
>
> (2002: 203)

At organizational level this could be seen in the School of Education. Those identified as 'researchers' were, in some respects, privileged at the expense of those cast as 'teachers'. But on the level of personal relationships there was no evidence of devaluing or of 'researchers' being considered 'superior'.

Barnett describes academic culture as:

> A shared set of meanings, beliefs, understandings and ideas; in short, a taken-for-granted way of life, in which there is a reasonably clear difference between those on the inside and those on the outside of the community. Part of the sharing and sense of community, resides in the taken for granted aspects of the culture.
>
> (1990)

While there were many different cultures within the School of Education, everyone appeared to share the view that the demands being made were conflicting, excessive and the consequence of the push for New University to compete with traditional universities.

Cultures, like identities, are created through the stories we tell to explain ourselves as collectives and individuals. It is in the telling of those stories about identity and culture that we begin to gain some sense of how individuals negotiate the structural conditions in which their lives are lived out and come to some awareness, if not understanding, of the complexities of what being an academic can mean at different times and in specific contexts and circumstances.

Notes

1   In the UK, the term 'new university' is used to refer to the former polytechnics and colleges of higher education, which were given university status in 1992. New universities have traditionally tended to focus more on teaching than research.
2   The RAE, which started in 1986, is undertaken on behalf of the UK higher education funding councils approximately every 5–7 years. Its purpose is to review the quality of research in UK universities and inform decisions about the allocation of funding for research.
3   The QAA (Quality Assurance Agency) is responsible for auditing teaching quality and standards in higher education in the UK.
4   Ofsted (Office for Standards in Education) is responsible for inspecting the quality of provision in schools and higher education teacher training programmes.
5   FENTO (Further Education National Training Organisation) is responsible for quality assurance in the further education sector.
6   In the 2008 RAE, individual research outputs were rated on a scale from 0 to 5*. In the previous RAE in 2001 academic units were rated on the same scale, with a 5* denoting the fact that the majority of research in the unit was judged to be of a world-leading standard.

References

Acker, S. and Armenti, C. (2004) 'Sleepless in academia', *Gender and Education*, 16 (1): 3–24.

Barnett, R. (1990) *The Idea of Higher Education*, Buckingham: Open University Press.

—— (2003) *Beyond All Reason: living with ideology in the university*, Buckingham: SRHE & Open University Press.

Becher, T. and Trowler, P. (2001) *Academic Tribes and Territories*, 2nd edn, Buckingham: Open University Press.

Beck, J. and Young, M. F. D. (2005) 'The assault on the professions and the restructuring of academic and professional identities: a Bernsteinian analysis', *British Journal of Sociology of Education* 26 (2): 183–197.

Butler, J. (1993) *Bodies That Matter*, New York: Routledge.

Chambers Twentieth Century Dictionary (ed. A. MacDonald) (1972), Edinburgh: W. R. Chambers.

Clegg, S. (2005) 'Academic identities under threat?'. Paper presented at British Educational Research Association Annual Conference, Glamorgan, September 2005.

Day, C., Kington, A., Stobart, G. and Sammons, P. (2005) 'The personal and professional selves of the teacher: stable and unstable identities', unpublished paper.

DfES (2003) *The Future of Higher Education*, London: HMSO.

Devos, A. (2004) 'Women researchers and the politics of professional development', *Studies in Higher Education*, 29 (5): 591–604.

Dreyfus, H. and Rabinow, P. (1982) *Michel Foucault: beyond structuralism and hermeneutics*, Chicago, IL: Harvester.

Ellis, C. and Bochner, A. (2000) 'Autoethnography, personal narrative, reflexivity: researcher as subject', in N. Denzin and Y. Lincoln (eds), *The Handbook of Qualitative Research*, 2nd edn, Thousand Oaks: Sage, pp. 733–768.

Foley, D. and Valenzuela, A. (2005) 'Critical ethnography: the politics of collaboration', in N. Denzin and Y. Lincoln (eds), *The Handbook of Qualitative Research*, 3rd edn, Thousand Oaks, CA: Sage, pp. 217–234.

Furlong, J. (2004) 'The 2008 RAE and beyond', *Research Intelligence*, 87: 2–3.

Greenwood, D. and Levin, M. (2005) 'Reform of the social sciences and universities through action research', in N. Denzin and Y. Lincoln (eds), *The Handbook of Qualitative Research*, 3rd edn, Thousand Oaks, CA: Sage, pp. 43–64.

Hartley, S. (2002) 'The impact of research selectivity on academic work and identity in UK universities', *Studies in Higher Education*, 27 (2): 187–205.

—— (2003) 'Research selectivity and female academics in UK universities: from gentleman's club and barrack yard to smart macho?', *Gender and Education*, 15 (4): 377–392.

Henkel, M. (1997) 'Academic values and the corporate enterprise', *Higher Education Quarterly*, 51: 134–143.

—— (2000) *Academic Identities and Policy Change in Higher Education*, London: Jessica Kingsley.

Lee, A. and Boud, D. (2003) 'Writing groups, change and academic identity: research development as local practice', *Studies in Higher Education*, 28 (2): 187–200.

MacLure, M. (1993) 'Arguing for yourself: identity as organising principle in teachers' jobs and lives', *British Educational Research Journal*, 19 (4): 311–322.

McNay, I. (1997) *The Impact of the 1992 RAE on Institutional and Individual Behaviour in English HE: the evidence from a research project*, London: HEFCE.

—— (1998) 'The paradoxes of research assessment and funding', in M. Little and B. Little (eds), *Changing Relationships Between Higher Education and the State*, London: Jessica Kingsley, pp. 191–203.

Marginson, S. (1998) 'Competition and diversity in the reformed Australian higher education system', in V. Meek and F. Wood (eds), *Managing Higher Education Diversity in a Climate of Public Sector Reform*, Canberra: Department of Employment, Training and Youth Affairs Evaluations and Investigations Programme Report 98/5, pp. 81–96.

Middleton, S. (2005) 'Disciplining the subject: the impact of PBRF on education academics'. Paper presented at British Educational Research Association Annual Conference, Glamorgan, September 2005.

Murray, J., Davison, J. and John, P. (2005) 'A little knowledge? – Perceptions of the professional knowledge base of teacher educators'. Paper presented at British Educational Research Association Annual Conference, Glamorgan, September 2005.

Morley, L. (2003) *Quality and Power in Higher Education*, Maidenhead: Open University Press and SRHE.

—— and Walsh, V. (eds) (1995) *Feminist Academics: creative agents for change*, London: Taylor & Francis.

Neumann, R., Parry, S. and Becher, T. (2002) 'Teaching and learning in their disciplinary contexts: a conceptual analysis', *Studies in Higher Education*, 27 (4): 405–517.

Nias, J. (1989) *Primary Teachers Talking*, London: Routledge.

Oancea, A. (2004) 'The distribution of educational research experience: findings from the analysis of RAE 2001 submissions – Part 1', *Research Intelligence*, 87: 3–8.

Rogers, A. (2005) 'Colleagues down under', *autLOOK*, January, 233: 8.

Rolling, J. (2004) 'Searching self-image: identities to be self evident', *Qualitative Inquiry*, 10 (6): 869–884.

Roth, W. (ed.) (2005) *Auto/Biography and Auto/Ethnography: praxis of research method*, Rotterdam: Sense.

Rowland, S. (2002) 'Overcoming fragmentation in professional life: the challenge for academic development', *Higher Education Quarterly*, 56 (1): 52–64.

Scott, D., Brown, A., Lunt, I. and Thorne, L. (2005) *Professional Doctorates: integrating professional and academic knowledge*, Maidenhead: Open University and SRHE.

Sikes, P., Measor, L. and Woods, P. (1985) *Teacher Careers: crises and continuities*, Lewes: Falmer.

Silver, H. (2003) 'Does a university have a culture?', *Studies in Higher Education*, 28 (2): 157–169.

Stronach, I., Corbin, B., McNamara, O., Stark, S. and Warne, T. (2002) 'Towards an uncertain politics of professionalism: teacher and nurse identities in flux', *Journal of Educational Policy*, 17 (1): 109–138.

Taylor, P. (1999) *Making Sense of Academic Life: academics, universities and change*, Buckingham: Open University.

Thornton, M. (2003) 'The Education RAE 2001: are there lessons 3bs can learn from 5/5*s?', *Research Intelligence*, 85: 10–15.

Part 3
Enhancing professionalism

12 Making teacher change happen

Paul Black

This chapter describes and discusses two quite different initiatives for teachers' professional development in which I was personally involved. The first, the Nuffield A-level physics project, dates from 1968 to 1972, when, as a university physicist, I was joint organizer of a project to develop and implement a radically new course for A-level physics.[1] The second dates from 1999 to 2002, and was a project based at King's College London which deployed broadly based research evidence to develop formative assessment within teachers' pedagogy. I shall describe these in turn, and then, in a closing section, compare and contrast them.

Nuffield A-level physics

The origin of this first project lay in the Nuffield Foundation's commitment to support the development of new courses in secondary science. The motivation and support for such changes had arisen earlier, and in sharper form, in the US. With the growing threats of the Cold War, and the fact that the US military found they could not meet their need for scientists, high school science education became a front-line resource (Rudolph 2002). Encouraged by government, a group of US physicists had gathered in 1956 to review school physics texts and design improved materials. They were already well ahead with this work when the launch of the Russian Sputnik in October 1957 triggered more funding for their efforts. While the motivation here was concern over the shortage of trained scientists, this was only one of the innovators' concerns. A second was the outdated picture of their subject presented by school texts that had hardly changed over fifty years (Haber-Schaim 2000). A Physical Sciences Study Committee (PSSC) was formed, which aimed to design a new course that would present a unified and coherent view of physics, based on a student text book, but also using new laboratory work and other learning aids. The course's emphasis on the inductive and deductive power of scientific thinking reflected the third concern – fear of the public mistrust of scientists, fuelled in part by Senator McCarthy's mission to label all liberals as communists. As one of the architects of the course said, 'I was impressed by the feeling of the early fifties that science and intellectual reason itself were not being given a fair chance in schools and in public life' (Morrison, quoted in Rudolph 2002).

The PSSC course was a one-year course requiring about five hours per week of study, which was the norm for high school physics in the USA. About 20 per cent of high school students studied physics, and about a quarter of these took PSSC physics. This inspired a further innovation which aimed to attract far more students by presenting a more humanistic view of physics, including topics about its history and about applications and social effects, thereby being less austerely academic (Holton 1969). This course, the Harvard Physics Project, appeared in 1970. However, while the PSSC book sold well over a million copies, many outside the US, with a seventh edition produced in the 1990s, the Harvard Project texts fared less well, with the last recorded publication in 1981.

Both of these projects had a powerful influence in the UK. The cold war pressure on labour power was less keenly felt, but many leaders in the school system deplored the moribund state of science texts and examinations (Jenkins 1979) reflecting the concerns of the US university academics. This led the Nuffield Foundation to set up reform projects, first in the science courses for all secondary pupils,[2] and later for the A-level sciences.

Given the national need to rejuvenate the curricula in order to offset the declining popularity of school science at A-level, and following as it did on the development of new pre-16 curricula, the A-level physics course was meant to offer a radical revision of the existing content and pedagogy so that students would become both interested and active participants in their learning. In planning this work, I and my fellow organizer eagerly studied both the PSSC and the Harvard Project materials, for while these were constrained by the need to offer a one-year course, and were at a level we judged to be between pre-16 and A-level work in England, they offered models both for the overall structure and for the treatment of several topics that were new at A-level. Moreover, the two different courses offered contrasts which illustrated the nature of the choices we had to make. We came to explain our task as follows:

> The construction of a course is itself a piece of engineering, a job to be done despite inadequate knowledge of how some of the basic components in the learning process work. We have conceived the task as one of weaving topics together to make a connected story which makes sense and arouses interest in its own right, which has discernible themes and connects these in fruitful ways, and which at the same time serves these deeper aims of learning in the future, of understanding physics, of understanding how physics works, of learning to inquire oneself, and of seeing applied and social implications. The success of the course will be judged, at least by its authors, by its success in achieving these aims, although we would also include one other, that of arousing interest and

enjoyment in the majority, and not just the able minority, of those who study it.

(Black and Ogborn 1970: 203)

A key feature was the intellectual excitement of putting, for the first time, some of the key ideas of twentieth-century physics into the A-level. This involved pedagogic transformation, that is finding ways to present advanced and complex ideas in ways that would be both authentic and intelligible. For example, a new way to teach the second law of thermodynamics in the Nuffield project involved consulting many sources to explore different approaches, setting up new visual aids (Black *et al.* 1972) and new methods that required expert theoretical validation (Black *et al.* 1971), then checking with several physics professors that the whole approach was authentic – all before any school trial could begin.

However, it took me some time to learn that there was more to this than a conceptual exercise. I had to learn that my vision of teaching, which focused on the clear and coherent lecture, was inadequate. I owe that learning to the other five team members who were experienced and outstanding as schoolteachers. Here there was a contrast with the US projects, in which the academic scientists were firmly in the driving seat, although they did consult teachers and were guided by feedback from school trials.

Work started in 1967, leading to school trials over the years 1968–1969 and 1969–1971, and then to publication in 1971–1972. The work involved about fifteen person-years and must have cost the equivalent of £1 million at present day prices.

In terms of the content, our declared aims meant that the course had to be designed to form a sequence in which each topic linked to others before it and after it, with the final topic serving as a grand finale, drawing together concepts developed in most of the earlier topics. This was physicists' physics, reflecting, in its web of connections, one of the most compelling features of the subject. Other topics led in other directions, principally to show how physics also produced technological and social effects.

In terms of the pedagogy, a core aim was that students should become independent learners. So the final publications did not include any pupil text-books. There were teachers' guides, and booklets for students of background reading and of questions, and teachers were asked to provide a range of existing textbooks for students to consult. Much of the learning work was laboratory-based, with experiments, many of them quite new, designed to provoke discussion rather than to 'prove' established results. There was variety in the student activity: one topic was studied by having different groups conduct one each of a suite of experiments, and then report to a plenary in which all could draw together the full picture. All were required to do two small independent investigations, each taking two to three weeks, with the second being teacher-assessed to contribute about 10 per cent of the A-level examination.

After developing the ideas and materials, the team had to train teachers, both for trials and later for dissemination, provide the range of resources that the teaching needed, and support teachers by creating the conditions needed to help them engage in a novel venture. Crucial to all of this was our success in arousing the enthusiasm of the participants, by connecting both with their enthusiasm for physics and with their commitment to involving their students. However, without the resources available to the team members, who could draw on resources of time and expertise that were beyond the reach of any teacher, and the legitimacy for new approaches that the Nuffield system guaranteed, such enthusiasm and commitment could not have established a radically new course.

This trio of training, provision and support implied many tasks. In order to set up trials of the ideas and materials we had to:

- recruit schools – initially 24, rising to 40;
- secure support from local authorities (LAs)[3] and school governors, including budgets for new equipment;
- design new experiments, make prototypes of new apparatus, then negotiate with manufacturers to make these in adequate numbers and in time for trials;
- prepare and provide printed guides and films for teachers and students;
- run one-week training courses each year for trial teachers.

During the trial years, the main task was to learn lessons from the trials and to modify, even abandon, some innovations. To do this, we had to:

- visit trial schools, collect observation and written feedback;
- prepare examination material, including mock test papers for schools;
- amend the plans and modify the timetables in the light of feedback.

These tasks overlapped for most of the time. So did further activities needed to ensure the future both of the students in the trials and of the course itself. We had to:

- negotiate a tailor-made examination with an A-level examination board[4] (Black and Ogborn 1977);
- secure acceptance of the new A-level from university admissions officers;
- report to, and satisfy, Nuffield's steering group for the project;
- negotiate with publishers to print revised material after trials;
- plan a dissemination programme and train future trainers.

Within three years of the completion of the trials, 6,000 students, about 15 per cent of all A-level physics candidates, were entering for the Nuffield A-level. The materials were revised and reprinted after a few years, and the course and its special examination continued for over twenty-five years until a quite new course replaced it. The new materials also had significant effects on the development of most conventional syllabuses and textbooks.

This was a systemic reform – the team had to foresee and provide all the support that teachers might need. While it was top-down, in that an expert team designed a system which teachers had to implement, there was strong interaction between the team and the trials teachers which led to plans being modified, and in some instances abandoned, in the light of the latter's practical experience.

Yet, apart from continuing to run the examination, the team soon went on to other things – the fate of the innovation was in the hands of those teachers who found it rewarding. Thus, the key to its success was the commitment of teachers to take on what it offered and make it their own. This in turn depended on the team's success in fashioning and presenting something new, attractive and feasible that teachers would choose in preference to conventional syllabuses and examinations.

However, what also mattered was the team's freedom at a time when the curriculum was not seen as an area for government control. One of the architects of PSSC (Haber-Schaim 1993, 1998) has argued that it worked because their team was free to innovate, and succeeded or failed by their power to attract voluntary participation. The more recent National Science Standards in the US (National Research Council 1996), being formulated by wide consensus, have led to vague and overloaded specifications, made precise through the state tests the limited validity of which means that they do not do justice to what was intended. Similar arguments could be made about innovations in the UK, although science educators have been allowed more freedom because government cannot, without them, solve the problems of poor recruitment to advanced studies leading to qualifications in science.

The Formative Assessment Project

The origins of this work lay in the concern of academics that the priority given to formative assessment in the recommendations for England's new national assessment system had been ignored by government (Harlen *et al.* 1992; Black 1997). This led to support for a review, conducted by Dylan Wiliam and myself, of 600 research studies, which yielded evidence that formative assessment approaches could raise pupils' test results, and which also provided a range of ideas about how formative feedback might be implemented (Black and Wiliam 1998a). The key idea was that teachers should evoke evidence from pupils to make clear their current state of understanding, and then use this feedback to help guide their teaching interventions.

In order to see how these potential benefits might be achieved, the King's group negotiated with two LAs, Oxfordshire and Medway, who selected and supported six schools altogether, and within each school two science and two mathematics teachers. Teachers of English and others were added later so that eventually forty-eight teachers were involved. The King's team had funding, first from Nuffield and later from the US (for a collaboration with a team at Stanford), of about £160,000. The time of the King's faculty and of the LA officers was not paid for: the funds were used to support one full-time researcher over three years, and to finance teachers' release so that they could attend project meetings at King's. The project adopted as its title the King's Medway Oxford Formative Assessment Project, which produced a clumsy acronym, KMOFAP, but did honour the collaborative ownership.

As they worked with the ideas from the research, the teachers came to change four aspects of their work. These aspects can be summarized briefly as follows:

- In *classroom questioning*, teachers learnt to ensure that their questions would promote thinking about key components of pupils' understanding, and to give pupils time to think about their answers, all of which were to be taken seriously: wrong answers, particularly, would help the teacher to identify learning needs.
- For the *marking of homework*, research had shown that giving comments produces substantial improvements, while giving either marks alone or marks with comments produces no improvement: teachers learnt to give only comments, designed to tell pupils what they needed to do to improve, and to ensure that pupils acted on these.
- *Peer- and self-assessment by pupils* were found to be productive, but pupils had first to grasp the purposes and criteria for the work, against which they could judge their attempts. Getting pupils to comment on each other's work helped them to understand the criteria for quality, and made it possible to involve all pupils in discussion.
- Formative assessment could also be deployed with teachers' own *summative tests*: peer- and self-assessment were used to help pupils to be more systematic in their prior revision, and were also used to involve pupils in marking their answers in small groups. Asking groups to invent a mark scheme focused attention on what the question required and on the criteria for a good answer.

These aspects have in common four features which are fundamental to effective teaching and learning – building on the initial ideas of learners and providing feedback in response to these ideas, involving learners in taking more responsibility for their own learning, helping them to understand the aims and criteria for the learning, and helping them to learn through active engagement in discussion. In addition, the formative approach was also important in its effects on *motivation and self-esteem*. Feedback that emphasizes to learners what they need to do to improve has been shown to improve these things, whereas feedback that emphasizes marks and competitive comparison between pupils is demotivating, and has been shown to lower performance (Dweck 2000).

In developing these new practices, teachers were expected to work within their normal curriculum plans and within the usual constraints of school-based and external summative testing: the King's-LA team did not attempt to change these.

A significant feature of the project was the role played by the King's team in working with the teachers. The guiding principle was that teachers cannot merely apply findings from research, but must rather create new knowledge in transforming any such input into that practical knowledge which each must construct to make things work in their context (see Hargreaves 1999). So, for example, in presenting the research findings to the teachers, we emphasized that we did not know what they should do about them – we offered no recipes, they had to work the practice out for themselves. We learned later from one LA adviser that some did not believe us at first, assuming that we knew what to do but were leaving them to work out 'the answers' for themselves.

Apart from this strategy of support, we provided two other resources. One was our status and that of King's, and the organization and resources to support the project, including our capacity to secure LA involvement and the support of each school's headteacher. The second was our knowledge of the research, which provided starting points for their innovations, with the reassurance that there was quantitative evidence that such innovations had improved pupils' attainments in the past (Black and Wiliam 2003).

A further source of support was the one-day meetings at King's which teachers attended about once every five weeks. These meetings featured inputs from us and from the teachers themselves, with the balance shifting from the former to the latter as the project progressed. Team members also visited schools, the visits providing opportunities to observe lessons, give feedback, discuss teachers' problems and collect research data. Teachers' opinions were also sought independently by the LA advisers. In planning these meetings, a steering group composed of the King's team, the LA advisers, and a Department for Education and Skills (DfES)[5] representative used this feedback to make these meetings responsive to emerging needs. Thus, after several teachers had raised questions about the principles of learning implied by their innovations, we spent some time at a meeting on a seminar about theories of learning. However, the most valued aspect of the meetings was that teachers of the same subject could discuss and exchange examples of their various attempts at innovation.

A further feature was that for the first six months (January to July 1999), the teachers were advised to start by trying one idea at a time and to report back on the experience. Thus at subsequent meetings they could hear what others had made of the same or different ideas, and decide whether to modify, add to, or abandon their developing portfolio of practices. Then in July each was asked to decide on their portfolio and to choose a specified target class, among Years 7 to 11[6] for the 1999–2000 school year. We placed no restrictions on the practices or the classes chosen. The record of these choices gave a list of 102 different ideas among twenty-four teachers, which could be grouped under the four main headings outlined above. The target classes ranged over all five years. In a subsequent school year we studied development with teachers of English and in-school dissemination.

Near the end of the 1999–2000 school year we collected pre- and post-test data, based on schools' own tests, Key Stage 2 or 3 results, or GCSE, as appropriate.[7] We also negotiated with each teacher a suitable control, a comparable class not involved in the project, for which comparable data were available. We were able to collect nineteen such sets of experiment–control data: these could show the innovations produced a clear net gain with effect size of the order of 0.3 – corresponding to about an average of half a GCSE grade[8] (Wiliam *et al.* 2004).

In addition to the research papers quoted above, both a booklet (Black *et al.* 2002) and a book (Black *et al.* 2003) for teachers have been published, each drawing on reflective writing collected from the teachers at the end of the project. Both have been, in sales terms, very successful. The members of the King's team have received numerous invitations to speak at conferences and to conduct professional development sessions in schools. Some of the findings were incorporated into the DfES initiatives to improve teaching and learning, without our direct involvement. The DfES strategy, based on one day of training and lengthy documentation, has been inadequate, so that superficial adoption has caused concern (Black 2007). Adoption has also been constrained because many teachers believe that they cannot explore new methods in the way that they desire because the importance of the national high-stakes tests constrains them to 'teach-to-the-test'.[9] By contrast, the Scottish executive replicated the KMOFAP process with two-year trials in pilot schools, with the King's team closely involved, and on this basis the national implementation of the process was successful.

Since the project ended, we have been studying the differences in implementation amongst different secondary subjects, the adoption of the process in primary schools, and the formative–summative interface. There have also been theoretical reflections (Black and Wiliam 2006), for we now see formative assessment as a way to strengthen a wide range of pedagogic practises.

The UK work on formative assessment has been a stimulus to comparable developments in the US. Two of the texts published by the King's group were published as articles in a US professional journal (Black and Wiliam 1998b; Black *et al.* 2004), while a project at Stanford, supported by the National Science Foundation, arose as a collaboration with the KMOFAP project. A broader review of educational assessment by that body (Pellegrino *et al.* 2001: 14) argued, in two of its twelve recommendations, for a shift, in resources and in provision of information, 'to increase emphasis on classroom formative assessment designed to assist learning'.

However, the impact in the USA has been uneven. Some texts which focus on classroom learning take 'Assessment during instruction' very seriously (Airasian 2005); others make no mention of formative assessment (McCombs and Millar 2007). One reason for this is that beliefs and practices in assessment do not exist in isolation from the broader culture of pedagogy; even the nearest US equivalent term, instruction, has a broader meaning, encompassing both teaching and learning. Just as the US innovation in physics, the PSSC course, could not have been adopted in England, but could only serve as a stimulus and a guide to a new course fashioned within the local professional culture, so the implementation of formative assessment in the UK can only serve a similar purpose in a country where both the culture of teaching and the processes for developing innovations are very different.

Contrasting stories but a common message

Table 12.1 summarizes the main differences between the two projects. While this description, albeit cursory, displays a range of contrasts, it is hard to argue that either project could have adopted the approach of the other. Each is a complex multifaceted story, and the metaphor of engineering is apt, for it emphasizes the need for careful and distinctive articulation of several types of resource to respond to the demands of each particular context. Yet, despite these contrasts, the two stories illustrate some common themes.

Table 12.1 Summary of differences between the two projects

Nuffield A-level Physics	*KMOFAP Formative Assessment*
1 Emphasis on subject content but pedagogy has to follow	Emphasis on pedagogy then content needs attention
2 Promises excitement and interest	Promises higher standards
3 Systemic reform – many contextual constraints had to be changed	Within existing curriculum and assessment, but radical in pedagogy
4 Subject experts develop with teachers feasibility of radically new approaches	Top-down impetus promotes teacher-led innovation, which then takes control
5 Expert contribution vital to create the core activity	Expert contribution vital as the catalyst and to validate experimentation
6 Builds on teachers' commitment to their subject	Builds on teachers' commitment to learning
7 Project meetings with teachers run by project team: weak collegiality	Meetings with teachers evolved to being teacher led: strong collegiality
8 Pupils see that content, pedagogy, assessment are all novel	Pupils see that pedagogy is novel – curriculum and assessment unchanged
9 Limited growth with definable market share, wider influence, lasts 25 years	Blossoms into widespread influence, with adoption superficial in England, sensitively professional in Scotland
10 Strong support from the professional science community	Weak support, and strong constraints, from government policies

Neither of them could have succeeded without the close involvement of teachers in the development and implementation of the innovations. This involvement helped to shape them so that they would be workable with most teachers, and helped them establish their credibility, both features that are critical for any innovation which seems likely to challenge existing practice. All of this makes clear that imposition of an innovation which has not been developed with, and by, some of the teachers for whom it is intended is likely to fail, for it will overlook some of the constraints and affordances of practice and will be offensive in undermining their status and responsibility. Thus, in these examples, our recognition of that aspect of teachers' professionalism, which calls for respect for, and trust in, their expertise was far more than an act of courtesy, it was a necessary condition for our work to succeed.

However, to infer from this that respect for teachers' professionalism implies that all innovations must arise from within the profession without external interference, is also unjustified. The physics story makes this clear in several ways, in that neither the social need, nor the allotment of resources, nor the vision arising from expertise in the subject, that this radical innovation required, could have been provided from within the profession. Likewise, the impetus for the formative assessment work arose from academic research, with such bodies as the King's team acting as brokers to summarise and articulate research findings and to set up a project to hand the next step over to the ownership of the professionals. The teachers involved with us had to be open to taking on influences from outside the boundaries of their community, so in this respect these stories illustrate another essential aspect of professionalism.

The impetus and support of agencies outside the profession is needed to achieve at least some possible and desirable improvements in teachers' work. Indeed this is inevitable, as education is not independent of the whole social fabric. What matters is that such impetus and support must be deployed in a manner sensitive to that complex expertise, which is needed for implementation and which teachers alone can provide. What also matters is that government should not be the sole agency for mediation between social needs and educational practice: neither of the two cases presented here were driven by government, and both benefited from their free and voluntary nature, and from the absence of the short-term pressures of politics.

Notes

1   In England, compulsory schooling ends at age 16. Students staying after that and aiming to take a university degree spend a further two years at school, during which, in the 1970s, the majority studied A-level courses in three subjects, reaching a level roughly equivalent to the end of a freshman course in the US.
2   Up to age 16, students took courses in at least five subjects and for most at least one of these was in science.
3   LAs are the regional governments in the UK. Each has an education department, which has oversight of state-funded schools, and many have specialist staff who advise schools, in particular subjects and in such issues as assessment and management.

4 The examinations in Advanced level subjects were conducted by several independent organisations, not-for-profit and, at that time, independent of publishers.

5 This was the title at the time of the central government ministry responsible for schools: it has since changed to Department for Children, Schools and Families.

6 Year 7 is the first year of entry to secondary schools in England with students of age 11–12; year 11 is the fifth year, with ages 15–16.

7 Key Stage 2 covers the last four years in primary schools; Key Stage 3 covers Years 7 to 9 in secondary: national tests in science are taken by all at the end of each of these stages. GCSE is the General Certificate of Education, the subject based examinations taken by most students at age 16.

8 In GCSE there are five passing grades, A to E, one 'near-miss', F, and one clear failing grade, G. Effect size is the ratio of any differential change to the spread in the student scores.

9 Pupils in secondary schools in England have to take national tests in English, mathematics and science at age 14 (called Key Stage 3 tests) in addition to the GCSE tests at age 16. In both cases, each school's overall results are published in 'league tables'.

References

Airasian, P. W. (2005) *Classroom Assessments: concepts and applications*, 5th edn, New York: McGraw Hill.

Black, P. (1997) 'Whatever happened to TGAT?', in C. Cullingford (ed.), *Assessment vs. Evaluation*, Cassell: London, pp. 24–50.

—— (2003) '"In praise of educational research": formative assessment', *British Educational Research Journal*, 29 (5): 623–637.

—— (2006) 'Developing a theory of formative assessment', in J. Gardner (ed.), *Assessment and Learning*, London: Sage, pp. 143–181.

—— (2007) 'Full marks for feedback', *Making the Grade (Journal of the Institute of Educational Assessors)*, Spring: 18–21.

—— and Ogborn, J. M. (1970) 'The Nuffield advanced physics course', *Physics Bulletin*, 21: 301–303.

—— and —— (1977) 'The Nuffield A-level physics examination', *Physics Education*, 12: 12–16.

—— and Wiliam, D. (1998a) 'Assessment and classroom learning', *Assessment in Education*, 5 (1): 7–74.

—— and —— (1998b) 'Inside the black box: raising standards through classroom assessment', *PhiDelta Kappan*, 80 (2): 139–148.

——, Davies, P. and Ogborn, J. M. (1971) 'A quantum shuffling game for teaching statistical mechanics', *American Journal of Physics*, 39: 1154–1159.

——, Hopgood, F. R. A. and Ogborn, J. M. (1972) 'Computer animation – chance and thermal equilibrium', *Some Research Applications of the Computer*, Didcot: Atlas Computer Laboratory.

——, Harrison, C., Lee, C., Marshall, B. and Wiliam, D. (2002) *Working Inside the Black Box: assessment for learning in the classroom*, London: GL assessment.

——, ——, ——. —— and —— (2003) *Assessment for Learning: putting it into practice*, Buckingham: Open University Press.

——, ——, ——. —— and —— (2004) 'Working inside the black box: assessment for learning in the classroom', *Phi Delta Kappan*, 86 (1), 8–21.

Dweck, C. S. (2000) *Self-Theories: their role in motivation, personality and development*, London: Taylor & Francis.

Haber-Schaim, U. (1993) 'National science education standards: an asset or a liability?', *The Physics Teacher*, 31: 220.

—— (1998) 'Reform in science education: then and now', *The Physics Teacher*, 36: 294–296.

—— (2000) *PSSC Physics: a personal perspective*. Online. Available www.aapt.org/publications/pssc.cfm (accessed January 2008).

Hargreaves, D. H. (1999) 'The knowledge creating school', *British Journal of Educational Studies*, 47 (2): 122–144.

Harlen, W., Gipps, C., Broadfoot, P. and Nuttall, D. (1992) 'Assessment and the improvement of education', *The Curriculum Journal*, 3 (3): 215–230.

Holton, G. (1969) 'Harvard project physics; a report on its aims and current status', *Physics Education*, 4: 19–25.

Jenkins, E. W. (1979) *From Armstrong to Nuffield: studies in twentieth-century science education in England and Wales*, London: John Murray. See Chapter 8.

McCombs, B. L. and Miller, L (2007) *Learner-Centred Classroom Practices and Assessments: maximising student motivation, learning and achievement*, Thousand Oaks, CA: Corwin Press.

National Research Council (1996) *National Science Education Standards*, Washington, DC: National Academy Press.

Pellegrino, J. W., Chudowsky, N. and Glaser, R. (eds) (2001) *Knowing What Students Know: the science and design of educational assessment*, Washington, DC: National Academy Press.

Rudolph, J. L. (2002) *Scientists in the Classroom: the cold war reconstruction of American science education*, New York: Palgrave Macmillan. (See also Rudolph's article online, available www.aapt.org/publications/pssc.cfm, accessed January 2008).

Wiliam, D., Lee, C., Harrison, C. and Black, P. (2004) 'Teachers developing assessment for learning: impact on student achievement', *Assessment in Education*, 11 (1): 49–65.

13 Improving schoolteachers' workplace learning

Heather Hodkinson

In many parts of the world improving the performance of teachers is a high policy priority, and improving teachers' learning is seen as a way of achieving this. In this chapter I argue for an approach to improving teachers' learning that is constructed upon a research-based understanding of how teachers learn. In claiming that teachers' personal professional development must be taken seriously, I endorse much existing teacher development research. However, that literature has not fully dealt with the significance of everyday working practices for teacher learning. Here I propose a mechanism for taking account of the role of teachers' dispositions and school and departmental working practices in improving teacher learning, drawing on a longitudinal qualitative research study of secondary school teachers' learning.[1] All names used are pseudonyms.

Approaches to teacher learning

There are three influential metaphors for learning used in recent academic literature. Sfard (1998) focuses on tensions between metaphors of *acquisition* and *participation*. Hager (2005) contrasts both of these with a third metaphor of *construction*. As I will show, English policy approaches have tended to assume a crude version of learning as *acquisition*. The teacher development literature critiques such approaches predominantly using a view of learning as *construction*, whereas the workplace learning literature largely develops a view of learning as *participation*. A combination of construction and participation provides a way of understanding teachers' learning that best fits the evidence of the research reported here.

Policy approaches: acquisition and technical rationality

The contemporary climate for educational policy in many parts of the world is linked to wider social and political movements. (See Helsby 1999, for a detailed analysis of these pressures within the English context.) Two major trends have been dominant in much Western practice over the last thirty years: the ideology of markets and competition, and the growth of 'the new managerialism' (Avis *et al*. 1996). The latter is related to an audit culture, with emphasis on financial accountability, measured outputs and value for money. It is within this twin ideological framework that the English government has tried to improve teacher learning. Two examples from within our research data illustrate that approach. One was the introduction of a performance management scheme. This involved each teacher agreeing measurable targets for development annually with a designated line manager. The second was a nationwide scheme to train teachers to make better use of computers in their work. Whatever their existing expertise all teachers had to go through a standardized training package, using computer-based distance-learning materials.

This policy approach was based upon a view of learning as acquisition. It focused on assumed deficits in the knowledge and skills of teachers, and saw what was to be learned as commodified content which could be identified, and the extent to which it had been successfully acquired measured. The problems with such a view of learning have been shown in a considerable literature that can only be briefly summarized here.

In this view, learning is seen as purely instrumental. The sense of learning as personal growth is lost. Further, by focusing on the content to be acquired, this approach epitomizes what Bereiter (2002) identified as the ubiquitous but inadequate 'folk theory' of learning, which involves placing 'stuff' into 'vessels'. It fails to take account of the many and complex processes by which teachers learn. It assumes that worthwhile learning is always intentional and planned, and focuses on content which is already known. Yet much learning in the workplace is unplanned and unintentional – a corollary to engagement in activities for which the prime purpose is not learning. Much learning is the on-going development and refinement of existing practice; and some involves doing something that has not been done before, meeting unforseen circumstances, challenges and problems. These shortcomings in understanding learning mean that such policy approaches to teacher development will have limited success.

The research literature: participation and construction

There is an extensive literature on teacher development or continuing professional development, which is paralleled by an established literature on workplace learning. As teacher learning is an example of workplace learning, a combination of the insights and strengths from both literatures can provide the foundation for a more productive approach to understanding and improving teacher learning.

Concepts of teacher development grew out of a view, expressed, for example, in the James Report (DES 1972), which focused on the in-service *education* of teachers, as a means of developing their knowledge and skills. This emphasized teacher learning, which took place away from work, on taught courses. On the other hand, the workplace learning literature tends to look upon formal learning as insufficient (for example, Lave and Wenger 1991) and concentrates on ways in which workers learn through more informal processes.

The two literatures intersect in the writings of Schon (1987) on reflective practice. For a significant period both literatures used these ideas to escape technically rational assumptions of planned learning. More recently, writers within both literatures have been more critical of Schon's work. For example, Day (1999) argues that reflection-in-action is too restrictive as a basis for teacher development, that reflection is never entirely rational, and that even reflection-on-action lacks a necessary critical edge, that comes best from sources external to the action. Beckett and Hager (2002), writing about workplace learning, argue that reflection is a predominantly backward-looking activity, and is too cerebral a concept. They argue that what they prefer to term 'judgement making' is embodied, entailing emotion and practice as well as reason, and involves a combination of reflection and anticipation. These literatures share a view of the learner as a holistic embodied person, for whom learning is essentially a matter of construction (Hager, 2005); and that learning is essentially concerned with changing the learner – constructing a developing and improving teacher through engagement in learning.

Both literatures are also striving to move beyond purely individual views of learning. This is less developed in the teacher literature, but some pointers have been established. Hargreaves (1994) explored ways in which different types of school culture influenced teacher development, concluding that collaborative cultures provided the richest developmental opportunities, but stressing that they could not be 'contrived'. Day (1999) builds upon Hargreaves's work, and goes on to advocate the value of networks in facilitating the development of the teacher's professional self. However, there remains a tendency to see teacher learning as an essentially individual act, albeit enhanced by collaboration and by external contacts.

None of these writers fully explores the processual links between cultures and learning. Two key ideas about the processes of learning in workplaces are under-used in the teacher development literature. The first is that learning is an integral part of everyday workplace practices, though it is richer in some workplaces than others, and richer for some workers than others. Thus, for example, Lave and Wenger (1991) and Billett (2001a) see participation in workplace communities and activities as the root of learning. The second key idea is that workplace learning is a predominantly social and cultural process, where individual learning is seen as a small integral part of something wider. Such participatory approaches are also problematic, for the individual learner is often lost. More recent workplace research has been trying to re-emphasize individual learning, but without losing the social and cultural perspective (Billett 2001b; Hodkinson and Hodkinson 2004). Our research findings suggest that combining the perspectives of learning as workplace participation and those of learning as personal construction points towards more effective ways of understanding and improving teacher learning.

The research project

The research investigated how some secondary school teachers in England learned at work, and consequently, ways in which that learning could be enhanced. We carried out longitudinal qualitative case studies between 2000 and 2003 of the teachers in four subject departments (Information Technology (IT), Art, Music and History) of two English secondary (11–18) schools. The research data included: documentary evidence; observation within the schools, particularly of the teachers working in their departments; and up to three semi-structured interviews with each teacher about their career history and learning as a teacher. Nineteen teachers, four student teachers and two middle managers were interviewed, providing a mix of age, gender, experience and commitment.

The research revealed many, varied and complex forms of teacher learning. We found three underlying dimensions, which exerted a major influence upon the nature of that learning, and upon the extent to which it was effective. They are: the dispositions of individual teachers; the nature of local working cultures; and the impact of policy and regulation frameworks and interventions.

The impact of individual teachers' dispositions

Throughout their careers, teachers develop an on-going sense of identity that influences their work and learning (Day 1999, Goodson 2003). To understand this, I use Bourdieu's concept of 'habitus' (Bourdieu and Wacquant 1992). Habitus consists of a battery of dispositions that orientate an individual in any situation and thus influence their actions and reactions. Dispositions are embodied, involving emotions and practices, as well as thoughts. Individuals are largely unaware of their dispositions, which develop throughout life, and are affected by their position in the world. Dispositions are relatively stable but can change, through gradual evolution or radical transformation. For example, Mary, head of art, wanted to be in control of her own learning. When there were unwelcome pressures to change she tried to transform them into something she could value. A requirement to teach literacy was initially problematic for the art teachers. However, Mary developed it to benefit the notes pupils had to produce for examinations. As a creative person, Mary was always looking for new ideas, sometimes in a planned way, sometimes opportunistically. Her learning was rooted in her initial teacher training and her early experience in progressive primary teaching. This could be seen in the ways artwork was developed as projects. An ongoing sharing of ideas between the art teachers aligned well with her dispositions, and led to effective teacher learning and teaching within the department.

Age and career stage are known to influence teachers' attitudes and practices (Huberman 1995), but dispositions go deeper. Malcolm and Steve were both mid-career, white, male teachers at the same school. Both were judged to be excellent teachers. But their dispositions towards their own learning were very different. Historian Malcolm was cynical, having suffered career setbacks. He was dismissive of courses and identified his learning as individual and occurring behind closed doors. Steve, head of music, was dynamic and enthusiastic. He worked and learned collaboratively whenever he could. Much of his learning was intentional, and he developed structured ways to improve his own learning, that of his colleagues, and that of student teachers. They reacted very differently to Performance Management. Steve used it as an opportunity to review his development. It had a negative effect on Malcolm who saw it as a tool for managerial control.

In a fuller discussion of teachers' dispositions and the significance for their learning Hodkinson *et al.* (2004) showed that the dispositions of teachers were significant for their learning in four overlapping ways:

- teachers' prior knowledge, understanding and skills can contribute to future work and learning;
- their dispositions influence how they construct and take advantage of opportunities for learning at work;
- working and belonging to a school and departmental community contribute to the developing habitus and sense of identity of teachers;
- the dispositions of individual teachers contribute to the co-production and reproduction of the cultures where they work.

The impact of departmental cultures

Academic subjects are important both in the English secondary school curriculum and in teachers' professional identities, and departmental cultures are significant in affecting teachers' learning. The departments in this study were similar in size and all were deemed successful by their schools. Nevertheless, they had very different cultures. They differed in the degree of internal collaboration and the style of leadership. These cultures were not a direct reflection of the schools. In one school the art department worked collaboratively with subtle leadership, whereas IT was more loosely integrated, with forceful leadership. In the other, the music department worked collaboratively with strong leadership, while history was loosely integrated, with subtle leadership.

Subtle heads of department advanced their ideas in low-key ways, while the forceful leaders had an explicit and intentionally strong influence. By 'loosely integrated', I mean to convey that staff in these departments got on with each other and worked together when there was a specific need, but the underlying tendency was for independent working and learning. They fell between Hargreaves' (1994) categories of collaboration and individualism.

There was effective teacher learning in all departments, but in collaborative departments teachers had an additional dimension to their learning. At its best, learning was ongoing whenever the teachers were together, through discussion, consultation and sharing of materials and ideas. In addition to using non-teaching time they were happy to visit and learn from one another's classrooms and lessons. The music teachers benefited additionally because of the explicit focus on their department's development, led by the head of department, and supported by all its teachers, including student-teachers.

Our data demonstrates complex interrelationships between individual teacher dispositions and departmental cultures. Each affects the other, and in turn affects teacher learning. A further influence on that learning comes from education policy and organizational regulatory practices.

The impact of national policy and regulation and school management

School management and national policy impact on teacher learning directly and indirectly. In the two schools, the approaches of management were slightly but significantly different. One had a successful and charismatic headteacher. Teachers there were happier with management than those in the other school. New initiatives were introduced more sympathetically causing less friction. Despite struggles for resources, both departments there felt valued and supported for much of the time. Teacher development was emphasized. In the other school, management had been criticized in an inspection report and although the problems were officially overcome, the head resigned, and was temporarily replaced by one of the deputies. Teachers grumbled more about management. The structure for professional development was similar to the first school, but the introduction of new initiatives and some in-service training generated antagonism that was counterproductive. These were differences of degree. Overall there was a similarity of approach that reflected the strength and frequency of government interventions.

There was frequent indirect pressure for teacher learning as a result of national policy. Government-led curriculum initiatives were common. For example, new curricula for older pupils caused changes that teachers had to learn to implement. Where policy affected teacher learning directly, it was usually based on the acquisition model. During the research there were various specific initiatives targeted at areas where (experienced) teachers' proficiency was deemed inadequate, like the compulsory computer training.

Skill deficits may be real, and teachers want to deal with such problems. The art teachers were aware of the potential of computers in their subject, but as novices, they were intimidated by the compulsory training sessions in the school's computer suite. They wanted to sort out specific applications relating to art in their own surroundings with focused support. They were looking for learning involving extended participation within their own established departmental practices. What they were given was a standardized online training course, without the facilities to use what they learned. One art teacher eventually progressed through buying her own computer and art software. She then helped her colleagues. By the end of the computer training initiative the level of IT competence had increased in the departments in our research, but rarely directly as a result of the imposed course, and not at a level commensurate with the high level of government expenditure.

Like Hustler *et al.* (2003) we found two pressures restricting formalized teacher learning. One was time. Teachers are reluctant to leave their classes for their own learning, especially in an era of outcome measurement, league tables and inspections. School management is reluctant to release them. Therefore, most planned teacher learning activity was located within five days a year designated for teacher development. Undertaking learning beyond these days often relied on teachers giving up their own time.

The second pressure was funding. During our study any money available had to be targeted at government-imposed priorities, and at the school's annual development plan (which in turn was government priority related). Teachers said there was no funding for learning that they wanted to do in their own time for their own professional purposes. This policy approach presented problems for experienced, successful teachers. There was little recognition of their wish to build on existing expertise, unless it fitted an official development priority.

Government interventions and management approaches did result in some effective learning. Teachers described how imposed curriculum change had led to learning and improved practice. Short in-service courses could be effective, where teachers personally valued the opportunity and were able to implement what they learned in practice. Offsite provision enabled collaboration with others with different experience. Sometimes success came through partial subversion of the system. In the IT initiative, the head of music negotiated permission for his teachers to spend the first training day at one of their homes, while everyone else took a school-based course. They used the expertise of the youngest music teacher to help them work through some of the required materials, digressing to relate to their departmental practices. They already had computers in the department, which allowed them to put into practice what they learned. Thereafter they persevered, using computers when other methods had initially seemed easier. The government initiative provided a trigger and an initial working day. The learning culture of the department, the willingness of one individual to share her skills and the determination of others to progress through practice led to success.

Improving teacher learning

This analysis demonstrates that teacher learning is complex and relational. There are many factors affecting the effectiveness of learning, each of which influences the others and is in turn influenced by them. Much of that learning is unplanned and does not have preset objectives or easily identifiable outcomes. Sometimes learning has significance only over a long timescale. This complexity presents difficulties for those striving to improve teacher learning. Hazardous oversimplifications include focusing on only a few of the factors affecting learning, and assuming that an initiative that works in 'x' place for 'y' teachers should work in all other teaching places for all other teachers. These problems were present in the performance management scheme and the IT training initiative. Both ignored learning which could not be measured although occasionally they may have triggered it. If our research findings relating to these two schemes were replicated nationally (Haynes *et al.* 2002 identified similar problems), then they represent an inefficient use of resources, for limited gain.

Our study of departmental cultures also illustrates the dangers of over-simplification. Teachers in the collaborative departments had a richer learning experience. One response might be to push all departments to work more collaboratively. But, as Hargreaves (1994) showed, collaboration cannot be forced. 'Contrived collegiality' results in the same forms of strategic compliance and resistance that we saw for performance management. The head of history in our study instigated changes to promote collaborative working. But as key staff were strong individualists, he had limited success and concluded that it was more important to support their autonomy.

In the light of such understandings, a different approach to enhancing teacher learning is required, one that maximizes the learning potential within the practice of teaching by improving opportunities to learn, incentives to learn and support for learning. This would increase the likelihood that more teachers will pursue learning and learn more effectively, while recognizing that different teachers will respond differently to similar circumstances, as each continues constructing his/her own professional habitus.

Expansive and restrictive learning environments for teachers

The concept of expansive and restrictive learning environments was developed by Fuller and Unwin (2003). They identified variations in what they termed the learning environment for apprentices in several steel companies. They defined an expansive learning environment as one presenting wide-ranging and diverse opportunities to learn, in a culture that values and supports learning. It increases what Billett (2001b) calls 'affordances' for learning while increasing the chances that workers will want to make the most of those opportunities. As we examined our school data, it became apparent that the expansive–restrictive model applied in a similar way. Table 13.1 gives exemplar factors that we identified from our data as important to the expansiveness of teacher workplace-learning environments. These features were important in our settings, and in related research (e.g. Hustler *et al.* 2003, Retallick *et al.* 1999).

Our research suggests that an effective way of improving teachers' learning is through encouraging expansive features of teachers' learning environments, appropriate to particular schools and departments. Table 13.1 represents a series of continua. The teachers, departments and schools in our study lay at various intermediate stages of the various continua. It would be difficult,

Table 13.1 Expansive–restrictive learning environments for teachers

<< *Expansive*	*Restrictive* >>
Close collaborative working	Isolated, individualist working
Colleagues mutually supportive of learning	Colleagues obstruct or do not support each others' learning
An explicit focus on learning as a dimension of normal working practices	No explicit focus on teacher learning, except to meet crises or imposed initiatives
Supported opportunities for personal development that goes beyond school or government priorities	Teacher learning mainly strategic compliance with government or school agendas
Out of school educational opportunities including time to stand back, reflect and think differently	Few out of school educational opportunities, only narrow, short training programmes
Opportunities to integrate off-site learning into everyday practice	No opportunity to integrate off-the-job learning
Opportunity to extend professional identity through boundary crossing into other departments, school activities, schools and beyond	Work restricted to home departmental team within one school. Opportunities for boundary crossing only come with a job change
Support for local variation in ways of working and learning for teachers and work groups	Standardized approaches to teacher learning are prescribed and imposed
Teachers use a wide range of learning opportunities	Teachers use narrow range of learning approaches

sometimes impractical or inappropriate, to have a completely expansive learning environment on all criteria, as teacher learning priorities cut across other school priorities. However, most schools, departments and teachers should be able to achieve a more expansive environment in relation to some criteria.

Some restrictions arise from the nature of English secondary teaching. At the time of the research the norm was individual teachers working in their own closed classrooms. Here much learning can take place through judgement making, but this setting does not encourage making that learning explicit, without additional activity, such as the use of reflective logs. Nor does it encourage sharing with and learning from others or broadening the scope of the learning. Opportunities to work with others beyond specific subject or responsibility groups were limited. There were few chances for the teachers to work with teachers of other subjects in their own schools or with fellow subject specialists elsewhere. There was little time for teachers to take part in relevant activities outside their lessons or their schools, or to stand back and take stock of situations, or to try to apply changes in practice. It was problematic for teachers to be away from their classrooms.

Other difficulties were rooted directly in the policy and management approaches already described. The *over*-emphasis on short-term and 'measurable' learning activity is restrictive, as is the *over*-emphasis on centralized learning priorities at the expense of those of the teachers themselves. Change would require a cultural and political shift.

As with most workplaces, the learning of staff is secondary to the prime productive activity (teaching pupils). This, combined with continual pressure on resources, means that some changes that might be beneficial for teacher learning will be difficult to accommodate. However, if there is a will to further enhance the learning of teachers as professionals, actions to increase the expansiveness of learning environments can be taken.

Actions to increase the expansiveness of teachers' learning environments

Individual teachers

As teachers are significant constitutive parts of the environment where they work, there are things they can do, individually or in collaboration with colleagues, to help increase the expansiveness of their learning environments. All the teachers in our study learned in some effective ways. We found many examples of dedication to personal and professional development, and to mutual support of colleagues. Some went further, looking to learn through mentoring others. Through fore-grounding their own learning, they helped create supportive conditions for colleagues. Others looked for ways to boundary-cross within and beyond the school, engaging with other teachers, groups and departments. Some engaged with longer courses, or engaged with action research, but such opportunities were rare. Most teachers can do some of these things, provided other aspects of the work environment are favourable. However, much depends upon the status, ambitions, identity and self-perception of the teacher.

Departments

Subject departments could regard teacher learning as one of their explicit purposes, integral to the ongoing improvement of their practice. Developing informal contacts, access to each other's lessons and work, team-teaching and team working are all potentially effective approaches. However, it may be necessary to balance the benefits of collaborative working with individual preferences for working more independently. Departments can also support staff members developing collaborative links elsewhere. Collaborative working and learning within a department need not preclude boundary crossing within and across schools.

Schools

Schools could plan strategically for the development and support of an expansive learning environment for teachers. This should recognize and work with everyday teaching practices as learning. Opportunities for collaborative learning, boundary-crossing and working in different teams can be constructed. Social procedures and physical structures can encourage teams of teachers to work cooperatively and spend non-teaching time together, providing opportunities for positive learning. While implementing government policy and fulfilling school development objectives are important, it is important to recognize that some teachers have other valid priorities. The five official staff development days in England are core time for (often more formal) teacher learning but they could be used flexibly, in terms of both time and content. Staff could be excused some attendance, in lieu of engagement with learning in their own time. Currently, longer off-site educational experiences are rare, but highly valued by those who access them, as they allow teachers to stand back and assess their practice. Managers need to look for imaginative ways to support such opportunities.

Government

At the time of our research, English policies for teacher learning did not seem to recognize teachers' professional attitudes, or support their judgements regarding their own learning. Instead they imposed universal schemes based on perceptions of deficit. The promotion of expansive learning environments would need a change in standpoint. One helpful change would be to reduce the focus on restrictive pre-specified objectives, instead helping schools enhance teacher learning by building on everyday practice. Beyond the school, support for attendance on longer courses would allow teachers to engage with different ideas and facilitate shifts in disposition. Another source of development for teachers can be working beyond their home department and school. Funding spare teaching capacity could benefit teachers and schools in these and other ways. Of course, teacher learning is only one educational policy concern and has to be balanced against other priorities. However, it should be possible to encourage good learning that is not target driven and does not meet measured objectives.

Conclusion

I have argued that to understand teacher learning better and then to enhance it, it is helpful to recognize a combination of learning as *participation* (as described in the workplace learning literature), and as an individual process of *construction* (from the teacher development literature). The concept of expansive and restrictive learning environments provides a way of combining these approaches. By making the learning environments of teachers more expansive, it is possible to increase the potential for effective learning, and increase the likelihood that more teachers will avail themselves of the opportunities that are available.

This chapter has illustrated some aspects of what an expansive approach to improving teacher learning might look like. It would mean changes in the ways that some teachers work, for their work is the major source of their learning. It would mean that planning and activity should be responsive to the micro-conditions of specific working groups and contexts, as well as to macro influences. To be successful, it will need to pay attention to power differentials and workplace inequalities, as well as individual dispositions. Our research suggests that such an approach will only have a partial impact, for any changes introduced will affect different teachers in different ways, and will result in differing responses from them. However, this partiality is true for all approaches to improving teacher learning. A strong conclusion from our work is that efforts to improve teacher learning will always impact unevenly, across schools, departments and individual teachers. In that situation, rather than imposing targets and compulsory training experience, a more helpful approach is to encourage and facilitate teacher learning through and beyond work: that is to construct an environment where learning and teacher professionalism can flourish.

Note

1   The project was part of the Research Network 'Improving Incentives for Learning in the Workplace', which was funded by the UK Economic and Social Research Council, as part of the Teaching and Learning Research Programme – award number L139251005. A longer version of this paper by Heather and Phil Hodkinson was published in *Research Papers in Education*, 20 (2) in June 2005. (Reprinted by permission of the publisher, Taylor & Francis Ltd, www.informa world.com.)

References

Avis, J., Bloomer, M., Esland, G., Gleeson, D. and Hodkinson, P. (1996) *Knowledge and Nationhood: education, politics and work*, London: Cassell.

Beckett, D. and Hager, P. (2002) *Life, Work and Learning: practice in postmodernity*, London: Routledge.

Bereiter, C. (2002) *Education and the Mind in the Knowledge Age*, London: Lawrence Erlbaum Associates.

Billett, S. (2001a) *Learning in the Workplace: strategies for effective practice*, Crows Nest, NSW: Allen & Unwin.

—— (2001b) 'Learning through working life: interdependencies at work', *Studies in Continuing Education*, 23 (1): 19–35.

Bourdieu, P. and Wacquant, L. J. D. (1992) *An Invitation to Reflexive Sociology*, Cambridge: Polity Press.

Day C. (1999) *Developing Teachers: the challenge of lifelong learning*, London: Falmer.

DES (Department for Education and Science) (1972) *The Education and Training of Teachers* [The James Report], London: HMSO.

Fuller, A. and Unwin, L. (2003) 'Learning as apprentices in the contemporary UK workplace: creating and managing expansive and restrictive participation', *Journal of Education and Work*, 16 (4): 407–426.

Goodson, I. F. (2003) *Professional Knowledge, Professional Lives: studies in education and change*, Maidenhead: Open University Press.

Hager, P. (2005) 'Current theories of workplace learning: a critical assessment', in N. Bascia, A. Cumming, A. Datnow, K. Leithwood and D. Livingstone (eds), *International Handbook of Educational Policy*, Dordrecht, Boston, London: Kluwer, pp. 829–846.

Hargreaves, A. (1994) *Changing Teachers, Changing Times: teachers' work and culture in the postmodern age*, London: Cassell.

Haynes, G., Chamberlin, R., Wragg, E. and Wragg, C. (2002) 'Being managed: performance management from the teachers' point of view'. Paper presented at the British Educational Research Association Annual Conference, September 2002.

Helsby, G. (1999) *Changing Teachers' Work*, Buckingham: Open University Press.

Hodkinson, P. and Hodkinson, H. (2004) 'The significance of individuals' dispositions in workplace learning: a case study of two teachers', *Journal of Education and Work*, 17 (2): 167–182.

——, ——, Evans, K. and Kersch, N., with Fuller, A., Unwin, L. and Senker, P. (2004) 'The significance of individual biography in workplace learning', *Studies in the Education of Adults*, 36 (1): 6–26.

Huberman, M. (1995) *The Lives of Teachers*, London: Cassell.

Hustler, D., Mcnamara, O., Jarvis, J., Londra, M., Campbell, A. and Howson, J. (2003) *Teachers' Perceptions of Continuing Professional Development*, DfES Research Report No. 429, London: HMSO.

Lave, J. and Wenger, E. (1991) *Situated Learning*, Cambridge: Cambridge University Press.

Retallick, J., Groundwater-Smith, S., Clancy, S. and Dunshea, G. (1999) *Investigating and Enhancing Teacher Learning in New South Wales Schools: research report*, WaggaWagga, NSW: Centre for Professional Development in Education, Charles Sturt University.

Schon, D. A. (1987) *Educating the Reflective Practitioner*, San Francisco, CA: Jossey Bass.

Sfard, A. (1998) 'On two metaphors for learning and the dangers of choosing just one', *Educational Researcher*, 27 (2): 4–13.

14 Research-based teaching

John Elliott

Introduction

The idea of 'research-based teaching' was originally shaped in the UK by 'Lawrence Stenhouse's compelling image of the "teacher as a researcher"' (Carr 1994: 428). As such it came to form part of what Carr depicts as a reformulation of action research that had emerged in the US during the 1940s. This reformulation in the UK occurred specifically in the field of education. In this chapter I will not only attempt to clarify the conception of 'research-based teaching', which emerged in the context of the British curriculum reform movement during the 1960s and 1970s, but also ask whether as a form of action research it is likely to suffer a similar fate to its predecessor in the US, and indeed to a parallel but quite separate development of action research in Germany, at the hand of a positivistic ideology. It will be argued that although such a fate is possible, the Stenhousian version of 'research-based teaching' has become sufficiently internationalized to render it improbable.

Historical context

In the US the term 'action research' is associated with Lewin's 'field theory', which formed the basis of the new discipline of social psychology. Lewin's 'field theory' provided an epistemology that directly linked a non-positivistic science of human behaviour with democratic social practices. Research into the dynamics of group and intergroup relations was seen to yield the kind of knowledge that empowered individuals to democratically participate in changing their social environment. Lewin cast his new science of human behaviour in the form of 'action science'. As Adelman (1993) points out, the 'fundamental tenet' of Lewin's view of action research was 'studying things by changing them – in "natural" situations'. His cyclical model depicts an interactive process in which research informs action and action informs research.

Although Lewin's account of action research posited a mutually dependent relationship between research and action, the location of the new behavioural science in academia tended to perpetrate a division of labour between researchers and practitioners. Lewin's insistence on methodological rigour, while requiring researchers and social practitioners to cooperate, was often seen as legitimating such a division. The new behavioural science became increasingly detached from contexts of action and was 're-interpreted from the perspective of the dominant research paradigm' that had emerged following the Second World War, with action research becoming 'repackaged as little more than a set of practical problem-solving techniques' (Carr 1994: 428). The old dualisms between theory and practice and research and action prevailed and Lewin's original idea of action research was distorted to accommodate a positivistic conception of social science. Such was the price of an attempt to institutionalize action research in academia.

In the wake of Lewin's work a 'teachers as researchers' movement emerged in the US, which included teachers beginning to publish their action research. However, it did not withstand the criticism of university-based educational researchers. They argued that teacher research lacked methodological rigour.

The emergence of action research as an alternative social science in Germany

Although Lewin developed his idea of action research as a democratic and inclusive process, he did not view it as a form of ideology critique. This was not the case with the idea of action research that emerged in German speaking countries towards the end of the 1960s. According to Altrichter and Gstettner (1993: 332) it was 'an idea born out of protest' against the 'growth society's immanent destructive potential'. Part of this protest focused on the role a mainly positivistic social science played in ideologically legitimating the power relations implicit in new social technologies that de-skilled individuals and devalued the knowledge they had accumulated from experience – hence, the search for an alternative paradigm of social science that would render the existing methods of social inquiry obsolete, and with it the separation between researchers and practitioners that gave control over knowledge construction to the former. The new action research paradigm would replace such methods with a form of inquiry that could not be pinned down in terms of any fixed methods, and was theoretically and practically more flexible. According to Altrichter and Gstettner (1993: 335) German action research aspired to break traditional methodological conventions, in order to reach human beings who were oppressed by capitalist forces and engage them in a 'process of socially relevant communication and self-reflection on the scene of action'.

Some of the initial German action research projects established themselves in the field of teacher education. One of the biggest of these – the Marburg Primary School Project – aims at enabling students to direct their own learning and to do so cooperatively by reflecting on the group interaction processes. The action research was envisaged as a cooperative venture between researchers and teachers, but aims at eventually enabling teachers to research and self-evaluate their teaching independently. It also aims at developing a wider public understanding and acceptance of the need for change both inside and outside the project schools.

From the start, according to Altrichter and Gstettner, there was controversy in the research team regarding the 'importance and feasibility of traditional methods for evaluating school innovation' (1993: 338), resulting in a compromise *multi-method system* embracing both quantitative and qualitative methods. They report Radtke's (1975) claim that the researchers used positivistically contaminated methods in the false hope that they could be subsequently cleansed by the use of a critical interpretative framework. Radtke cast doubt on this aspiration by arguing, first, that a positivistic outlook was embedded in the project's concept of *pragmatic-flexible task differentiation* that referred to variable strategies governing the interactions between researchers and teachers at different phases of the project while leaving the basic division of labour untouched. Second, Radke argued that some of the methods employed by the researchers separated the research from the values pursued in the action context of the practitioners in order to guarantee 'objectivity'. Finally, he contended that insights from the research were detached from the particular contexts of reflection and action in which they made sense in order to give them the appearance of generalizable findings. Ironically, he argued that in doing so they failed to provide the kind of information that is needed to transfer the insights gained in one action context to another.

Altrichter and Gstettner report (1993: 341) that by the early 1980s the term 'action research' had largely disappeared from the discourse of German social science. As perhaps the Marburg project illustrated, action research, while springing out of a critique of positivistic social science, failed to establish itself as a truly alternative social science. Some may argue that it had more success in this respect within Latin America where Fals Borda (1979, 1988) has been one of the leading figures attempting to redirect social science as a form of participatory action research (PAR) aimed at engaging the poor in improving the conditions of their existence. Fals Borda argues that it was heretical in 1970 'to preach horizontal relationships in the research adventure' (1997: 108). However, whereas today his work may no longer be regarded as heresy, one might still question the extent to which PAR is working with, rather than against, the cultural grain of Latin American social science.

Carr (1994) has argued that the emergence of action research movements may be little more than moments in the development of a more sophisticated and all-embracing form of positivism. The implication is that, rather than setting a new direction, action research has become a means by which the general outlook and assumptions of positivism embedded in academic culture can come to penetrate the everyday life-world in a form that defines what counts as commonsense. However, both Carr (1994: 428–429) and Altrichter and Gstettner (1993: 351–352) regarded the British version of action research that stems from Stenhouse's image of 'teachers as researchers', and was further developed by this author (Elliott 1978, 1991), more promising in terms of its prospects of forging new directions for educational research. This is because they saw it emerging in response to practical problems experienced by teachers as they tried to initiate curriculum and pedagogical change in their classrooms and schools. Indeed, this author argues (Elliott 1991) that his experience of action research stemmed from his engagement as a teacher in school-based curriculum development during the 1960s. He claims that Stenhouse tapped into and articulated the logic of a research process that was already emerging in innovatory schools. This contrasts significantly with the circumstances that characterized the emergence of the action research movements described above. They directly challenged, rather than side-stepped, the positivistic assumptions that frame the behavioural and social sciences in order to forge a new academic paradigm.

Certainly the assumptions of positivism had not as yet permeated the wider social and political culture to frame what might be called 'scientific management'. Hence, as Altrichter and Gstettner (1993) point out, the decentralized administrative culture in the UK that was conducive to small-scale locally negotiated initiatives, together with a relatively strong professional teacher culture, provided a context in which a form of educational action research could emerge that was relatively free from contamination by positivism.

Unlike the German version the English version of action research rapidly internationalized. Altrichter and Gstettner (1993) describe its impact on the widespread development of school-focused action research in Austria during the 1980s, which owed very little to the German version. They also refer to the large-scale spread of this form of action research in the context of the OECD/CERI curriculum development project 'Environment and School Initiatives' involving schools from nineteen countries (Posch 1990; Elliott 1995). Carr (1994: 429) refers to this author's paper, 'What is action research in schools?' (Elliott 1978) as a seminal contribution to the development of 'nothing less than a full-blown movement' that spread to Australia, continental Europe and the US. Even more recently this movement can be traced to parts of the Far East, such as Hong Kong, where recent curriculum reforms have created more space for school-based curriculum development initiatives. However, as Carr points out, the widespread enthusiasm for an action research paradigm freed from the constraints imposed by a traditional academic discipline has increasingly resulted in a lack of shared understandings of how action research is to be interpreted. It has come to mean different things to different people and as a result the movement 'often appears to be held together by little more than a common contempt for academic theorizing and a general disenchantment with "mainstream" research' (1994: 429).

What follows is an attempt to re-articulate the form of action research that stemmed from Stenhouse's notion of 'research-based teaching'. In the process I shall examine other trajectories of meaning that have emerged over the course of time, with a view to assessing the future prospects of this form of action research at a time when a version of positivism is being confidently reasserted in the context of educational research and its assumptions have successfully invaded the educational system generally and its policy context.

Research-based teaching as a pedagogical innovation

The idea of 'research-based teaching' (Stenhouse 1975, 1979) emerged in the context of Lawrence Stenhouse's Humanities Curriculum Project (HCP) (1967–1972). The project, jointly funded by the Nuffield Foundation and the UK Schools Council for Curriculum Reform and Examinations, was briefed to address the problem of large-scale disaffection from the humanities subjects on the part of 'average and below average ability' students as they approached the raising of the school leaving age from 15 to 16 years (Stenhouse 1968, 1971).

The Humanities Project cast the curriculum solution to the problem of widespread disaffection in the form of a pedagogical experiment. It re-described the objects of learning in the humanities as those human acts and social situations that posed controversial value issues about the conduct of human affairs, and proceeded to categorize curriculum content in these terms – for example, 'War and Society', 'The Family', 'Relations between the Sexes', 'Poverty', 'Law and Order'. This was a significant departure from the traditional objects of learning that had been largely conceived in terms of factual knowledge. For Stenhouse it had radical implications for pedagogy, and implied a shift away from a traditional instruction-based towards a more discussion-based pedagogy.

Since the professional knowledge of humanities teachers was largely confined to knowing how to teach factual knowledge, the realization of discussion-based classrooms would require a great deal of pedagogical experimentation on their part in order to develop new knowledge – hence, the idea of 'research-based teaching'.

The curriculum change context is important. Stenhouse (1975) did not associate 'research-based teaching' with mere refinements and improvements in teachers' technical knowledge about how to transmit traditional subject matter. The idea implied a more radical shift in the conceptualization of the objects of learning that constitute a curriculum. Moreover, it implied a different view of the relationship between these objects and the teaching-learning process. Whereas instructional processes are contingently related as means to the learning outcomes they are intended to bring about, in the discussion-based classroom learning outcomes will be inherently unpredictable and variable. The objects of learning – human acts and situations – are appropriately objects of free and open discussion between people holding different evaluative outlooks. In the course of learning through discussion individuals will modify and extend their understanding of acts and situations as they examine them in the light of each other's evaluative outlook as well as their own. Mutual learning in the form of a growth of understanding takes place, but what this growth consists of cannot be predicted in advance of the process. Nor can it be presumed that the process will necessarily result in the elimination of all individual differences in understanding. Through open and free discussion participants may arrive at understandings which reflect a greater degree of overlapping consensus (Rawls 1993/1996) while at the same time differing in some respects.

For Stenhouse the quality of discussion can only be defined in terms of standards that are internal to this process – for example, ensuring that students had freedom to express their views regardless of majority opinion, were open to views that differed from their own, and had regard for reasons and evidence when defending their views and critiquing those of others. Standards like these cannot be defined independently of the learning process. Hence, Stenhouse evolved a 'process' as opposed to an 'objectives' model of curriculum development.

For Stenhouse the transformation of the culture of teaching and learning that prevailed in the field of humanities education, and which he believed to be the primary source of students' disaffection, depends upon the capacity of teachers to adopt a research stance towards their practice. He did not view this capacity in purely individualistic terms. Cultural transformation depends on teachers cooperating together across classrooms and schools to identify and diagnose common problems they experience as they attempt to realize the standards implicit in their pedagogical aim and to devise experimental strategies for resolving such problems.

Research-based teaching and the generalizability of findings

The concept of 'generalization' in the context of the Stenhousian idea of 'research-based teaching' takes on a different meaning to the positivistic conception embedded in the teacher effectiveness research which has recently been promoted as a basis for 'Evidence-Based Teaching'. Teacher effectiveness research abstracts variables from particular contexts of practice in order to discover co-relational regularities that can be couched as statistical probabilities. Its findings are then used as evidence in support of claims that 'if teachers do X rather than Y in their professional practice, there will be a significant and enduring improvement of outcome' (Hargreaves 1997). The aspiration is to furnish teachers with general principles for rationally determining what will in all probability be the most instrumentally effective means of bringing about the desired learning outcomes. The cost of this kind of generalization is a loss of information about the particularities of teaching situations that teachers need to take into account in developing their teaching strategies.

The primary context in which Stenhouse developed the idea of 'research-based teaching' was that of a curriculum innovation where it is inappropriate for teachers to evaluate their teaching in terms of its instrumentality as a means of achieving pre-determined learning outcomes. In this context 'standards' refers not to measures of learning outcomes but to qualities that are inherent in the process of learning itself. Hence HCP's pedagogical aim of 'developing understanding' could not be specified independently of the learning process by which it is realized. In HCP the appropriate focus for research is the *ethical consistency* of teachers interventions with the process standards implied by the project's pedagogical aim. For example, Stenhouse regarded the following situations to be ethically inconsistent with the standards inherent in the process of 'developing understanding':

- where teachers used their authority position in the classroom to promote their personal views;
- where teachers failed to protect divergence in discussion;
- where teachers allowed a student to disregard reasons and evidence in support of a view different to their own.

HCP teachers were asked to collaborate with the external team in systematically identifying, in and across classrooms, patterns of interaction with and between students that were inconsistent with the standards implied by the project's pedagogical aim. This was done by studying triangulation data drawn from observations and recordings, from teachers' self-accounts and from students' accounts of their classroom experience. Teachers were then asked to adopt and test a set of experimental teaching strategies designed to change the salient patterns of classroom interaction into ones that are more consistent with the pedagogical aim of the project. For example, one common pattern that was identified involved the teacher asking students whether they agreed with a particular point of view expressed in the group. Students invariably interpreted this pattern as 'pressurizing for consensus' around a view endorsed by the teacher, and tended to respond with silence. Teachers were then asked to test the 'action hypothesis' that divergence in discussion is best protected if they refrain from asking 'Do you agree?' and instead ask 'Does anyone disagree?' Those 'action hypotheses' that were confirmed by the majority of teachers were then incorporated into a set of general findings that other teachers of controversial issues in the humanities were invited to test and further develop in their particular classroom settings. As a body of new professional knowledge to support curriculum change teachers presented the project's generalizations as provisional and open to continuous re-assessment. Their role was not so much to prescribe practice as to build capacity for research-based teaching on a sustainable basis within a curriculum field.

The difference between the kinds of generalization that issue from teacher effectiveness research and those that issue from research-based teaching is well captured in Martha Nussbaum's (1990) distinction between *general rules* and *universal rules*. A *general rule*, Nussbaum argues, not only covers many cases, 'it applies to them in virtue of some rather non-concrete characteristics'.

In other words it originates from a process of abstraction from the particularities of time and circumstance. *Universal rules*, on the other hand, apply to all particular cases 'that are in the relevant ways similar'. Nussbaum argues that the latter may play an important role in practical reason without being prior to particular situations of choice. She views them as summaries of good concrete judgements in situations that are similar in all relevant respects. As such they are useful as guides to perception, to discerning the practically/ethically relevant features of particular concrete and complex situations that tend to repeat themselves from one situation to another. This is quite different from the normative function of *general rules* as 'the ultimate authorities against which the correctness of particular choices is assessed'. *Universal rules*, captured in summaries of good concrete judgements in similar cases, represent the 'voice of concrete practical experience'. Yet at the same time they open one to the experience of surprise. Our capacity to recognize the unique and novel features of a case that are nevertheless ethically significant depends on our use of universal 'rules of thumb'. In other words a capacity to recognize the unanticipated depends on the anticipations provided by universal principles. Viewed in this light the generalizations about teaching and learning that issue from research-based teaching, and that are grounded in the comparison of cases, support reflection about the complex particularities of life in classrooms. Even in a situation where they are found not to apply they nevertheless have the important function of sensitizing the teacher to practically relevant features of that situation. From the standpoint of Stenhouse's idea of research-based teaching there is no contradiction involved in the use of a case study approach and the search for generalizations about teaching and learning. The often-expressed view that one cannot generalize from case study research stems from a positivistic conception of generalization that restricts inquiry to the search for *general rules* as opposed to *universal rules*.

Research-based teaching as a generic approach to curriculum reform

Stenhouse's vision of curriculum reform was ultimately grounded in a general epistemological stance, a view of knowledge as provisional and open to questioning and discussion. Such a vision radically challenged the epistemological assumptions that underpin traditional curriculum structures as classifications of indubitable truths for the purpose of authoritative transmission. The idea of research-based teaching therefore presumed a backdrop of shifting conceptions of educational knowledge and pedagogical aims. Via a process that fused teaching and research teachers could develop new professional knowledge and skills, which enabled them to meaningfully engage students with new objects of learning. For Stenhouse the notion of research-based teaching forged an inextricable linkage between curriculum development and the professional development of teachers.

Shifting conceptions of educational knowledge were embedded in a number of curriculum development projects sponsored by the Schools Council for Curriculum Reform and Examinations during its lifetime (Plaskow 1985). These projects, however, failed to make explicit the standards inherent in the teaching and learning process that was being advocated as the context of use for their curriculum materials. It was assumed that general notions of pedagogical aims, such as 'inquiry' or 'discovery' learning, provided sufficient direction for teachers. In 1972 the Ford Foundation awarded the author a grant to cooperate with teachers to develop a cross-curricula pedagogy for Inquiry/Discovery Learning through action research. In doing so Adelman and I involved teachers in a process of clarifying these conceptions of the learning process and their pedagogical implications (Elliott 1976/77). An overlapping consensus evolved around the view that these concepts referred to a process of self-directed learning as a pedagogical aim. From this aim a framework of values and procedural principles was derived to enable teachers to reflect critically about and test the theories of Inquiry/Discovery Teaching often tacitly embedded in their practice.

In the light of the procedural principles teachers were able to identify constraints they imposed in common on their students' freedom to direct their own learning and to experiment with strategies for removing and replacing them with strategies that were more consistent with such freedom. They also developed and tested action hypotheses about ways in which they could positively intervene in the learning process to foster their students' capabilities at directing their own learning. At the end of the project participating teachers chose to use the framework of values and principles as a basis for systematically organizing their general findings about the problems of realizing an inquiry/discovery learning process in classroom settings and strategies for resolving them. These findings were couched in the form of diagnostic and action hypotheses for other teachers engaged in curriculum reform to test in their classrooms.

Research-based teaching as the linkage between theory and practice

Stenhouse's idea of 'research-based teaching' emerged as a way of linking the world of the educational theorist in the university with that of the teacher. It is the means by which the development of theory is disciplined by the problems of practice and places theorists under an obligation to translate their ideas into a *form* that can be tested in practice (Stenhouse 1980). Busy teachers needed theorists as a source of new ideas and theorists needed teachers to test and develop them further. The bridges between the two worlds of theory and practice were to be curricula that opened up spaces for teachers to re-theorize their practice and theorists to 'practicalize' their theories through research-based teaching.

The problem with many curricula designed by academics in the light of shifting conceptions of educational knowledge and the process of learning is that they did not go far enough in building the bridge between theory and practice. This resulted in a failure of curriculum projects to demonstrate how the ideals and theories that underpinned them might be translated into concrete classroom practice. If the design of many of these projects had followed Stenhouse and provided more support for research-based teaching the UK's curriculum reform movement of the 1960s and 1970s might have become more sustainable – in which case it would not have been so easily replaced in the late 1980s by a state-driven, outcomes-based and highly prescriptive national curriculum.

Different trajectories of meaning: 'research-based teaching' and 'practitioner research'

The 'teachers as researchers' movement in the UK persists but it has tended to be reconstituted along a different trajectory of meaning to the one depicted above by an outcomes-based national curriculum and the 'science of measurement' associated with it. What is now called 'practitioner research' tends to be understood as an inquiry into how to drive up standards in the classroom. 'Standards' in this context refer to what standardized tests of attainment measure rather than qualities inherent in learning processes that are deemed to be educationally worthwhile in themselves. 'Practitioner research' of this kind is shaped by an objectivist and instrumentalist rationality as opposed to the deliberative and democratic rationality embedded in the idea of research-based teaching to improve the ethical quality of teacher's interactions with students in the teaching–learning process.

'Practitioner research' tends to be viewed as a form of inquiry carried out by teachers, on their own or sometimes with peers, rather than as an integral part of a collaborative process of curriculum development between groups of teachers and educational thinkers in the university. Academics may provide advice on research methods but the relationship is no longer that of a curriculum development partnership. Both educational academics and the teaching profession have become cast out of the curriculum field. Whereas curriculum development provided a context for the idea of 'research-based teaching', this context need no longer exist for the practitioner–researcher who has little generative role with respect to the curriculum. Her role is to implement and deliver the prescribed curriculum rather than to test a curriculum against the problems of practice and contribute to its further development.

The idea of 'research-based teaching', therefore, carries a set of meanings that the 'teachers as researchers' movement has tended to cast off in the course of its adaptation to the logic of instrumental rationality that currently prevails in education in the UK. Practitioner research has accomplished a marriage of convenience with a renewed positivist paradigm of educational research, and has a wide measure of acceptance and support in the policy context.

Research-based teaching in the context of globalization: an example from Hong Kong

Stenhouse's idea of 'research-based teaching' has globalized and is now circulating in transnational space. It no longer depends on conditions in the UK to survive. This does not imply that it does not acquire new meaning as it interacts with other ideas from different cultural settings. One striking example is its spread to the Asian Pacific region where sweeping curriculum reforms have been underway, and the encounter with a Confucian version of action research entitled 'Lesson Study' (Matoba *et al.* 2006). The latter involves a group of teachers collectively developing a lesson through experimental cycles of action and reflection. An initial lesson plan is constructed together and then taught in succession by each teacher with his or her peers observing. At the end of each lesson peer observations are pooled and discussed and modifications to the lesson agreed prior to it being taught by the next teacher.

The 'Lesson Study' is a more specifically focused and tighter procedural package than Stenhouse's idea of 'research-based teaching', which is more generally focused on transforming the culture of teaching and learning by employing a variety of methods for gathering and interpreting data. 'Lesson Study' also operates with a more collectivist notion of the teacher's professional self. The action research procedures give less space for the expression of a teacher's individuality in 'discerning the practically salient features of the teaching situation'. Such discernment becomes the collective responsibility of the professional peer group.

However, the Stenhousian version of 'research-based teaching' and 'Lesson Study' have much in common. Both emerged from the context of teaching to address the problems that arise in it, rather than emerging to address problems arising in the academic context of social inquiry. The possibility of achieving a synthesis between the two versions is evidenced by the development of 'Learning Study' in Hong Kong (Lo *et al.* 2005). Here the post-changeover from British colonial rule in 1997 saw the emergence of a national curriculum framework of aims, values and principles that gave spaces for teachers to play a generative role in developing curriculum programmes that are disciplined by the problems of practice (Hong Kong Curriculum Development Council 2001).

'Learning Study' in Hong Kong retains the focus of the 'Lesson Study' on specific lessons, and although the procedural package remains tight it has been extended to accommodate the triangulation methods used in the Stenhousian version by incorporating the perspectives of students and academic curriculum expertise. It has also introduced a more controversial (among teachers) use of pre-post testing to demonstrate the potential of Learning Studies to reduce the learning gap between high and low achievers. However, what characterizes the major difference between 'Learning' and 'Lesson Study' is a shift in the aims of the research towards enhancing the quality of the learning process that the teacher mediates, as opposed to simply improving the effectiveness of teaching methods. In this respect, 'Learning Study' embraces a pedagogical perspective that is not too dissimilar from Stenhouse's concern for the quality of the learning process. However, whereas Stenhouse espoused a philosophically informed 'process model' of curriculum development based on the specification of process values and principles of procedure for handling subject matter, the 'Learning Study' draws on a psychological theory of learning, known as 'variation theory' (Marton and Booth 1997). This theory is used to inform the way teachers mediate the relationship between the subject matter and the learning process of students, inasmuch as it sensitizes teachers to the different ways students experience and understand the subject matter and guides pedagogical experimentation aimed at enriching and extending their understandings.

It remains to be seen whether 'Learning Study' shaped by 'variation theory' is compatible with a version of action research that is shaped by an educational philosophy. There is an issue about the extent to which variation theory is being used to shape pedagogy according to a more sophisticated and refined logic of technical rationality – in which case the transformation of the 'Lesson Study' into the 'Learning Study' inside Hong Kong signals the development of a positivistic, albeit sophisticated, technology of teaching. This raises questions about the extent to which the current widespread use of 'Learning Study' is distorting the aims, values and principles that underpin the curriculum reform framework in Hong Kong. On the other hand, it might be claimed that the proponents of 'Learning Study' and the Stenhousian approach to action research have much to learn from each other. Currently the two approaches are interacting in a curriculum reform context where Eastern and Western ideas are in circulation and often collide. There is a strong prospect of a distinctively Hong Kong version of 'research-based teaching' emerging as a synthesis between the two approaches.

The problem of disaffection from learning remains on a grand scale in the UK. The time has now come when new curriculum solutions are required as an alternative to the social engineering that has characterized the past two decades. The national curriculum is currently, at the time of writing, being reviewed and teachers are beginning to reclaim a more generative role in curriculum development. The idea of 'research-based teaching' expounded in this chapter may shortly re-emerge in the UK and be embraced by the teaching profession on an even larger scale than before. After all, teachers have learned a bitter lesson in recent years concerning how the profession needs to position itself to meet the challenges of educational reform.

References

Adelman, C. (1993) 'Kurt Lewin and the origins of action research', *Educational Action Research Journal*, 1 (1): 7–25.

Altrichter, H. and Gstettner, P. (1993) 'Action research: a closed chapter in the history of German social science', *Educational Action Research Journal*, 1 (3): 329–360.

Carr, W. (1994) 'Whatever happened to action research?', *Educational Action Research Journal*, 2 (3): 427–436.

Elliott, J. (1976/77) 'Developing hypotheses from teachers' practical constructs: an account of the work of the Ford Teaching Project', *Interchange*, 7 (2): 2–22.

—— (1978) 'What is action research in schools?', *Journal of Curriculum Studies*, 10: 355–357.

—— (1991) *Action Research for Educational Change*, Milton Keynes, and Philadelphia: Open University Press.

—— (1995) 'Environmental education, action research, and the role of the school', in *Environmental Learning for the 21st Century*, Paris: CERI-OECD.

Fals Borda, O. (1979) 'Investigating reality in order to transform it: the Colombian experience', *Dialectical Anthropology*, 4 (March): 33–55.

—— (1988) *Knowledge and People's Power: lessons with peasants in Nicaragua, Mexico, and Colombia*, New York: New Horizons Press.

—— (1997) 'Participatory action research in Columbia: some personal feelings', in R. McTaggert (ed.), *Participatory Action Research: international contexts and consequences*, Albany, NY: State University of New York Press, pp. 107–120.

Hargreaves, D. (1997) 'In defence of research for evidence-based teaching: a rejoinder to Martyn Hammersley', *British Educational Research Journal*, 23: 405–419.

Hong Kong Curriculum Development Council (2001) *Learning to Learn: life-long learning and whole-person development*, Hong Kong Special Administrative Region of The People's Republic of China: Curriculum Development Institute.

Lo, M. L., Pong, W. Y., Pakey, C. P. M. (eds) (2005) *For Each and Everyone: catering for individual differences through learning studies*, Hong Kong: Hong Kong University Press.

Marton, F. and Booth, S. (1997) *Learning and Awareness*, Mahwah, NJ: Lawrence Erlbaum Associates.

Matoba, M., Crawford, K. A. and Sarkar Arani, M. R. (eds) (2006) *Lesson Study: international perspective on policy and practice*, Beijing: Educational Science Publishing House.

Nussbaum, M. (1990) 'An Aristotelian conception of rationality', in *Love's Knowledge*, Oxford: Oxford University Press.

Plaskow, M. (1985) *The Life and Death of the Schools Council*, Lewes: Falmer Press.

Posch, P (1990) 'Educational dimensions of environmental school initiatives', *Australian Journal of Environmental Education*, 6: 79–91.

Radtke, F. (1975) 'Wider ein restringiertes Verstandnis von Aktionsforschung – Bermerkungen zu Klafkis Schilderung des "Marburger Grundschulprojekts"', *Beltrage zur Bildungstechnologie*, 1: 11–25.

Rawls, J. (1993/96) *Political Liberalism*, New York: Columbia University Press.

Stenhouse, L. (1968) 'The Humanities Curriculum Project', *Journal of Curriculum Studies*, 1: 26–33.

—— (1971) 'The Humanities Curriculum Project: the rationale', *Theory into Practice*, 10: 154–162.

—— (1975) *An Introduction to Curriculum Research and Development*, London: Heinemann Educational.

—— (1979) 'Research as a basis for teaching'. Inaugural lecture at the University of East Anglia, Norwich. Subsequently published in Stenhouse, L. (1983) *Authority, Education and Emancipation*, London: Heinemann.

—— (1980) 'Curriculum research and the art of the teacher', *Curriculum*, 1, Spring: 40–44.

15 Values and ideals in teachers' professional judgement

Gert Biesta

It has been argued many times that we should see teaching as an art and not, or not exclusively, as a science. Teaching is not about the simple application of decontextualized knowledge and abstract rules, but entails sensitivity for the teachable moment and an ability to make appropriate decisions in situations which, in some respect, are always new and unique. When William James reflected on the relationship between the science of psychology and the art of teaching in his *Talks to Teachers* (1899), he put it as follows:

> Psychology is a science, and teaching is an art; and sciences never generate arts directly out of themselves. . . . To know psychology, therefore, is absolutely no guarantee that we shall be good teachers. To advance to that result, we must have an additional endowment altogether, a happy tact and ingenuity to tell us what definite things to say and do when the pupil is before us. That ingenuity in meeting and pursuing the pupil, that tact for the concrete situation, though they are the alpha and omega of the teacher's art, are things to which psychology cannot help us in the least.
>
> (James 1899: 14–15)

Many teachers connect their sense of professional identity precisely with the idea of the art of teaching and thus strongly resent policies which aim to specify the 'what' and 'how' of their work. Such policies restrict the space for professional judgement and hence limit the scope of teachers' professional agency.

In this chapter I want to take a closer look at the specific nature of teachers' professional judgement. I will argue that the judgements teachers make are not merely of a technical nature but necessarily involve values. Teachers' value judgements are, in turn, informed by underlying educational ideals. In the context of this chapter I will focus on three questions: (1) How should we understand the role of educational ideals in teachers' work and, more specifically, in their professional judgements? (2) How can teachers be supported in the development of the normative dimensions of their professionality? (3) What can we say about the conditions under which teachers can make normative judgements? My argument is partly of a theoretical nature and partly draws from a project conducted in the Netherlands with teachers from primary, secondary, further and higher education.

Judgement in teaching

What kind of judgements do teachers make? The most ardent supporters of the idea of a science of teaching would probably argue that there is no need for teachers to make any judgements at all. They should simply put into practice the strategies and teaching scripts that research has proven to be the ones that work. Yet even if it were possible for research to tell us 'what works' (for a critique see Biesta 2007), putting such knowledge into practice already requires judgements about how research knowledge can be applied in situations that, in some respect, are always unique and that are different from the contexts in which the research was conducted.

The notion of a science of teaching resonates with Aristotle's definition of science (*episteme*) as the knowledge of 'the necessary and the eternal' (Aristotle 1980: 140). In the domain of human action we are, however, not dealing with the necessary and the eternal but with what Aristotle referred to as 'the variable' (1980: 142). Education is a form of *social* interaction and is therefore fundamentally different from interaction in the physical domain. It is not a process of 'push and pull', but of meaning and interpretation and can therefore best be characterized as a process of symbolic interaction (Vanderstraeten and Biesta 2006). What kinds of judgements are therefore required in the domain of education?

Part of the professional expertise of teachers lies in their ability to make judgements about the most effective ways of securing certain ends with particular students in particular situations. What is the best way to teach this student how to read? How can this student be supported to become a good hairdresser? This suggests that the professional expertise of teachers is first of all of a *technical* or *instrumental* nature; it is about identifying the most effective means for achieving particular ends. Although this is an important dimension of teachers' professional judgements, it is important to see that 'effectiveness' as such is not a sufficient criterion on which educational judgements can be based (see Bogotch *et al.* 2007). This is because effective strategies are not automatically also desirable. Administering electric shocks may well be an effective way for modifying someone's behaviour, but it is generally not considered to be an acceptable educational technique. Taking young children away from their parents may well be an effective intervention for securing future educational success, but it is generally not considered to be a desirable educational strategy.

This shows that the judgements teachers make are not simply of a technical or instrumental nature, that is, they are not simply about finding the most effective means to achieve certain ends; they always also involve an *evaluation* of the means themselves and hence require *value judgements* about the desirability of the ways in which particular aims and ends might be achieved. Sometimes such judgements are clear-cut (although ideas about what is acceptable do change over time). Often the question will be whether the ends justify the means. The values that inform such judgements are of a general nature, that is, they are about what is considered to be acceptable in human interaction more generally. In this respect education is not different from other professions, as doctors, therapists and judges also need to decide whether the means they wish to deploy are justified by the ends they aim to achieve. However, the specific nature of education adds a further dimension to teachers' professional judgement which has to do with the fact that in the case of education we always also need to consider the impact of the means we use on our students' learning.

The point is that even if we were to decide that physical punishment is the most effective way to control particular behaviour, and even if we would feel that the harm done by a particular form of punishment is justifiable, we may still have *educational* reasons that prevent us from using it, for example, because the use of punishment 'teaches children that it is appropriate or permissible in the last resort to enforce one's will or get one's own way by the exercise of violence (Carr 1992: 249). What this shows is that the means we use in education are not neutral with regard to the ends. The means we use in education 'contribute qualitatively to the very character . . . of the goals which they produce' – which is why education is at heart a moral and not a technological endeavour (see Carr 1992: 248). There is, in other words, an *internal* or *constitutive* relationship between the means and ends of education. This implies that teachers' professional judgement is not only about whether particular means are desirable but also about whether they are *educationally* desirable. In order to make such judgements teachers not only need to have general ideas about what is acceptable in human interaction. They also need to have particular ideas about what is *educationally* worthwhile. They need to have ideas about what it means to be an educated person; they need to have ideas about the good society and the good life. What they need, in other words, are *educational values and ideals*.

The arts of education: *poiesis* and *praxis*

The foregoing discussion suggests that the more important question is not whether teaching is an art or a science, but about what kind of 'art' teaching actually is and what kind or judgements are involved in the 'art' of teaching.[1] It is here that a further distinction made by Aristotle is helpful, namely, between two modes of human action in the domain of the variable: *poiesis* and *praxis* or, in Carr's (1987) translation, 'making action' and 'doing action'. *Poiesis* is about making things. It is about 'how something may come into being which is capable of either being or not being' (which means that it is about the variable, not about what is eternal and necessary), and about things 'whose origin is in the maker and not in the thing made' (which distinguishes *poiesis* from biological phenomena such as growth and development) (Aristotle 1980: 141). *Poiesis* is, in short, about the creation of something that did not exist before. The kind of knowledge we need for *poiesis* is *techne* (usually translated as 'art'). It is, in more contemporary vocabulary, technological or instrumental knowledge, 'knowledge of how to make things' (Aristotle 1980: 141). Aristotle comments that *poiesis* 'has an end other than itself' (1980: 143). The end of *poiesis* is *external* to the means, which means that *techne*, the knowledge of how to make things, is about finding the means that will produce the thing one wants to make. *Techne* is therefore concerned with judgements about effectiveness.

Praxis is everything that *poiesis* is not. It is not instrumental, it is not about making things, and it does not require technical or technological knowledge. *Praxis* is 'about what sort of things conduce to the good life in general' (Aristotle 1980: 142). It is about good action, but good action is not a means for the achievement of something else. '[G]ood action itself is its end.' The kind of judgement we need here is not about *how* things should be done; we rather need judgement 'about what is to be done' (Aristotle 1980: 143). Aristotle refers to this kind of judgement as *phronesis*, which is usually translated as practical wisdom. Phronesis is a 'reasoned and true state of capacity to act with regard to human goods' (1980: 143).

In terms of the distinction between *poiesis* and *praxis* we can conclude that education is not only *poiesis* – making action – but necessarily involves *praxis* – doing action. Teachers' professional judgements are not only about what is most effective, but have to include judgements about what is *educationally* desirable. This means that teachers not only need *techne*, knowledge of how to make or produce things (including such immaterial things as 'learning outcomes'); they also need *phronesis*, the practical wisdom that allows them to make judgements about 'what is to be done', judgements about what is educationally desirable and worthwhile.

Can practical wisdom be taught?

If it is granted that teacher's professional judgement necessarily involves a normative dimension, the question to ask next is how teachers can develop their capacity for making such judgements. How, in other words, can teachers acquire practical wisdom? How can they be supported in the development of the normative dimensions of their professionality?

Aristotle makes two interesting points in relation to this. First, he emphasizes that *phronesis*, practical wisdom, is itself not an art (*techne*) but a virtue (*arete*) (1980: 143). It is a 'characteristic' of the practically wise person (or in Aristotle's case: the practically wise man, the *phronimos*), the one who is capable of judgements about what is to be done. Aristotle writes: 'It is for this reason that we think Pericles and men like him have practical wisdom, viz., because they can see what is good for themselves and what is good for men in general' (1980: 143). Second, Aristotle points out 'that a young man of practical wisdom cannot be found' (1980: 148).

At first sight these observations appear to be rather unhelpful if we want to find out how practical wisdom can be acquired and cultivated. Yet the point of saying that *phronesis* is a virtue and not an art (*techne*), is meant to highlight that making judgements about what is desirable is not about the application of general rules or principles. There is real, 'fresh' judgement involved each time we are required to judge what is to be done in a particular situation. *Phronesis* is therefore not a competence or skill but is more akin to a way of being. Aristotle's reason for saying that 'a young man of practical wisdom cannot be found' has to with the fact that 'such wisdom is concerned not only with universals but with particulars, which become familiar from experience, but a young man has no experience, for it is length of time that gives experience' (1980: 148). This also shows that practical wisdom is not about the application of rules, but about 'seeing' and responding to situations in a particular way, with an eye on what is to be done. Viewed in this way, Aristotle's comments are more helpful, since they indicate that practical wisdom has to do with ways of understanding – or 'seeing,' as Aristotle emphasizes – and ways of being that engage with the particularities of unique situations with a focus on what is to be done. This suggests that the cultivation of practical wisdom requires an engagement with particular situations (case studies) and seeing those situations through a particular 'lens,' that is, the lens of educational values and ideals. The 'man of practical wisdom', Aristotle writes, must not only know 'particular facts' since 'understanding and judgement are also concerned with things to be done', and these, Aristotle writes, 'are ultimates' (1980: 153).

Learning to see from an educational point of view

It was precisely the combination of case-study work and the clarification of the role and function of educational values and ideals in teachers' thinking and doing that was central to a project we conducted in the Netherlands with a group of teachers from primary and secondary schools and further and higher education (Biesta *et al.* 2002).[2] The main aim of the project was to develop a methodology for supporting beginning and experienced teachers in the enhancement of their 'educational professionality', that is, their ability to make judgements and decisions about what is educationally desirable. The focus of the project was on the role of educational ideals and the book we wrote about the project (in Dutch) got the title *Pedagogisch Bekeken* – which literally means: to *see* in an educational way.

What we tried to do in the project is support teachers in getting a better understanding of the ways in which educational values and ideals function in their everyday practice, so that they might be able to use such values and ideals in a more reflective and deliberate manner. This already reveals an important assumption of the project, in that we started from the assumption that *all* teachers have educational values and ideals, albeit that for some such values and ideals are far more implicit than for others (and in some cases such values and ideals are almost invisible). We shouldn't think, therefore, of educational values and ideals as something teachers explicitly hold and endorse. Educational values and ideals 'happen' or 'occur'. They are part of what teachers do and think, they guide teachers' action, they support their decisions, they inform a particular, educational way of seeing and under-standing, and they provide inspiration and motivation. Educational values and ideals are not only about *what* teachers do; they are also about *why* they do it – and why they continue doing it.

Such an 'embedded' view of educational values and ideals immediately raises a problem (which is well known to those who study tacit knowledge): How can we make what is implicit (more) explicit? How can we make educational values and ideals as they function in teachers' everyday work visible? We addressed this issue in the first part of our project where we asked the teachers to write two short stories: one about an experience in their work about which they were very happy/satisfied, and one about an experience that had made them very unhappy/dissatisfied. We then asked them to help each other in exploring these contrasting stories in order to find an answer to the question *why* they felt about these situations as they did. This proved to be an effective way for getting an understanding of teachers' motivations, values, convictions and ideals. By focusing on more 'extreme' cases – stories of success and stories of failure – and by accessing these examples through teachers' feelings and emotions, teachers were able to articulate what literally 'moved' them.

While the first step in our project helped our teachers to get a better understanding of the range of educational values and ideals they held, we also felt that it was important to examine the relationships between such values and ideals. Are some ideals more fundamental or more encompassing than others? Do all values and ideals go together or is there potential for conflict? Which ideals are central and which are more peripheral? To work on these questions we asked the teachers to write their values and ideals on pieces of cardboard and represent them in a spatial manner. (We called this task 'bricklaying' but not all teachers in the project ended up with a 'wall'. Some, for example, put their values and ideals in a circle, with some in the centre and some in the periphery; others grouped their values like a tree, with roots, a trunk and branches.) The spatial representation of values and ideals helped the teachers to 'sort out' their priorities, that is, to better understand the often-complex relationships between their motivations, convictions, values and ideals. Some were indeed able to identify core values and, when asked to talk through the configuration of their pieces of cardboard and provide examples, were able to show an underlying 'logic' in their thinking and doing. Others did not identify core values, but did gain a much better understanding of the range of values and ideals that was important to them and were able to indicate, through examples and discussion, how different (sets of) values and ideals hung together and how they informed different aspects of their professional practice.

In the second phase of the project we continued with a smaller group of teachers who were all interested in developing and enhancing their ability to make educational judgements about (aspects of) their work. The approach we took centred on the tried and tested idea of the circle or spiral of action–reflection–action. According to this approach, reflection is often triggered by a problem or, to be more precise, by the experience of a problem, by the awareness that action has been interrupted, by the experience that it is not completely clear what to do, how to respond, how to act. We asked the participating teachers to write fairly detailed case studies about a particular problem they were currently struggling with, a situation that had confronted them and where it was really not clear how they should respond. Interestingly – but perhaps not surprisingly given the nature of our project – the case studies did not focus on 'technical' problems but all dealt with discrepancies between what the teachers tried to achieve with particular students or groups of students, and the ways in which they were not able to achieve what they hoped and wanted to achieve. We then asked the teachers to help each other to analyse the case studies, focusing both on their own ideas, perceptions and feelings and on their understandings of the students' ideas, perceptions and feelings. By analysing the stories in this way, some teachers became aware that they had clear ideas about the students, but were far less articulate about their own feelings and thoughts. Others found out that they had a fairly good understanding of thoughts and actions, but not of their own and the students' feelings. In still other cases the original case study was mainly about feelings, and the systematic investigation of the problem helped them to better understand *why* they felt about the situation as they did. We then asked the teachers to explore why things were important for them, both positively (that is, in terms of what they wanted to achieve) and negatively (that is, in terms of where their frustrations and feelings of failure came from). This allowed for a clarification and exploration of underlying educational values and ideals. Finally, we asked the teachers to develop suggestions for action, for a way forward, a way to address the problem they had identified in their case studies. By now they were able to use their understanding of the educational ideals and values that were at play in the particular problem in a more positive and constructive way. It informed their suggestions for action.

In many cases the systematic group-work we did on the case studies indeed resulted in useful suggestions for action, although in one case the participating teacher came to the conclusion that the best way forward for him was to quit his job. He had come to the conclusion that the gap between his educational ideals and more systematic features of his educational practice had become (almost) unbridgeable. For one of the other teachers, participation in our project had the opposite result. For him the exploration of the way in which his educational ideals figured in his thinking and doing had allowed him to reconnect with what really mattered to him; it had allowed him to find again what had motivated him to become a teacher in the first place, as a result of which he was able to return to teaching after a long and stressful break. Other teachers indicated that they had become much more aware of their own educational values and ideals and had gained a better understanding of how these figured in their doing and thinking which, indeed, had helped them to make them part of their professional judgements. All teachers reported that the most important aspect of the whole process had been the fact that they were able to devote time to reflect on their work in a systematic way and, even more importantly, that they were able to do so in collegial dialogue with other teachers. The fact that the teachers in our group came from quite different sectors of the educational spectrum did not really matter for this.

A final point to make is that in this particular project our focus was predominantly on the clarification of teachers' educational values and ideals so that these could become a more explicit part of their professionality. It is, of course, one thing to clarify values and ideals but quite another to make (value) judgements about the appropriateness of certain values and ideals. In the way in which teachers interrogated each other's values and ideals, this was, however, an important issue as well. Quite often the question was raised why particular values or ideals were important, why teachers were giving them priority, and what the effect of such prioritization was, both on their practice and on themselves. In this way the project had an impact that went beyond just becoming aware of one's values and ideals. It helped the teachers to evaluate what moved them and in this regard there was real change and learning as a result.

Conclusions

In this chapter I have argued that value judgements should be seen as an integral part of teachers' professionalism and I have provided an overview of a way in which teachers can be supported in enhancing the normative dimensions of their professionality, that is, their ability for *phronesis*. The experience from our project suggests that practical wisdom can be learned. It also supports the assumption that the ability to make normative judgements, that is, judgements about what is educationally desirable, is not a rule-based skill, but is more akin to a complex disposition – a way of seeing and being – which can be developed over time through systematic reflection on the normative dimensions of one's professional practice and a systematic exploration of the educational values and ideals at stake.

The most important conditions that the teachers in our project identified for their own learning in this domain were *time* and *collegiality*: time to pay attention to the role of educational values and ideals and time to do this together with other teachers. Time is surely a scarce commodity in many educational settings. This is partly because there is always the 'pressure of the immediate' in teachers' work. It is also because of the increasing intensification of teachers' work in many educational settings around the world (something which the other chapters in this collection document in more detail). However, the conditions under which teachers can exert professional judgement are not only about *time* – and in a sense it is significant that the teachers who participated in the project only mentioned time as a constraint. This seems to suggest that they did not experience any other constraints on their ability to exert professional judgement. It seems to suggest, in other words, that they felt able to make both technical and normative judgements in their professional settings which, in turn suggests, that at least to some extent the system and professional culture they worked in provided them with opportunities for professional agency in the broad sense outlined in this chapter. The constraints they felt were mainly pragmatic – which is not to suggest, of course, that they were not real.

One question this raises is whether the Dutch experience is significantly different from the situation in other countries. Answering this question requires detailed comparative research into the cultures and practices of teachers' work – something which is well beyond the scope of this chapter. Whether there is more space for professional judgement in particular countries will partly depend on *cultural* issues, such as the availability of traditions of educational reflection and theorizing – and it is clear that different countries and cultures do have different ways to understand and approach education. There are, however, also *structural* and *systemic* issues at stake, such as the extent to which teachers' work is subjected to top-down control and regulation. This, in turn, suggests that the extent to which values and ideals can play a role in teachers' professional judgement not only relies on their own ability for doing so but also crucially depends upon cultural conditions and structural constraints.

Note

1   I put 'art' in quotation marks because in the English translation of Aristotle's work 'art' is the translation of 'techne', the knowledge involved in making (*poiesis*).
2   The project was conducted together with Fred Korthagen and Hildelien Verkuyl of the IVLOS Institute of Education, Utrecht University, The Netherlands.

References

Aristotle (1980) *The Nicomachean Ethics*, Oxford: Oxford University Press.
Biesta, G. J. J. (2007) 'Why "what works" won't work: evidence-based practice and the democratic deficit of educational research', *Educational Theory*, 57 (1): 1–22.
Biesta, G. J. J., Korthagen, F. and Verkuyl, H. (2002) *Pedagogisch Bekeken: de rol van pedagogische idealen in het onderwijs* [*From an educational point of view: on the role of educational ideals in teaching*], Baarn: Nelissen.
Bogotch, I., Mirón, L. and Biesta, G. (2007) '"Effective for what; effective for whom?" Two questions SESI should not ignore', in T. Townsend (ed.), *International*

Handbook of School Effectiveness and School Improvement, Dordrecht, Boston: Springer, pp. 93–110.

Carr, D. (1992) 'Practical enquiry, values and the problem of educational theory', *Oxford Review of Education*, 18 (3): 241–251.

Carr, W. (1987) 'What is an educational practice?', *Journal of Philosophy of Education*, 21 (2): 163–175.

James, W. (1899) *Talks to Teachers on Psychology: and to students on some of life's ideals*, New York: Henry Holt.

Vanderstraeten, R. and Biesta, G. J. J. (2006) 'How is education possible? A pragmatist account of communication and the social organisation of education', *British Journal of Educational Studies*, 54 (2): 160–174.

16 Education and the public good
The integrity of academic practice

Jon Nixon

> The university . . . is a kind of utopian state . . . It's a grandiose idea, because most of us tend to think of the university as a place where one has a career, which is certainly true, and there's nothing wrong with that; but if you wanted to you could have a somehow more extended idea of what the university is . . . something of this sort is at least useful to get discussion started. And it can be done by individuals.
>
> (Said 2004: 190)

This chapter is written as a kind of open letter to colleagues and fellow scholars working in higher education: hence the somewhat repetitive use of the first person plural. Of course, this 'we' is an imagined community of occupational groups that are increasingly atomized through the fractionalization and stratification of the institutional contexts within which their members work. This rhetorical device is not intended to iron out these differences and inequalities, but to highlight the need for academic workers to develop what Taylor (2004: 23) has termed a 'social imaginary': 'that common understanding that makes possible common practices and a widely shared sense of legitimacy'. The resources necessary for developing and consolidating such an imaginary, I argue, include certain dispositions that are intrinsic to academic practice: dispositions towards truthfulness, respect, authenticity and magnanimity. It is these virtues that provide academic practice – across its constituent activities of research, scholarship and teaching – with its moral integrity.

Reclaiming a public language for education

In recent years universities in particular, and the non-profit-making sector in general, have become increasingly dominated by a language that fails to recognize the rich unpredictability of learning: a language of cost-efficiency, value for money, productivity, effectiveness, outcome-delivery, target-setting and auditing. We are increasingly encouraged, as scholars, teachers and researchers, to think in business terms. Indeed, it is difficult to think outside this terminology, given its all-pervasive dominance. On occasion, we have little option other than to speak its language in order to fulfil the requirements of the internal and external accountability and funding mechanisms that ensure our survival.

We ought not to be sanctimonious about this. We have all, as intellectual workers, in varying degrees had to learn to be bilingual: to utter the standard platitudes of managerialism, while adopting within our own street culture of academic journals and collegial dialogue an older demotic. We cannot afford to ignore the language of managerialism, but nor can we afford to ignore its deep ideological drift. The language of inputs and outputs, of clients and products, of delivery and measurement, of providers and users, is not just a different way of talking about the same thing. It radically alters what we are talking about. It constitutes a new way of thinking about teaching and learning. Ultimately, it affects how we teach and how we learn. It has designs upon us and upon what we understand by educational studies.

What universities can do – must do – is forge a public language which has the capacity to affirm and construct an educated citizenry. The dominant language currently at our disposal is emphatically *not* directed towards such ends and purposes. For all its insistence on 'user relevance', it is an exclusive language of technocrats and bureaucrats, the ideological purpose of which is to endorse technocratic and bureaucratic ways of thinking about education. Against these ways of thinking universities must seek to open up the debate regarding the ends and purposes of education, to expand and render more inclusive its civic spaces, and to recognize the diversity of human presence that comprises those spaces. That is the prime task of any university seeking to reclaim its civic leadership: to reclaim, that is, a public and inclusive language for higher education.

The second task is to provide an inclusive forum for deliberative debate within the public domain. As Said (2004: 181) puts it:

> The academy is ... *not* a place to resolve socio-political tensions ... but it is a place to *understand* them, to understand them in their origin, to understand them in the way in which they are going, in which what is brought to bear is intellectual process.

By that I take Said to mean that the academy should not seek to be dispassionate, but it should insist upon its disinterestedness: it exists, in other words, to provide a civic space within which vested interests are acknowledged and called to account. Government and privately sponsored think tanks for all their bright ideas cannot perform this function. I am not suggesting that such bodies perform no useful function. A good case could be made out for the various quasi-non-government organizations that dominate the policymaking scene having made a valuable, if limited, contribution to the debate on higher education. But that contribution carries with it no obligation to critically scrutinize the interests they and their sponsors have invested in the knowledge they produce and propagate.

Of course, the university sector has its own interests, some of which are admittedly self-serving. Universities have, after all, to survive in an increasingly market-led policy context. But they have one defining interest which is institutionally unique: an interest, that is, in the intrinsic goods of learning and in the critical examination of particular programmes and agendas of change in the light of a relentless examination of those goods. The purpose of any university is not only to bring society back to the questions it needs to ask of itself but to insist that those questions are formulated and addressed, as MacIntyre (1990: 22) puts it, 'in the best rationally defensible way'.

Management, money and marketing!

> ... the three horsemen of the new apocalypse – management, money and marketing.
>
> (Eyre 2003)

The new public management of education was driven by the resurgence of neo-liberal market ideologies that dominated the last quarter of the last century and continue to exert an influence on the way in which universities are managed. It was based on the assumption of a general breakdown of trust in the public and non-profit making sectors and on the further assumption that public trust is best regained through systems of accountability that support competition across these sectors. If only the public and non-profit making sectors could learn from, and behave as if they were a part of, the private sector, all would be well! From that forlorn hope unravelled the endless palaver of performativity – target setting, league tables, inspection regimes – that now characterizes the university sector and dominates the working lives of those located within that sector.

As O'Neill (2002) pointed out in her BBC Reith Lectures, this widely endorsed mode of institutional management is itself part of the problem, not part of the solution. Far from reinstating public trust in public institutions, it has encouraged what she calls a 'culture of suspicion' which is then used to justify the centralized control of those institutions:

> *In theory* the new culture of accountability and audit makes professionals and institutions more accountable *to the public*. This is supposedly done by publishing targets and levels of attainment in league tables, and by establishing complaint procedures by which members of the public can seek redress for any professional or institutional failures. But underlying this ostensible aim of accountability *to the public* the real requirements are for accountability *to regulators, to departments of government, to funders, to legal standards*. The new forms of accountability impose forms of central control – quite often indeed a *range of different and mutually inconsistent* forms of central control. [Author's italics.]
>
> (O'Neill 2002: 52–53)

This statement constitutes a serious indictment of the new public management of higher education. The charge against that management regime is its lack of both transparency and internal consistency. It fails, according to O'Neill, to declare its underlying purposes and to render those purposes coherent in organizational practice. It is a fudge: a muddle masquerading as a serious response to a problem it fails to address, let alone analyse.

Far from encouraging institutions within the public and non-profit making sectors to engage with their publics, the new public management of higher education has served to render them defensive and inward looking: 'we are heading towards defensive medicine, defensive teaching and defensive policing' (O'Neill 2002: 50). The moral trajectory of professional practice towards public service through the exercise of professional judgement brought to bear on highly complex, indeterminate problems has been deflected. Both the professionals and their publics are thereby the poorer. The accountability regimes that characterize the new public management of education have scored an embarrassing 'own goal'. In a bureaucratic effort to open up institutions, they have managed to close them in culturally.

The increasing reliance on mechanisms of accountability and audit in the management of universities is complemented by the increasing reliance of universities, and indeed other institutions within the public and non-profit-making sectors, on commercial funding. Shumar (1997) refers to this same process in terms of 'the commodification of higher education'; Slaughter and Leslie (1997) see it culminating in what they call 'the entrepreneurial university'; while Aronowitz (2000) labels what he calls 'the corporate university' as 'the knowledge factory'. Each of these writers provides different explanations for the rapid acceleration of the process of commercialization, but they broadly agree on what is at stake: namely, that the academic practices associated with the university have 'come to be valued in terms of their ability to be translated into cash or merchandise and not in other ways, such as aesthetic or recreational pleasure. Eventually the idea that there are other kinds of value are lost' (Shumar 1997: 5). That loss of all values other than the values of the marketplace further erodes public trust in the universities by restricting the notion of public concern to the narrow self-interests of the commercial sector.

Bok (2003) analyses this process of commercialization from the perspective of a seasoned senior academic, and respected legal scholar, within American higher education. Pointing to the 'rapid growth of money-making opportunities provided by a more technologically sophisticated, knowledge-based economy' (2003: 15), Bok cites as an example the fact that, in the USA, 'corporations doubled and redoubled their share of total academic research support, increasing it from 2.3 percent in the early 1970s to almost 8 percent by the year 2000' (2003: 12). 'Within a few short decades', he maintains, 'a brave new world had emerged filled with attractive possibilities for turning specialized knowledge into money' (2003: 13–14). Williams (1995: 177) points to a similar trend within the UK. 'The transformation has been dramatic', he argues: 'within ten years, students have been metamorphosed from apprentices to customers, and their teachers from master craftsmen to merchants'.

The future to which such a process is likely to lead is, argues Bok (2003), a bleak one:

> One can imagine a university of the future tenuring professors because they bring in large amounts of patent royalties and industrial funding; paying high salaries to recruit 'celebrity' scholars who can attract favourable media coverage; admitting less than fully qualified students in return for handsome parental gifts; soliciting corporate advertising to underwrite popular executive programs; promoting Internet courses of inferior quality while cancelling worthy conventional offerings because they cannot cover their costs; encouraging professors to spend more time delivering routine research services to attract corporate clients, while providing a variety of symposia and 'academic' conferences planned by marketing experts in their development offices to lure potential donors to the campus.
>
> (Bok 2003: 200–201)

At issue are the underlying purposes of professional practice and the capacity of professionals to reach out to a wide and diverse public. The choice, as Reid (1996) puts it, is 'higher education or education for hire'. The complex societal forces operating in the late-modern age require a radical reappraisal of those purposes and a radical redefinition of what we understand by the increasingly differentiated and stratified public sphere. However, the ways in which we have set about that reappraisal and that redefinition, through the mechanisms of new public management and a collapse into wholesale commercialism, presage an ideological dead-end. The endemic problem of the redistribution of power across new force fields of difference cannot be resolved through piecemeal measures that seek to reconcile centralized control with an over-reliance on unmediated market forces. As Bok (2003: 208) concludes, 'universities will find it difficult to rebuild the public's trust . . . In exchange for ephemeral gains in the continuing struggle for progress and prestige, they will have sacrificed essential values that are all but impossible to restore'.

A consequence of this Faustian exchange of 'ephemeral gains' for 'essential values' is, among other things, the low morale among academic workers: the sense of being under-valued and of having no effective input into the way in which universities are run or the direction in which they are heading. However, if loss of values is part of the problem, then the sense academics have of their own professional identity must be part of the solution. Any serious attempt at institutional change necessarily involves a commitment to professional reconstruction. Without that commitment, institutional change (and, indeed, broader policy change) lacks all substance.

The moral bases of academic reconstruction[1]

Universities, as we academic practitioners are constantly reminded, undoubtedly contribute to wealth creation and the economic regeneration of the regions within which they are located. They provide skills and understandings, without which an advanced society could not hope to compete within the global market. They are key partners in economic regeneration schemes that benefit regions and help locate those regions within a broader frame of economic competition. They are part of the complex infrastructure of global capitalism, which relies increasingly on the recognition of knowledge transfer as a key component of economic well-being. Their trade is knowledge; and they have undoubtedly become increasingly successful in this entrepreneurial endeavour. Some universities, at least, have grown up and got wise to the economic reality of late capitalism; and the more grown-up and wised-up they have become, the greater their competitive edge.

Economic growth, however, is not the prime purpose of the university. Universities exist to hold the mirror up to society and, in so doing, ask it to examine its assumptions and its underlying logic. It must be emphasized that this is not necessarily an either/or. Sometimes, happily, the university and society can have it both ways. But when 'the chips are down', as Arendt put it, hard decisions have to be taken. Then the question of what universities are for re-surfaces and has to be addressed. Sometimes, in the interests of learning, universities have to take a stand against what is seen to constitute progress or growth (as when, for example, the imposition of managerial structures threatens the very practice of learning). Because of this possible eventuality, universities have to sustain their underlying purposefulness as a resource for an indeterminate future. The university must be a repository of these other, sometimes oppositional, ways of thinking about why we do what we do.

The university is above all a civic space: a space where people come together with the purpose of learning together, with a respect for the practices that sustain such learning, and with a sense of there being dispositions that have to be achieved in order for learning to take place. This claim can, however, no longer be taken for granted. Like all claims regarding the purpose of the university it is increasingly contested and has to struggle for recognition within a policy context that is fraught with competing priorities and agendas. To insist upon the primacy of that claim is not to deny the complexity of the context within which academic workers forge their moral careers and seek to define for themselves a new academic professionalism. It is merely to insist that, in positioning itself within that context, the university needs to affirm as a condition of its survival the centrality of learning as a civic necessity.

Williams (2002) reminded us, in the last book of his published during his lifetime, of the importance to the continuation of learning of the notion of *truthfulness*. In that sense a university might be seen as an extension of a good home – a space within which we learn to tell the truth within these 'domestic' parameters. To claim that the university is a 'civic' space is to assume that the university exists to search for ways of speaking the truth within a wider forum. The possibility of learning and of their being a civic space within which we can, in difference, learn together is itself a condition of hope. The university is a space within which that condition can be realized. It is not the only space, but it remains a significant space to which those of us who acknowledge the authority of truthfulness may, and indeed do, return in troubled times.

Truthfulness relies upon a commitment to *accuracy* in respect of belief and *sincerity* in respect of professing those beliefs that we hold to be accurate. Learning how to learn is in large part a matter of acquiring those dispositions that make such a commitment possible. Truthfulness does not presuppose an ultimate truth; it aspires towards a set of practices that limit the potential violence of untruth. Truthful people may sometimes deceive, tell lies; but they acknowledge the troubling and disabling impact of their deceptions and lies both on their own lives and on the well-being of others. To seek to be accurate in respect of the beliefs one holds and sincere with regard to the professing of those beliefs is intrinsic to becoming a good academic practitioner. In that sense we might say that accuracy and sincerity are the virtuous dispositions associated with truthfulness.

Learning presupposes, in its emphasis on truthfulness, *respect* for the other. Sennett (2003) reminds us that respect necessarily takes as its starting point a deep *attentiveness* to difference. That attentiveness involves identification through sympathy and empathy, but must move beyond those sentiments to an *honesty* regarding the difficulty of practising respect within a deeply unequal world. We cannot collapse the self into the other. The civic space provided by the university allows us to grow into respect through a process of painful standing back – through deliberation, argumentation and an acknowledgement of the deep disagreements which may, ultimately, be the only common ground we share.

There is, Sennett (2003) goes on to argue, a kind of phasing into respect through identification and then through recognition. What might then emerge is respectful distance: the respect accorded to those we know to be different, but have learnt are part of whatever (Arendt's phrase again) 'care for the world' might mean. What respect does is weld our recognition of difference and our commitment to a more socially just society into a kind of morally functional disunity – an openness to difference, while trying to work through the quite specific and always culturally-specific social justice project. Living life purposefully for the betterment of an imagined good society, which is precisely what the university exists for, is a matter of entertaining that disunity – that openness – and privileging it against the symbolic violence of premature foreclosure. The virtuous dispositions of accuracy and honesty implicit in the traditions of teaching, learning and humanistic scholarship are crucial means by which, as academic practitioners, we set about that task.

Learning presupposes, also, the possibility and, indeed, as Taylor (1991) would have it, the necessity of *authenticity*. It provides the potential for living life in such a way that truthfulness and respect become what we are in our relations with one another. Authenticity is the public face of truthfulness and respect and involves the additional virtuous dispositions of *courage* and *compassion*. Judged by the strictest standards of authenticity none of us can claim to be a moral success. Insofar as some of us do we risk the eventual accusation of hypocrisy. But we may rightly think of authenticity as a kind of journey; and, in so far as we do so, the university is one of the institutions through which we may choose our long march. It is not the only institutional route any of us will take, but it is an important one and one which we must keep open for others.

Authenticity is not an end-point. In a tangled world of interrelated privacies, it may even seem a chimera. But it is a notion to which the university must hold fast. The idea is that life can be lived all of a piece for ourselves and others; that truthfulness can become a way of life for ourselves and others; and that respect can become part of that life for ourselves and others. It is a near impossibility, but not quite impossible. We must begin, at precise points and within specific sectors, the task of recreating from an increasingly alienated workforce the possibility of a new academic professionalism. It is, I am arguing, only from within our own academic practice that we can discover the virtuous dispositions of courage and compassion to set about that task.

Finally, learning involves *magnanimity*. Magnanimity points to the generous, unselfish, kind and benevolent aspects of human nature. To describe learning in terms of magnanimity suggests a similar reaching out to the unknown – and to what is different – in a spirit of generosity, altruism, kindness and benevolence. The moral endpoint of magnanimity, to borrow Berger's (2007) phrase, is to 'hold everything dear'. Learning necessarily involves this kind of reaching out: to new forms of understanding; to different points of view; to new situations; to new media and new ways of saying whatever it is one came to say. It is not just that magnanimity is a useful optional extra for successful learners to acquire, but that it is central to whatever it means to be a learner. Without magnanimity one simply cannot learn or be open to learning.

The unfamiliar and strange are everywhere: no longer a world apart, but part of our world of difference. We are all becoming increasingly familiar with what is unfamiliar and strange. Within this world of difference magnanimity is of the utmost importance. While outward looking, magnanimity relies on a strong sense of selfhood: a sense, that is, of one's own *autonomy* and capacity for self-determination. Only an autonomous person can *care* for the autonomy of others; without autonomy, care is likely to collapse into dependency. Similarly, only a caring person can ensure that autonomy is disposed towards magnanimity; without care, autonomy collapses into self-regard. Autonomy and care are the complementary and constitutive dispositions comprising magnanimity.

Conclusion

Research, scholarship and teaching share a necessary relationship based upon the virtuous dispositions implicit in academic practice. The increasing tendency to distinguish institutions of higher education in terms of either their research capacity or their teaching capacity certainly reproduces deep inequalities within the system. It also, however, fractures the moral coherence of the academic practice comprising those activities. Research, scholarship and teaching do not simply hang together instrumentally. They are dependent upon, and at the same time help sustain, a moral framework the pivotal points of which are truthfulness (accuracy/sincerity), respect (attentiveness/honesty), authenticity (courage/compassion) and magnanimity (autonomy/care). The university, viewed as a 'utopian state' (which is precisely how Said suggests we should view it), is a civic space within which these particular virtues, and the dispositions associated with them, are allowed to flourish.

Although research, scholarship and teaching are clearly very different kinds of activity, each requires a dispositional orientation towards these virtues. That moral orientation is a defining feature of the field of academic practice within which these various activities are located. As activities each is clearly very different and involves a differing range of skills and understandings. However, as moral endeavours, these activities have much in common; and what they have in common is, in part at least, a sense of moral purposefulness in respect of the virtues of truthfulness, respect and authenticity. Those involved in these different activities share what Pring (2003: 64) has called 'the deep down *feeling* concerning how they ought to act' (original emphasis).

It is important to insist upon the moral coherence of academic practice precisely because of the increasing stratification of the higher education sector, whereby deep divisions of labour are being systematically engineered and then justified on the spurious grounds of consumer choice. Within this context the notion of 'widening participation' becomes meaningless, since what students will be participating in at different points within the system will not just be different (in the naively benign sense of that term) but will differ *qualitatively*. The reclamation of the moral bases of academic practice, by us as academic practitioners, is essential if universities are to contribute to the building of the good society. 'It can', as Said insists, 'be done by individuals': by people like ourselves who, through our academic practice, are continuing to learn how to be accurate and sincere, attentive and honest, courageous and compassionate, autonomous and caring. How we practice as academic professionals, and how we conceptualize our ends and purposes as academic practitioners, can and does make a difference.

Note

1   This section presents a much-abbreviated form of an argument elaborated in Chapters 4–7 of Nixon (2008).

References

Aronowitz, S. (2000) *The Knowledge Factory: dismantling the corporate university and creating the higher learning*, Boston: Beacon Press.

Berger, J. (2007) *Hold Everything Dear: dispatches on survival and resistance*, London and New York: Verso.

Bok, D. (2003) *Universities in the Market Place: the commercialization of higher education*, Princeton, NJ, and Oxford: Princeton University Press.

Eyre, R. (2003) 'The BBC is one of the few things in Britain that works', *The Guardian*, 27 September: 22.

MacIntyre, A. (1990) *Three Rival Versions of Moral Enquiry: encyclopaedia, genealogy, and tradition* (Gifford Lectures delivered at the University of Edinburgh in 1988), London: Duckworth.

Nixon, J. (2008) *Towards the Virtuous University: the moral bases of academic practice*, London and New York: Routledge.

O'Neill, O. (2002) *A Question of Trust* (BBC Reith Lectures), Cambridge: Cambridge University Press.

Pring, R. (2003) 'The virtues and vices of an educational researcher', in P. Sikes, J. Nixon and W. Carr (eds), *The Moral Foundations of Educational Research: knowledge, inquiry and values*, Maidenhead and Philadelphia: Open University Press/McGraw-Hill Education.

Reid, I. (1996) *Higher Education or Education for Hire? Language and values in Australian universities*, Rockhampton, Queensland: Central Queensland University Press.

Said, E. (2004) *Power, Politics and Culture: interviews with Edward W. Said* (ed. G. Viswanathan), London: Bloomsbury.

Sennett, R. (2003) *Respect: the formation of character in an age of inequality*, London: Allen Lane/The Penguin Press.

Shumar, W. (1997) *College for Sale: a critique of the commodification of higher education*, London, and Bristol, PA: Falmer Press.

Slaughter, S. and Leslie, L. L. (1997) *Academic Capitalism: politics, policies, and the entrepreneurial university*, Baltimore, MA: Johns Hopkins University Press.

Taylor, C. (1991) *The Ethics of Authenticity*, Cambridge, MA, and London: Harvard University Press.

—— (2004) *Modern Social Imaginaries*, Durham, NC, and London: Duke University Press.

Williams, B. (2002) *Truth and Truthfulness: an essay in genealogy*, Princeton, NJ, Oxford: Princeton University Press.

Williams, G. L. (1995) 'The "marketization" of higher education: reforms and potentials in higher education finance', in D. D. Dill and B. Sporn (eds), *Emerging Patterns of Social Demand and University Reform: through a glass darkly*, Oxford, New York and Tokyo: Pergamon Press/The International Association of Universities Press.

17 Leadership for professional practice

Eric Hoyle and Mike Wallace

We argue in this chapter that the accountability movement of the late 1970s onwards succeeded in its tacit intention to curtail the power of the public service professions, including teaching. Professionalism was reconceptualized as the efficient delivery of a client demand-led service. It also became substantially *incorporated* into the process of managing public service organizations such as schools. This incorporation had two aspects. The structural aspect entailed headteacher and teacher roles and tasks becoming increasingly managerial. The cultural aspect entailed the incorporation of headteachers and teachers into the ideology of managerialism, particularly through their internalization of the emerging language of management. However, despite this incorporation, there are indirect indications that headteachers and teachers are maintaining more longstanding professional values in the interstices of managerial structures, and the chapter adopts an ironic perspective to capture this process. We will assert that, although there is a case for a collective, principled defence of professionalism, there is also a case for fostering a client-centred professionalism at the school level. The success of this endeavour depends on temperate school leadership supporting a pragmatic professionalism.

Challenging professions

The traditional conception of a profession became, from the mid-1960s, subject to critique challenging the central tenets of what it meant to be a professional. Initially this critique stemmed largely from a political-left perspective. It held that the idea of a profession was essentially an ideology of 'providerism', serving the interests of members rather than those of clients. Thus professional knowledge, credentials, practitioner autonomy, self-regulation, political voice and codes of professional ethics were recast as strategies to strengthen professional boundaries. The late 1970s saw the emergence of a further critique, now from a political-right perspective, driven by the burgeoning costs of the professionally staffed public services. The latter critique was characterized by a desire for greater political control over professional practice, the creation of a more cost-efficient and educationally effective market for professional services, and a greater voice for clients. *Professionalization* can be regarded as having two dimensions: enhancing the standing of a profession, and enhancing the quality of professional practice (Hoyle 1974). The unfolding critique claimed that the former had become too dominant over the latter.

Critiques from left and right generated the accountability movement. Its strategy entailed centralizing policy, devolving to local managers the task of implementing these policies, and creating a series of quasi-governmental audit agencies to ensure implementation (Clarke and Newman 1997; Power 1997). The underlying function of these strategies is interpretable as the elimination of *ambiguity*. Central to the traditional idea of a profession had been the view that professional practice was endemically 'indeterminate', requiring practitioners to be accorded a level of autonomy allowing them to make judgements in 'uncertain situations'. Critics regarded this view as a self-serving exaggeration, since professional practice is more routine and guided by 'recipe' knowledge than proponents of professional autonomy acknowledged. Teaching was particularly vulnerable to this critique, since educational goals had long been regarded as diverse and diffuse (Hoyle 1986), with pedagogy presented as largely contingent rather than universal. This degree of ambiguity was deemed inimical to service efficiency, and the accountability movement in education sought to reduce ambiguity of professional practice through such policies as establishing national standards and measurable outcomes of schooling, the publication of comparative achievements, and surveillance through inspection.

The accountability movement (subsequently labelled the educational reform movement) has profoundly affected the professional work of teachers. Key impacts are the expansion and intensification of the teacher's role, the reduction of teachers' jurisdiction over professional work, and the incorporation of teachers into management (Hoyle 2001a). These changes in practice have been accompanied by a semantic shift. The term *profession* became less widely used – and then primarily by occupational elites pursuing enhanced status. The key term became *professional*. As noun and adjective, this concept now connotes a no-nonsense efficiency and detachment and, as such, has come to share the same domain as the metaphors of management (Hoyle and Wallace 2007a). Thus the reconfiguration of the teaching profession has been occurring at the institutional and cultural levels, both characterized by *incorporation*.

The institutional incorporation of teaching

Incorporation entails assimilating the professional mode of organizing work into the managerial mode of organizing work, such that the previously existing boundary between the two is now more permeable. Moreover, managerialism – which we define pejoratively as excessive leadership and management – has been a key strategy whereby successive governments have sought to ensure the implementation of state-determined policies. Thus professionalism can also be regarded as having been increasingly incorporated into the political domain. This form of incorporation has generated relatively little overt teacher resistance because legislation has reduced the power of the teacher unions as the major agencies of resistance, and there are also strong imperatives for headteachers and teachers to accept incorporation of teaching into management.

Early studies of organizations staffed by professionals noted the inherent conflict between bureaucratic and professional modes of organizing work, and their temporary and unstable accommodation (Davies 1983). Schools were thus marked by a 'structural looseness' (Bidwell 1965) and pre-reform studies noted the contingent, ambiguous and negotiated nature of bureaucratic-professional relationships in schools. This negotiated boundary became the target of reform and was thereby eroded. The term 'bureaucracy' slipped out of the discourse, probably because of negative connotations surrounding its everyday usage, to be replaced by the more positive-sounding concept of 'management'. Professionalism and management were no longer competing modes of controlling work but overlapping, with unclear boundaries.

Managerialism ostensibly represents a solution to the management-professional tension through the incorporation of professionals into the management process. A central task of headteachers is now implementing national policy to the satisfaction of the agencies of audit. Senior staff are incorporated into this process through membership of senior leadership teams. Likewise middle managers and most teachers are involved in some way in meeting managerialist expectations. The incorporation of the teaching profession is mirrored in other public services (Causer and Exworthy 1999). There have been three major pressures towards the incorporation of teachers: career, entrepreneurship and the professionalization of management.

It has long been the case that a 'successful' teaching *career* eventually took teachers out of the classroom and into a headship, or an educational role outside schools. A 'successful' career in education now entails passage through succeeding roles where the management component becomes increasingly more salient. In addition to conventional managerial positions, there are a growing number of adjunct posts in auditing, appraising, mentoring and quality assurance. Moreover, the growth of these functions has stimulated the emergence of new quasi-professions of audit, creating new career opportunities in associated agencies and consultancies. That headteachers and teachers have pursued these new career opportunities is understandable. It is now difficult for even the moderately ambitious teacher to avoid incorporation, even though work satisfaction for most teachers still derives largely from teaching.

The reform movement has also created opportunities for *entrepreneurship* with the emerging pre-eminence of the market. For public service institutions marketization has taken the form of internal markets, largely generated by requiring schools to compete for students, grants and other resources. It has also been fostered through allowing schools to achieve and to exercise their independence (for example, in England initially through the grant-maintained schools initiative and latterly through other diversification patterns such as specialist secondary schools, and academy status) (Woods *et al.* 2007). Many headteachers and teachers now recognize that a display of entrepreneurial spirit contributes to professional success.

Since managerialism was introduced into education specifically to curtail the power of the professions, it is ironic that educational management has itself been *'professionalized'*. Educational management is now marked by credentialism, a clear career structure, a body of research and scholarship underpinning management programmes in higher education, and a discourse of managerialism as arcane as the discourse of professionalism which had been accused of sustaining professional power by confusing clients.

We have considered incorporation as largely a matter of institutions, role and structures. But we have also hinted at a cultural assimilation of professionalism into managerialism, to which we now turn.

The cultural incorporation of teaching

We fully support efforts to improve the management of schools. The problem is not management but the culture of *managerialism* – management to excess. In the UK developments to improve school management were initiated in the 1960s by a group of academics, leaders of teachers' unions, local inspectors and advisers and practitioners. Despite some interest among HMI there was little government initiative. Those interested in developing programmes of training for headteachers used the term *educational administration* (as employed in the USA), since linking *management* with *education* was regarded as unseemly. Headteachers were regarded as 'traditional' rather than 'bureaucratic' leaders in the Weberian sense, and as 'leading professionals' with additional administrative functions (Hughes 1973). However, a culture and an ideology of managerialism developed during the 1980s. Its credo is that not only *can* everything be managed but that everything *ought* to be managed: in the mantra of the McKinsey Corporation 'Everything can be measured and what can be measured can be managed'. The culture of managerialism led to management becoming a solution in search of a problem. Managerial resources could not be allowed to stand idle and management became, in part, a search for problems, with meetings becoming a major form of work.

Of course, there are endemic limits to managerialism in education because management is not teaching and teaching still essentially entails a teacher working with a group of pupils. Nevertheless education became permeated by managerialist values. What had previously been professional problems of curriculum, pedagogy and socialization were transformed into management problems to be solved by structures, procedures and reporting.

The cultural incorporation of professionalism into managerialism is evidenced by change in educational discourse and its metaphors. In the

1960s educational discourse was dominated at the political level by the language of *equality* and at the level of curriculum, pedagogy and assessment by the language of *child-centredness*. The two domains remained loosely coupled, a situation sustained by the successful resistance of the teaching profession to political encroachment (Lawn 1987; Dale 1989). Thus the term *educational management* was little used before the late 1970s. When school management became an instrument of reform, the metaphors of management, adopted from the private sector, came to dominate educational discourse – as in this quotation:

> Good management requires the identification of management units for which objectives can be set and resources allocated; the unit is then required to manage itself within these resources in a way which seeks to achieve the objectives; the performance of the unit is monitored and the unit held to account for its performance and its use of funds. These concepts are just as applicable to the public sector as the private sector.
>
> (Coopers and Lybrand 1988)

Metaphors such as the above were inescapable and became universal among educationists. They were disseminated through management texts and teaching materials generated by specialists in educational management in higher education, dominating educational discourse throughout the 1980s.

However, during this period the metaphors of management became overlaid by a different set of metaphors centred on 'leadership' (Hoyle and Wallace 2007b). In the early 1980s there occurred 'the cultural turn' in management theory whereby organizational effectiveness was held to be a correlate of organizational culture. Also, a major shift in leadership theory occurred with the emergence of *transformational* leadership. The two developments coalesced to produce today's dominant discourse, summarized by us as:

> Effective organizations have transformational leaders who generate a strong, shared culture, which underpins a compelling vision which, in turn, yields a distinctive mission; such leaders create a learning organization through which members internalise the vision and are empowered to work collegially in order to bring it to fruition.
>
> (Hoyle and Wallace 2005)

This discourse was given added power because of its congruence with the new political discourse of New Labour (Fairclough 2002). The metaphors of management and leadership have thus now become so embedded that they inform the language of all who work in education and fluency in the language has become essential to promotion.

However, we do not know how far the language of management has been internalized by headteachers and teachers and now shapes their cognition. Some educationists will have fully internalized the language, but many headteachers and teachers may employ it in professional contexts only as a matter of convention and remain capable of switching to other registers. For some, the language may be used only in a tone of discreet irony. The incorporation of teachers as professionals may not yet be complete, as indicated by the endurance of an independent form of professionalism.

The persistence of professionalism

Here we speculate that despite the advance of managerialism there survives in schools a professionalism which sustains some of the worthwhile elements of the traditional idea of a profession. In essence this professionalism entails giving priority to the needs of immediate clients – pupils and their families – even where doing so runs counter to policy.

We have sought to capture the persistence of professionalism through the trope of *irony* (Hoyle and Wallace 2005, 2007a). In its everyday usage, irony connotes a figure of speech whereby an intended meaning is conveyed by a statement of the opposite. But we take irony much more seriously and we are influenced by the ironic strain in philosophy from Socrates, Kierkegaard, Schlegel and Nietzsche to Rorty. We are more interested in *situational* than in *literary* irony. Our views on situational irony have been strongly influenced by the idea of *ambiguity*, as developed in the work of March (1999) and March and Olsen (1976). We have noted how an underlying intent of the reform movement was the reduction of ambiguity. This has undoubtedly occurred in education and has most probably had a beneficial effect on the quality of schooling. But again the problem lies in excess. Ambiguity is endemic in education. Irony resides in the fact that an over-zealous preoccupation with 'driving up standards' has ensured that, while explicit targets are being met, the diffuse goals of education would not be met unless teachers pursued them within the interstices of the structures of accountability. In short, managerialism has generated *unintended consequences*, the paradigm form of situational irony.

While we cannot firmly demonstrate the persistence of professionalism we are reasonably confident that it can be inferred from a variety of sources, particularly from professional workplace studies (including Woods *et al.* 1997; Helsby 1999; and McCulloch *et al.* 2000). In essence, our argument is that there is a reciprocal relationship between the irony of policy and the irony of practice.

Although there are endemic ironies in all organizations, we believe that endemic irony has been aggravated by the reform movement. The unintended consequences of targets are now a matter of public experience and political concern. The aggravated irony of policy has evoked an ironic response from headteachers and teachers. Of perhaps three major modes of response to the ironies of policy – acceptance, resistance and mediation – *mediation* is the characteristic form. It entails adapting policy to contingent circumstances (Pollard *et al.* 1994; Osborn *et al.* 2000). Interviews with headteachers and teachers reported in professional workplace studies suggest that notwith-standing official policies their primary concerns remain with the interests of the pupils. The pursuit of pupil interests necessitates strategies whereby accountability requirements are ostensibly met but surreptitiously 'worked round' – mediated. We have referred to such practices as *principled infidelity*: infidelity because policies are not implemented as strictly intended and principled because they are infused with a professional concern with clients' interests.

Our argument is open to challenge, in that research has yet to explore the incidence of principled infidelity in schools. Maybe only a minority of teachers adopt this perspective while others will comply or leave teaching altogether. Some teachers will undoubtedly be unprincipled, incompetent and unprofessional (in the everyday connotation of the latter term). It was ever thus and we do not idealize teaching, but we anticipate that there is a critical mass of teachers who continue to prioritize professionalism over managerialism.

The professionalism that we have in mind acknowledges the inevitable ambiguity, complexity and irony of teaching. It has these characteristics:

1   *Contingency* – although there are legitimate national policies, and although there exist general principles that inform teaching and learning, the professional recognizes that the contingent features of pupils, schools, families and communities must be taken into account in shaping practice.
2   *Pragmatism* – closely related to contingency – informing professional practice by helping to determine the balance between principles and realities. Targets may be alien to one's principles, so they should be accepted as an imperative but then means sought to compensate for their effects. Moore *et al.* (2002) write of the 'pragmatism-with-principles' that they found in the responses of headteachers in their study.
3   *Constructivism* – following from the two preceding principles. Pragmatic practice in contingent conditions requires the construction of solutions drawing on principles and bodies of knowledge to address local problems.
4   *Scepticism* – teachers have long treated educational theory with scepticism and may be even more sceptical of today's policy initiatives. Yet scepticism is not to be confused with cynicism nor does it underplay the importance of research: it takes research seriously enough to entail weighing competing bodies of evidence.
5   *Reflexiveness* – widely accepted as an aspect of professionalism since Schon (1983) introduced his notion of 'the reflective practitioner'. Egan (1997: 155) notes that 'the central constituent of irony is a high degree of reflexiveness on our own thinking and a refined sensitivity to the limited and crude nature of the conceptions and resources we can deploy in trying to make sense of the world'.
6   *Collaboration* – teachers report one of the few benefits of the reform movement to be increased opportunities for professional collaboration,

and there is a substantial associated literature. However, there is a danger that this becomes incorporated into the management process in the form of 'contrived collegiality' (Hargreaves 1994).

A paradox lies at the heart of our view of professionalism. It is modest and lacks the force of a grand statement in defence of the professions. Yet it is perhaps more demanding since it could easily slip into a relativistic localism. We must concede this as a danger. And yet it would seem from studies of teachers' professional practice that many bring this thoughtful professionalism to their work. We believe that preservation and enhancement of this form of professionalism lies largely in the hands of school leaders.

Temperate leadership and professional practice

Improving the professionalism of teachers is perhaps best undertaken at the school level, building on the spirit of professionalism which has been sustained by many teachers in the face of permanent 'reform'. We also believe that headteachers need to play a key role in sustaining and enhancing this professionalism, and in doing so, they will need to reconsider their own professionalism.

The metaphor of transformational leadership conveys an inappropriate message in relation to professionalism. However 'transformational' is used, it would seem to connote radical change. Yet school leaders have little opportunity to act 'transformationally' since they are tightly constrained by national policies and the procedures of accountability – the more appropriate descriptor would be 'transmissional' leadership. When we read of school leaders who have been 'transformational' it usually emerges that their exceptional success lies in getting teachers to achieve improvements in schooling by doing the normal things better. It is tempting to use the term 'improvement' rather than 'transformation' to describe what they do, but some aspects of what is termed 'school improvement' differ little from managerialism (Thrupp 2005).

Temperate leadership is 'managerial' in relation to some areas of professionalism such as ensuring that teachers 'do things professionally' concerning the routines of schooling – marking work, being punctual – and 'act professionally' in relation to pupils, colleagues and parents. School leaders will, of course, model this behaviour. Moreover, the temperate leader will where possible take the strain and ease the stress for teachers, thus helping them to focus on their core professional tasks. Ironically, such actions are likely to entail minimizing the incidence of management, reducing the number of meetings, and simplifying procedures. But more fundamentally, temperate leadership entails finding and nurturing teacher professionalism. A difficult endeavour, since it entails engaging with endemic dilemmas. We list three.

Accountability versus responsibility. The imperative of accountability has certainly improved practice and given a voice to clients, but responsibility reaches the parts that accountability cannot reach. A sense of responsibility cannot be preordained. It is essentially contingent and entails making judgements in uncertain and changing circumstances (Hoyle and John 1995).

Structure versus emergence. Managerialism exhibits a preference for predetermined structures according to which work is organized. Professionalism is to an important degree emergent from practice. Its emergence is highly dependent on practitioner autonomy – a key component of the traditional idea of profession – which temperate leaders need to foster. Communities of practice can play a significant role in fostering professionalism (Wenger 1998, Bolam *et al.* 2005). They are inherently temporary, protean and have an evolving membership. The success of such communities leads to the managerialist temptation to transform them into formal components of the organization. Temperate leadership would foster rather than incorporate them.

Rules versus trust. Bureaucracy was predicated on rule-following behaviour and the limitation of discretion. Managerialism likewise assumes rule-following behaviour, notwithstanding the *empowerment* strain in the new rhetoric of leadership. There are powerful imperatives inducing risk-averse behaviour in educational leadership: principally the tyranny of targets and league tables, but also the increased trend towards litigation. This increase in risk has led to a decrease in trust. Discussion of the decline of trust in relation to the professions (O'Neill 2002) including teaching (Bottery 2003) indicates that there are no easy solutions. Our proclivity is towards 'trust-with-verification': promoting the willingness to trust professional colleagues alongside unobtrusive monitoring, linked to *emergence* and the cultivation of *responsibility* as complementary characteristics of temperate leadership.

Towards an enhanced teacher professionalism

The professions have been on the defensive for thirty years. Freidson (1994) has argued for a principled defence of the professions that is 'offensive as well as defensive'. We are in sympathy with a collective response to political efforts to convert professionalism into managerialism. The case made by Sachs (2003: 33) for an 'activist teaching profession' sees such activism as potentially occurring at all levels. But she notes that 'activism is probably safer as a collective activity than as an individual one'.

Our appeal is pitched at the school level: at individual teachers, groups of teachers and headteachers. It is subversive rather than militant but it expects much. It would seek to reduce levels of management, increase levels of trust, and discourage the banalities of managerial language. It is a stance that hardly stirs the blood. Nor is it a path which would enhance the status and prestige of teaching according to conventional measures. Yet it would enhance the *esteem* of teachers (Hoyle 2001b). We suggest that this approach to enhancing teacher professionalism deserves prominence in programmes of leadership and management development and training. Since it is predicated on empathy with the experienced realities of teaching it surely offers a better prospect for improving education than yet more managerialist reforms.

References

Bidwell, C. E. (1965) 'The school as a formal organization', in J. G. March (ed.), *Handbook of Organizations*, Chicago, IL: Rand McNally, pp. 972–1022.

Bolam, R., McMahon, A., Stoll, L., Thomas, S. and Wallace, M. (2005) *Creating and Sustaining Effective Professional Learning Communities*, Research Report 637, London: Department for Education and Skills.

Bottery, M. (2003) 'The management and mismanagement of trust', *Educational Management and Administration*, 31 (3): 245–261.

Causer, G. and Exworthy, M. (1999) 'Professionals as managers across the public sector', in M. Exworthy and S. Halford (eds), *Professionals and the New Managerialism in the Public Sector*, Buckingham: Open University Press, pp. 83–101.

Clarke, J. and Newman, J. (1997) *The Managerial State*, London: Sage.

Coopers and Lybrand (1988) *The Local Management of Schools*, London: HMSO.

Dale, R. (1989) *The State and Educational Policy*, Milton Keynes: Open University Press.

Davies, C. (1983) 'Professionals in bureaucracies: the conflict thesis re-visited', in R. Dingwall and P. Lewis, (eds), *The Sociology of the Professions*, Basingstoke: Macmillan, pp. 189–201.

Egan, K. (1997) *The Educated Mind: how cognitive tools shape our understanding*, Chicago, IL: University of Chicago Press.

Fairclough, N. (2002) *New Labour, New Language*, London: Routledge.

Freidson, E. (1994) *Professions Reborn: theory, prophecy and policy*, Chicago, IL: Chicago University Press.

Hargreaves, A. (1994) *Changing Teachers, Changing Times*, London: Falmer.

Helsby, G. (1999) *Changing Teachers' Work*, Buckingham: Open University Press.

Hoyle, E. (1974) 'Professionality, professionalism and control in teaching', *London Education Review*, 3 (2): 13–19.

—— (1986) *The Politics of School Management*, London: Hodder & Stoughton.

—— (2001a) 'Teaching as a profession', in N. J. Smelser and P. Balthes (eds), *International Encyclopaedia of the Social and Behavioural Sciences*, Amsterdam: Elsevier, 536–547.

—— (2001b) 'Teaching: status, prestige and esteem', *Educational Management and Administration*, 29 (2): 139–152.

—— and John, P. (1995) *Professional Knowledge and Professional Practice*, London: Methuen.

—— and Wallace, M. (2005) *Educational Leadership: ambiguity, professionals and managerialism*, London: Sage.

—— and —— (2007a) 'Educational reform: an ironic perspective', *Educational Management, Administration and Leadership*, 35 (1): 5–25.

—— and —— (2007b) 'Beyond metaphors of management: the case for metaphoric re-description in education', *British Journal of Educational Studies*, 55 (4): 426–442.

Hughes, M. (1973) 'The professional as administrator: the case of the secondary school head', *Educational Administration Bulletin*, 2 (1): 11–23.

Lawn, M. (1987) *Servants of the State: the contested control of teaching*, London: Falmer.

McCulloch, G., Helsby G. and Knight, P. (2000) *The Politics of Professionalism*, London: Continuum.

March, J. G. (1999) *The Pursuit of Organizational Intelligence*, Oxford: Blackwell.
—— and Olsen, P. (1976) *Ambiguity and Choice in Organizations*, Berger: Universitetsforlaget.
Moore, A., George, R. and Halpin, D. (2002) 'The developing role of the headteacher in English schools: management, leadership and pragmatism', *Educational Management and Administration*, 30 (2): 175–198.
O'Neill, O. (2002) *A Question of Trust*, Cambridge: Cambridge University Press.
Osborn, M., McNess, E. and Broadfoot, P., with Pollard, A. and Triggs, P. (2000) *What Teachers Do. Changing policy and practice in primary education*, London: Continuum.
Pollard, A., Broadfoot, P., Croll, P., Osborn, M. and Abbott, D. (1994) *Changing English Primary Schools: the impact of the Educational Reform Act at Key Stage One*, London: Cassell.
Power, M. (1997) *The Audit Society: rituals of verification*, Oxford: Oxford University Press.
Sachs, J. (2003) *The Activist Teaching Profession*, Buckingham: Open University Press.
Schon, D. (1983) *The Reflective Practitioner*, New York: Basic Books.
Thrupp, M. (2005) *School Improvement: an unofficial approach*, London: Continuum.
Wenger, E. (1998) *Communities of Practice*, Cambridge: Cambridge University Press.
Woods, P., Jeffrey, B., Troman, G. and Boyle, M. (1997) *Re-structuring Schools, Re-structuring Teachers: responding to change in the primary school*, Buckingham: Open University Press.
Woods, P. A., Woods, G. J. and Gunter, H. (2007) 'Academy schools and entrepreneurialism in education', *Journal of Education*, 22 (2): 263–265.

Conclusion

18 Teachers for the future

What have we got and what do we need?

Ian Menter

A review of the chapters in this book provides a clear indication that the nature of teachers' work has been changing rapidly during the first part of the new century. These changes can be related to a number of factors, including, for example, technological developments, globalization or public sector reform. They can also be related to curriculum and pedagogical developments and the increasing significance of the 'knowledge economy' as a major influence on education systems.

In this concluding chapter my intentions are threefold. First I wish to identify common threads that emerge from the contemporary study of teachers, their work and their identities. Second, I wish to assess the significance of some of these patterns and the ways in which they may indicate how teaching is continuing to change. Third, I offer some reflections on what these insights may tell us about the positioning of teachers as actors within twenty-first century democratic societies.

In order to fulfil these three intentions, I commence with the briefest overview of the history of teachers as a significant public sector workforce, including some reflections on questions of identity, values and motivations. Then, drawing both upon the earlier chapters in this volume, as well as on a range of other sources, I consider the key changes that have been occurring in the recent period. This leads to a somewhat polemical conclusion in which I express concern about the ways in which it appears that teachers may be in the process of becoming, once again, 'servants', no longer of the state, but of the global economy.

In the development of state education systems of the 'advanced' nations during the nineteenth and twentieth centuries, the training of teachers was based very much within the national systems of each country. A key concern of this chapter is to examine how the forces of globalization, which are judged to have impinged on schooling and education policy across the world, have influenced the work and identities of contemporary teachers. In a wide range of national contexts, teachers have been key players in 'nation building', through ideological and economic means. If the significance of nations has now been reduced through the impact of globalization, then what are the implications for teachers and their work?

Teachers as public servants

Raymond Williams' account of the forces which competed with each other during the emergence of a public education system in Britain (especially England) has some correspondence with the main motivations and interests of those who sought to work as teachers within that system. In *The Long Revolution*, Williams (1961) suggests that the way in which the state education system in England developed and evolved during the twentieth century reflected the changing fortunes of three major sets of influences:

- the 'old humanists', with a belief in the inherent value of a rounded education for the betterment of the learner;
- the 'public educators', with a belief in the right of all people to achieve literacy and numeracy in order to play their part in a democratic society;
- and the 'industrial trainers', who saw public education as a necessity for economic development, in the preparation of a suitably equipped workforce.

As Williams wrote, 'In general, the curriculum which the nineteenth century evolved can be seen as a compromise between all three groups, but with the industrial trainers predominant' (1961: 163).

Each of these traditions has continued to be present in the development of state education in the second half of the twentieth century and into the current one. And, each of those traditions plays some part in the construction of the professional identity of teachers, in whichever country they are working.

In an important series of 'critical policy studies', Gerald Grace (1978, 1987, 1995) has tracked some of the ideological commitments and motivations of teachers in the public sector. He shows that many of them are driven by a deep commitment, sometimes religiously driven, other times not, to 'service', to the improvement of the life chances of young people. Yet he demonstrates how this commitment, which may be seen as altruistic and democratic, simultaneously serves the interests of the state, for example in reproducing a differentiated (by class, gender, ethnicity, and so on) workforce. This paradoxical positioning of teachers as a force for social development and for social reproduction has been at the core of many of the tensions within the workforce and in the relations between teachers and their employers throughout the twentieth century.

Another defining feature of the development of the teacher workforce during the twentieth century was the way in which collective organization came to be significant, especially through the emergence of a number of trade unions specifically serving teachers. Teachers became an industrial workforce of considerable power and influence until a point towards the last quarter of the century, when – along with many other public sector workforces – they experienced a major onslaught from governments, especially in the US and England (Compton and Weiner 2008).

If this potted history of teachers draws mainly on British, especially English, experience, there are certainly some similarities with the history of education and teachers in most 'Western' nations. The public service ethic is a common theme in north America and Australasia. It may take a different form in mainland European countries where teachers are classed as civil servants, but nevertheless teachers do tend to be seen as servants of the community in which they work. We may also note that in developing countries and countries going through major transitions (for example, South Africa and former states of the USSR) the ways in which teachers are perceived and the ways in which they talk about their roles has some similarities with the discourses surrounding the early phases of state education in the developed world (see Poppleton and Wubbels 2000 and Harley and Wedekind 2004, for example).

However, the bigger question that must arise in the increasingly globalized world is whether the balance between Williams' three main interest groups has shifted significantly. Certainly in the discourse deployed by politicians and policymakers education policy is increasingly driven by economic values. Key words are modernization, competitiveness and standards. The language of liberal humanism has largely disappeared, although of course it thrives in some parts of private sector education as well as in elite universities. In Williams' terms, the dominant discourse around the world, especially within 'advanced' societies, is that of the industrial trainers, albeit with a new emphasis on communication and advanced technologies. The public educator discourse is more notable in its deployment within nations that are in transition (as indicated above) although it is still deployed through the social justice rhetoric and policies that derive from concerns about social inclusion and exclusion, such as '*No Child Left Behind*' in the USA or '*Every Child Matters*' in England.

Teachers and education reform

At the turn of the twentieth century, Smyth *et al.* (2000) wrote of 'a crisis in teachers' work'. While their empirical work was carried out in the context of Australia, nevertheless they were claiming that this crisis, as they saw it, was identifiable across the world. To some extent this crisis is a correlation of the shift in policy drivers referred to above. As the shaping of education policy is increasingly driven by economic priorities, so the way in which teachers' work is shaped and controlled has changed significantly. The economic drivers have created pressures for schools to behave like businesses:

> Teachers are increasingly expected to follow directives and become compliant operatives in the headlong rush to encase schools within the ideology, practices and values of the business sector – never mind that they have histories, aspirations and professional cultures that make them decidedly different to car plants, breweries or fast-food outlets.
>
> (Smyth *et al.* 2000: 1)

Indeed, throughout the Western world, and especially in North America, Australasia and the UK, there was a very significant tightening of control of teachers' work during the last fifteen to twenty years of the twentieth century. This could be seen very clearly through the growth of state and national accreditation procedures for teacher education and through the emergence of sets of performance standards defining entry into the profession across most of these countries (Mahony and Hextall 2000). While these standards had many differences, they nevertheless shared the common purpose of setting out some minimal achievements that were required in order to be recognized as a qualified teacher in a particular context.

It has been suggested that the overall effect of these moves has been to 'technicize' the work of teachers and to increasingly define teaching as a craft, rather than as a profession. As Morrow and Torres put it:

> What underlies this model is the reduction of teaching to the model of the industrial workplace. Many critics of neoliberal policies have ... shown how standardization of teaching and curriculum is closely linked to de-skilling of teachers and the logic of technical control of education.
>
> (Morrow and Torres 2000:47)

Very frequently it is suggested that the autonomy of the teacher has been seriously reduced, so that the scope for judgement and decision making is tightly constrained by an externally imposed framework which sets out the key elements of professional activity.

Drawing on experiences in the US and Australia, Loomis *et al.* (2008) have written of the 'flattening' of the education landscape and of teachers through these processes of standardization (although aspects of their views are challenged by Nagel 2008 and Ladwig 2008). There is also some scope for arguing that even if there has been a major convergence between nations, nevertheless some of the differences between states/nations are still very significant and do reflect the cultural traditions of each nation and are an expression of some divergence of values. The term invoked by Lingard and others to describe such a phenomenon is 'glocalization' – or 'vernacular globalization' (Ozga and Lingard 2007).

Moves such as these raise very serious issues about the role of the university in the preparation and support of teachers. Much has been made of the significance of 'partnership' between schools and universities in debates on teacher education in recent years. However, if teaching is no longer an intellectual activity that requires pedagogical understanding and knowledge as well as technical teaching skills, then the role of the university may be severely limited. Furthermore, the contribution of research in the development of the teaching workforce may be much reduced under this dispensation, yet further diminishing the role of the higher education sector. To resist the demoralizing effects of such technocratic modernization of teacher education Young argues instead for a 'reflexive modernization', which would reverse the trend to dissociate universities from schools but would be reflected in 'new forms of partnership between schools and universities' (1998: 166).

Developments such as these have also affected the work of teachers in the recently developed economies of the Pacific Asia region, according to Cheng (2008) (President of the Asia-Pacific Educational Research Association), who suggests that teaching has a declining status, competent teachers are being lost and the quality of teaching and learning is being damaged. He lists the following factors as contributing to this:

*   marketization
*   competition
*   excessive management control
*   close monitoring
*   deprofessionalization
*   increasing work pressure
*   ambiguities and inconsistencies in policies.

Such factors, Cheng argues, are damaging teachers' well-being and working conditions, leading to depression and burnout.

Across much of the world then, the twin urges in New Right ideology of moral authoritarianism and economic libertarianism gave rise to the curious mix of centralizing and decentralizing tendencies that were played out through this neo-liberal assault on education policy (Olssen *et al.*, 2004). At the same time as national curricula have been increasingly closely prescribed, so the quality of teachers and teaching was being called into question, with increasing encroachment of government into the management of the process of entry into the profession and the development of highly interventionist accountability procedures. Ball's description of a 'discourse of derision' directed at teachers (Ball 1990) was coined in the UK context but is applicable in many contexts. More recently, Ball has succinctly identified the triumvarate of 'markets, management and performativity' as being the dominant tendencies of this neo-liberal education agenda (Ball 2008) that have so transformed the working lives of teachers. The deep irony of these processes of curtailing the independence and autonomy of teachers is that they are usually presented within a discourse of 'professionalization'.

One of the best examples of the particular dualism referred to above, between performativity and enhanced professionalism in teaching, is seen in Scotland. There, an agreement entitled *A Teaching Profession for the 21st Century* (Scottish Executive 2001) was adopted in 2001 by the teaching unions, the teacher employers and the government. As has been argued elsewhere, this set the scene for a much more 'balanced' approach than that seen in England at the time (see Menter *et al.* 2004). Although there were some performative elements to it, including attempts to pin down the working time of teachers within a 35-hour working week, there were also many attempts within the agreement to foster the professional autonomy and responsibility of teachers. One example of this would be the innovative scheme for the creation of Chartered Teachers (see Reeves in this volume). Scotland thus provides an example where there is an apparent balance between performativity and enhanced professionalism. In other settings there may be a stronger emphasis on performativity and it may be that in some, and perhaps Northern Ireland would be the best UK example, there is a stronger emphasis on enhanced professionalism (Hulme and Menter 2008).

Nevertheless, it remains the case that, in many parts of the world, teachers have entered a new era of accountability and standards. The impact of this on the identities of teachers has been considerable, as demonstrated in many of the chapters in this book. As teaching has been defined increasingly explicitly, through the drawing up of standards or competences, it has been very interesting to see how different national versions of standards have positioned the question of values that may underlie teaching (see chapters by Biesta and Cribb in this volume; and Hulme and Menter 2008).

It is in the relationship between 'the professional' and 'the personal' dimensions of teacher identity that the psychic and emotional conflict generated by performativity has been most evident. In the rolling out of new approaches, whether it be performance related pay or new accountability regimes, there has been no evidence at any time that policymakers have taken any significant cognisance of the enormous and deep commitment felt by many teachers towards their work or to the personal investment involved for many teachers. Nevertheless a range of research studies over the same period has shown just how severe the impact of such policies has been, at least on some teachers (for example, Hargreaves 1998; Mahony *et al.* 2004).

The performative agenda has been based on a technical rationalist view of the nature of teaching that has had a strongly reductionist tendency, with the teacher being seen as a technician, 'delivering' a national curriculum. However, the tendency has not been left unchallenged. Indeed it is something of a paradox that there has been a simultaneous growth of interest in more expansive views of teaching during the same period.

There has been something of a renaissance of a commitment to a form of more fully engaged professionalism, through the resurgence of interest in such notions as the 'teacher as researcher' (see Elliott's chapter in this volume) or in the development of 'professional learning communities' (Hargreaves 2003). Support for the development of practitioner research has emerged in a number of schemes across the world. Tatto's (2007) international collection of studies contrasts reforms that emphasize 'teachers' professional knowledge and discretion' in Mexico, Chile, Japan, the Philippines and Guinea with reforms 'emphasising increased control over teachers work and performance' in China, Germany, Bulgaria, Ontario and the USA.

While some of the initiatives that seek to enhance professionalism might be criticized for lacking the radical edge of some earlier approaches to teacher activism (Sachs 2003), they do nevertheless represent a form of 'extended professionalism' that locates teaching as an intellectual occupation.

It has been noticeable however that these initiatives have tended to be short term and localized in their impact. While they may have led to a sense of enhanced professionalism, they may not have led to much change in policy or practice. They tend to take a functionalist or managerialist approach to action research – and can sometimes be associated with the school effectiveness movement – rather than an approach that sets out to bring about wider change and development of the kind proposed in the works of, for example, Stenhouse (1975), Carr and Kemmis (1986) or Simons (1987).

What does the education workforce look like in the twenty-first century?

In addition to the reshaping of teachers' work through the redefinition of the nature of the occupation, there are at least two other significant processes that are reshaping teaching workforces at present. One is the increasing differentiation or segmentation within the school workforce. There is a trend towards increasing numbers of ancillary staff (such as people who are not qualified as teachers) playing a part in the provision of school education. Governments often present this as creating a more flexible workforce that will help to reduce the bureaucratic load on teachers thereby enabling 'teachers to teach'. Teacher unions, on the other hand, have been deeply suspicious of these developments, suspecting that these less well-paid staff may be deployed to replace teachers.

The other process that has been evident is the emergence of a growing cadre of education workers, largely former teachers and school principals, who are working on a commercial basis within the sector, carrying out a range of activities, such as consultancy, training and quality assurance. In the US there is also a significant private publishing industry involving former teachers. The emergence of these new fractions of the education workforce has been a significant part of the privatization of education during the last decade of the twentieth century and into the new century (see Molnar 2006; Ball 2007).

But there is also a third change process of a rather different kind that is taking place. The teaching workforce is significantly being affected by processes of migration. In the large metropolitan areas of the US, increasing numbers of teachers are drawn from the same minority groups as the pupils in schools. The number of Latino (usually bilingual) teachers has been increasing, while the number of African American teachers has apparently been fluctuating (Gordon 2000; Zumwalt and Craig 2004), and is certainly not yet meeting the proportions of those groups among the pupil population. In the former case this is a reflection of recent phases of migration from southern and central America. In the latter case, where progress is made, it represents a long overdue redressing of earlier extreme segregation.

To take another example, schools in London have long depended on an international labour market. During the most severe teacher shortages of the

1990s, employment agencies were sending staff to a number of countries, including South Africa and Australia, to seek to increase the inflow of overseas trained teachers to London (Hutchings *et al.* 2002). Although the need for such teachers has reduced over recent years, there continues to be a significant inward flow of teachers from overseas. Some arrive seeking to spend a relatively short time in the UK while others are economic migrants who will seek to stay in the UK for much, if not all, of their lives. There is also a significant number of teachers who arrive as asylum seekers and may become refugees. It is estimated that there are perhaps 150 teachers among the asylum seeker and refugee communities in Scotland, although at present very few of them are actually employed in schools in Scotland.

That we are witnessing the development of some form of global market in teachers is further demonstrated by considering the impact of some of the migrations referred to above on countries which are still at an early stage of developing national education systems. For example, in the Maldives as many as 50 per cent of secondary school teachers are described as 'expatriates' coming to work there from their homes in India and Sri Lanka, where there is no employment available for them (Anwar 2008).

The point that arises from this discussion of teacher mobility is that in the past it has been common for 'teacher identity' to be closely linked to some notion of 'national identity'. Teachers are trained within a specific context and, at least within Europe, that is usually a national context. (In the US or Australia, training is accredited at state level.) When a teacher migrates therefore – even within the UK – it is likely that significant processes will ensue that affect her professional identity.

All of these changes indicate a growing complexity in relation to teacher identity. If the service ethic principally informed teachers throughout most of the twentieth century, then the public sector reforms referred to throughout this chapter have meant that there are other identifiable identities, sometimes supplanting the service-based identity, sometimes complementing it, though often accompanied by some tension or conflict. Sachs (2003: 127ff.) talks of 'new professional identities for new times', contrasting an entrepreneurial identity with a transformative identity. Robertson (2000: 209–210) suggests that there are at least five identifiable teacher identities, each with their short-hand depiction:

- teacher bricoleur – problem solving
- teacher manager – social efficiency
- teacher entrepreneur – doing well
- temporary teacher – filling in
- service teacher – doing good.

To this list, in the light of the discussion above, we might add:

- travelling teacher – moving practice.

Teachers for nations or teachers for a global economy?

So, if the late 1990s and early parts of the twenty-first century saw an increasing technicization and deskilling of teaching in many countries, and also a changing profile of the education workforce, to what extent can we now suggest that rather than teachers being servants of the (national) state (Lawn 1996; Grace 1987), they are now becoming servants of a global economy, indeed servants of globalization (see Robertson 2000; Smyth *et al.* 2000; Burbules and Torres 2000)? Paradoxically, as suggested above, the rhetoric of national governments commonly invokes economic competitiveness as one of the key drivers for the modernization of education systems. As I suggested earlier, in Williams' terms, one could say that the 'industrial trainer' lobby is once again significantly in the ascendancy. However the terms used to describe this force would need to be adapted to the new times, perhaps to a 'global economy' lobby. Indeed such a shift in language does reflect the way in which information and knowledge have become the new cutting edge of economic growth and development; there is indeed a sense in which the knowledge economy has taken hold in 'advanced societies'. The contradictions that such a perspective reveals are very powerful, however. How can it be that the wealthiest societies that generate the flows of capital around the world associated with this knowledge economy are also societies where inequality is greater than it has ever been and where real poverty is still a major factor and significant sections of society have very limited life chances?

An overriding emphasis on creating a 'knowledge-based', 'world class' education system can all too easily reduce the expectation and responsibility of teachers to address inequality and social injustice in their work (orientations that might be associated with Williams' public educator lobby). 'Making a difference' has long been an important motivational ideology for many teachers working in state schools. The old questions about the purposes of education still lie very close beneath the surface of teacher identity. If education cannot compensate for society, nevertheless is it not still reasonable to expect teachers to be working for social development and for the improvement of the life chances of those who are most disadvantaged in society? Certainly, economic success and social development within a society are closely linked, but the way in which the former is so frequently emphasized above the latter leads to a restricted view of the work of teachers and furthermore needs to be problematized in itself. To assert that economic development is a primary function of education must be seen as raising far more questions than it answers. What do we mean by economic development in a world where human activity is bringing about climate change and expendable resources are diminishing rapidly? This is a world where war and conflict appear to be endemic features of the economy. How highly is human life valued in this economically driven culture?

It is at this juncture and at the risk of being interpreted as romantic, or even sentimental, that it is important to draw the oldest of Williams' ideological drivers into the equation – that of education for the development of the human spirit and intellect, what he described (even then) as the old humanist tradition. This tradition indubitably did grow out of elitist sections of European society, where education was valued for its 'civilizing' influence. This background does not make this tradition necessarily invalid, however, as one can see by considering some of the advances in culture and art that have actually had their origins among very oppressed and poor peoples (one of the best examples being the creation of jazz and blues in the US). Furthermore, the significance of adult education in radical working-class or peasant movements in many parts of the world represents additional evidence to support this view – with the most well known example here being the work of Paolo Freire (1972).

Teachers for the future

In reflecting on the continuing role of teachers in this rapidly changing world where so much is influenced by global economics, how can we develop a sense of what reasonable expectations of teachers might be and how does that connect with the questions around identity and professionalism that have been the major concerns of this book?

To the extent that we do now experience an 'information society' and a 'knowledge-based economy', then the roles and responsibilities of teachers would seem to be as great, if not greater, than ever. But, given that the learning of young people, while being a predominantly social process, involving language and interaction, is associated with the individual destiny of each and every young person, then a standards-based, technicized approach is unlikely to be responsive either to social contexts or to individual needs.

In this light it is more important than ever that teachers are seen to be workers whose judgements and actions are of great social significance. Teachers will need skills of enquiry and evaluation, skills of analysis, synthesis and action. They will need to be able to contribute significantly to the development of education policy and practice, through networks of professional discourse, research and development (see Edwards *et al.* 2002). Few, if any, would question the principle of accountability in teaching, but accountability can take many forms other than simplistic inspection systems or regimes of performativity. Accountability within democratic societies must start from a shared commitment to challenging assumptions and asking critical questions, questions based on the values of a democratic society, including social justice, and the valuing and sustaining of human life.

Such a call does not make teaching an easy occupation, indeed quite the reverse. The challenges for all stakeholders, including teacher unions, teaching councils, governments (local, national and transnational), communities and teacher education institutions, are considerable. And the challenges for teacher educators and for teachers themselves are also greater than ever. If during the nineteenth and twentieth centuries teaching could be seen as playing a key role in the project of modernity that emerged with industrialization, then teaching in the twenty-first century, a century characterized (so far) by uncertainty and change and instability, must be seen as a complex, multilayered and multifaceted occupation where responsiveness and flexibility, the ability to make informed judgements and to apply imagination, are all essential requirements.

References

Anwar, A. (2008) 'Problems of teacher supply in the Maldives in relation to their work, status and the market situation', unpublished Ed.D. thesis, University of Bristol.

Ball, S. (1990) *Politics and Policymaking in Education*, London: Routledge.

—— (2007) *Education plc*, London: Routledge.

—— (2008) *The Education Debate*, Bristol: The Policy Press.

Burbules, N. and Torres, C. (eds) (2000) *Globalization and Education*, London: Routledge.

Carr, W. and Kemmis, S. (1986) *Becoming Critical: education, knowledge and action research*, London: The Falmer Press.

Cheng, Y. C. (2008) 'Reform syndrome and educational research in the Asia-Pacific region'. Paper presented at the Annual Meeting of the American Educational Research Association, New York, USA, 28 March.

Compton, M. and Weiner, L. (eds) (2008) *Global Assault on Teaching, Teachers and their Unions: stories for resistance*, New York: Palgrave.

Edwards, A., Gilroy, P. and Hartley, D. (2002) *Rethinking Teacher Education: collaborative responses to uncertainty*, London: Routledge/Falmer.

Freire, P. (1972) *Pedagogy of the Oppressed*, Harmondsworth: Penguin.

Gordon, J. (2000) *The Color of Teaching*, London: Routledge.

Grace, G. (1978) *Teachers, Ideology and Control*, London: Routledge & Kegan Paul.

—— (1987) 'Teachers and the state in Britain: a changing relation', in M. Lawn and G. Grace (eds), *Teachers: the culture and politics of work*, London: Falmer Press, pp. 193–228.

—— (1995) *School Leadership*, London: Falmer Press.

Hargreaves, A. (1998) 'The emotional politics of teaching and teacher development: with implications for educational leadership', *International Journal of Leadership in Education*, 1 (4): 315–336.

—— (2003) *Teaching in the Knowledge Society: education in the age of insecurity*, Maidenhead: Open University Press.

Harley, K. and Wedekind, V. (2004) 'Political change, curriculum change and social formation, 1990 to 2002', in L. Chisholm (ed.), *Changing Class: education and social change in post-apartheid South Africa*, London: Zed Books.

Hulme, M. and Menter, I. (2008) 'Learning to teach in post-devolution UK: a technical or an ethical process?', *Southern African Review of Education*, 14 (1–2): 43–64.

Hutchings, M., Menter, I., Ross, A. and Thomson, D. (2002) 'Teacher supply and retention in London – key findings and implications from a study carried out in six boroughs in 1998/9', in I. Menter, M. Hutchings and A. Ross (eds), *The Crisis in Teacher Supply – research and strategies for retention*, Stoke-on-Trent: Trentham Books.

Ladwig, J. (2008) 'Response to Loomis *et al.*: Information flows, knowledge transportability, teacher education and world culture', *Teaching Education*, 19 (1): 13–15.

Lawn, M. (1996) *Modern Times? Work, professionalism and citizenship in teaching*, London: Falmer Press.

Loomis, S., Rodriguez, J., Tillman, R. and Gunderson, J. (2008) 'The logic of convergence and uniformity in teacher production', *Teaching Education*, 19 (1): 1–10.

Mahony, P. and Hextall, I. (2000) *Reconstructing Teaching*, London: Routledge/ Falmer.

Mahony, P., Menter, I. and Hextall, I. (2004) 'The emotional impact of performance-related pay on teachers in England', *British Educational Research Journal*, 30 (3): 435–456.

Menter, I., Mahony, P. and Hextall, I. (2004) 'Ne'er the twain shall meet? The modernisation of the teaching workforce in Scotland and England', *Journal of Education Policy*, 19 (2): 195–214.

Molnar, A. (2006) *School Commercialisation: from democratic ideal to market commodity*, London: Routledge.

Morrow, R. and Torres, C. (2000) 'The state, globalization and education policy', in N. Burbules and C. Torres (eds), *Globalization and Education: critical perspectives*, London: Routledge.

Nagel, N. (2008) 'Response to Loomis *et al.*: convergence and uniformity in teacher production: a catalyst to create individualistic teacher education programs', *Teaching Education*, 19 (1): 11–12.

Olssen, M., Codd, J. and O'Neill, A.-M. (2004) *Education Policy*, London: Sage.

Ozga, J. and Lingard, B. (2007) 'Globalisation, education policy and politics', in B. Lingard and J. Ozga (eds), *The Routledge/Falmer Reader in Education Policy and Politics*, London: Routledge.

Poppleton, P. and Wubbels, T. (2000) 'Educational change and its impact on the work lives of teachers in eight countries', in R. Alexander, M. Osborn and D. Phillips (eds), *Learning from Comparing: new directions in comparative educational research, Volume 2, Policy, Professionals and Development*, Oxford: Symposium Books.

Robertson, S. (2000) *A Class Act: changing teachers' work, the state and globalisation*, London: Falmer Press.

Sachs, J. (2003) *The Activist Teaching Profession*, Buckingham: Open University Press.

Scottish Executive (2001) *A Teaching Profession for the 21st Century: agreement reached following recommendations made in the McCrone Report*, Edinburgh: Scottish Executive.

Simons, H. (1987) *Getting to Know Schools in a Democracy*, London: Falmer Press.

Smyth, J., Dow, A., Hattam, R., Reid, A. and Shacklock, G. (2000) *Teachers' Work in a Globalizing Economy*, London: Falmer Press.

Stenhouse, L. (1975) *An Introduction to Curriculum Research and Development*, London: Heinemann.

Tatto, M. (ed.) (2007) *Reforming Teaching Globally*, Oxford: Symposium Books.

Williams, R. (1961) *The Long Revolution*, London: Chatto & Windus.

Young, M. (1998) *The Curriculum of the Future*, London: Falmer.

Zumwalt, K. and Craig, E. (2004) 'Teachers' characteristics: research on the demographic profile', in M. Cochran-Smith. and K. Zeichner (eds), *Studying Teacher Education*, Mahwah, NJ: Lawrence Erlbaum.

Index